Thomas More

ALISTAIR FOX

Thomas More

History and Providence

Yale University Press
New Haven and London

First published in the United States in 1983 by
Yale University Press.

*Library of Congress Cataloging in Publication
Data*

Fox, Alistair
  Thomas More, history and providence.

  Bibliography: p.
  1. More, Thomas, Sir, Saint, 1478-1535.
  I. Title
DA334.M8F68 1983   942.05'2'0924   82-11178
ISBN 0-300-02951-9
ISBN 0-300-03415-6 (pbk.)

10 9 8 7 6 5 4 3 2

Printed in Great Britain

Contents

PART THREE The Tower Works

Preface

Throughout this study I have quoted from More's works frequently, and often extensively, for much of his meaning resides in tone and nuance which is difficult to paraphrase and even more dangerous to ignore. This is particularly true of the Latin works, and because most modern translations reproduce the interpretative bias of the translator, I have usually given the Latin original either in the footnotes, or, where convenient, in the text itself. Translations are normally those of the Yale edition, but occasionally I have emended them or given my own. I would stress that in all cases where a translation is quoted the reader should consult what More actually wrote, which is the Latin.

For More's English works I have used the 1557 edition for works that have not yet appeared in the modern Yale edition. In referring to 1557, I cite by page and marginal letter, not by signature, because finding a reference in double-column folio pages of commonly 1,000 words or more is otherwise like searching for a needle in a haystack. Rastell's compositors occasionally misnumbered pages, but this causes no serious difficulty, and where it has occurred I have noted the correct page number in square brackets.

My practice in transcribing is conservative, but not as conservative as that of the Yale edition: contractions and the ampersand have been silently expanded, but otherwise spelling and punctuation are those of the original.

Many of the most relevant critical studies on More are now reprinted in *Essential Articles for the Study of Thomas More*, edited by R. S. Sylvester and Germain Marc'hadour, and because this volume is widely and readily available, I have therefore cited articles appearing in it there, rather than in their original locations; the original sources, however, can be found enumerated in the bibliography.

I wish to acknowledge my debt to the University of Otago for its generous research grants and provisions for sabbatical leave: the former allowed me to gather indispensable material while still in New Zealand, and the latter made possible the year spent in Cambridge during which I wrote the book. I should also like to thank the Nuffield Foundation for the assistance of its Travelling Fellowship, the members of Clare Hall for welcoming me as an Associate, Professor G. R. Elton for his hospitality, astute advice, and the stimulation of his Tudor seminar, and Professor J. B. Trapp for guiding me through the resources of the Warburg Institute. Finally, I should like to thank Mrs Mary Sullivan for proofreading my typescript and checking the quotations, Mrs Lynnsay Francis for patiently typing corrections to the final draft, and Mrs Anaig Fenby for assisting me in checking the proofs.

Acknowledgement is made to the respective editors and translators and the Yale University Press for permission to quote from *The Yale Edition of the Complete Works of St Thomas More*.

Alistair Fox
Dunedin

For Ana

Abbreviations

Allen	*Opus epistolarum Des. Erasmi Roterodami.* 12 vols. Ed. P. S. Allen, H. M. Allen and H. W. Garrod (Oxford, 1906–58)
Bradner and Lynch	*The Latin Epigrams of Thomas More.* Trans. and ed. L. Bradner and C. A. Lynch (Chicago, 1953)
CW	*The Complete Works of St Thomas More.* 14 vols. (New Haven and London, 1963–):
CW 2	*The History of King Richard III.* Ed. Richard S. Sylvester (1963)
CW 3	*Translations of Lucian.* Ed. Craig R. Thompson (1974)
CW 4	*Utopia.* Ed. Edward Surtz and J. H. Hexter (1965)
CW 5	*Responsio ad Lutherum.* Ed. John M. Headley (1969)
CW 6	*A Dialogue Concerning Heresies.* Ed. Thomas Lawler, Germain Marc'hadour and Richard Marius (1981)
CW 8	*The Confutation of Tyndale's Answer.* Ed. Louis A. Schuster, Richard C. Marius, James P. Lusardi and Richard J. Schoeck (1973)
CW 9	*The Apology.* Ed. J. B. Trapp (1979)
CW 12	*A Dialogue of Comfort against Tribulation.* Ed. Louis L. Martz and Frank Manley (1976)
CW 13	*Treatise on the Passion, Treatise on the Blessed Body, Instructions and Prayers.* Ed. Garry E. Haupt (1976)
CW 14	*De Tristitia Christi.* Ed. Clarence H. Miller (1976)

Essential Articles	*Essential Articles for the Study of Thomas More.* Ed. R. S. Sylvester and G. P. Marc'hadour (Hamden, Conn., 1977)
EW 1931	*The English Works of Sir Thomas More, Reproduced in Facsimile from William Rastell's Edition of 1557 and Edited with a Modern Version of the Same by W. E. Campbell.* 2 vols. (London, 1931)
EW 1557	*The Workes of Sir Thomas More Knyght, Sometyme Lorde Chauncellor of England, Wrytten by Him in the Englysh Tonge.* Ed. William Rastell (London, 1557)
LP	*Letters and Papers, Foreign and Domestic, of the Reign of Henry VIII.* 21 vols. Ed. J. S. Brewer et al. (London, 1862–1932)
Rogers, *Correspondence*	*The Correspondence of Sir Thomas More.* Ed. Elizabeth F. Rogers (Princeton, 1947)
Rogers, *SL*	*St Thomas More: Selected Letters.* Ed. Elizabeth Frances Rogers (New Haven and London, 1961)

Introduction

Several decades ago an eminent critic concluded of More that 'what is actually expressed in most of his work is a third More, out of whom both the saint and the humanist have been made'.[1] The saint and the humanist have each been amply described, the former in a long line of hagiographies beginning with William Roper's *Lyfe of Sir Thomas Moore* and culminating in the recent books of E. E. Reynolds,[2] and the latter in a host of studies focusing upon *Utopia*.[3] The two Mores, however, never seem happily to coincide, in spite of determined efforts to make them do so.[4] Emphasis on the humanist produces an anachronism,[5] and attempts to depict the saint produce only a plaster saint.

Both More the saint and More the humanist as scholarship has so far presented them are fictions: convenient, yet increasingly unsatisfying. The recent findings of historians, in particular, suggest that

[1] C. S. Lewis, *English Literature in the Sixteenth Century* (Oxford, 1954). Lewis' comments on More are reprinted in *Essential Articles for the Study of Thomas More*, ed. R. S. Sylvester and G. P. Marc'hadour (Hamden, Conn., 1977), pp. 388–401.

[2] *Saint Thomas More* (London, 1949) and *The Field is Won* (London, 1968). These and similar works by Christopher Hollis (*Saint Thomas More* (London, 1961)), E. M. G. Routh (*Sir Thomas More and His Friends, 1477–1535* (Oxford, 1934)) and R. W. Chambers (*Thomas More* (London, 1935)) are essentially refinements of T. E. Bridgett's *Life and Writings of Sir Thomas More* (London, 1891).

[3] These works are too numerous to catalogue at length. Notable among them are Frederic Seebohm, *The Oxford Reformers, John Colet, Erasmus, and Thomas More* (3rd edn, London, 1911), R. P. Adams, *The Better Part of Valour: More, Erasmus, Colet and Vives on Humanism, War, and Peace, 1496–1535* (Seattle, 1962), E. L. Surtz, *The Praise of Wisdom* (Chicago, 1957), and J. H. Hexter, *More's Utopia: The Biography of an Idea* (Princeton, 1952), together with the same author's Introduction, *CW* 4: *Utopia*.

[4] Chiefly by Chambers and Surtz.

[5] The problematic nature of More's humanism is reiterated by Craig R. Thompson, 'The Humanism of More Reappraised', *Thought: Fordham University Quarterly*, 52 (1977), pp. 231–48.

1

the saintly image that so impressed More's own family masked a deeply involved political activism of which they were barely aware.[6] As the Yale edition has made More's polemical writings more readily accessible, scholars have also discovered unresolved problems not only in his doctrinal convictions,[7] but also in his personality.[8] In short, the mounting evidence means that neither of the received myths will any longer do; the study of More must find some way of freeing itself from the impasse into which it has wandered.

Scholarship finds itself in such a position because the third More has never been properly assessed. In one respect this is astonishing, because he is indeed expressed in his works, which provide a more extensive body of evidence than exists for most other figures of the period. In another, it is not at all surprising, for until recently the vast bulk of More's works, the Latin and English controversies, was available only in the original editions of the 1520s and 1530s, William Rastell's 1557 black-letter edition of the English works, and the Louvain *Opera omnia* of 1565. Apart from that, these polemical writings are almost unreadable *in toto* for the modern reader: prolix and tedious, exhaustive and exhausting.

Yet they are, nevertheless, essential to a sound understanding of More. *Utopia* at one end of his career and the Tower works at the other have always been reasonably well served, but to understand the former one must approach it by way of the earlier English and Latin works, and to understand the latter one must grasp the contents and import of the controversies. It is little wonder, then, that scholarship has tended to dismember More into parts that seem not to relate when

---

[6] I refer to the studies of G. R. Elton ('Sir Thomas More and the Opposition to Henry VIII', *Essential Articles,* pp. 79–91), and John A. Guy (*The Public Career of Sir Thomas More* (Brighton, Sussex, 1980)).

[7] Chief among these is the question of his papalism versus his conciliarism, which has occasioned a lively debate between two of the Yale editors. See Richard C. Marius, 'Thomas More's View of the Church', *CW* 8, III, pp. 1309–15, John M. Headley's reply in *Moreana,* 41 (1974), pp. 5–10, Francis Oakley, 'Headley, Marius and the Matter of More's "Conciliarism"', together with the rejoinders of Headley and Marius, in *Moreana,* 64 (1980), pp. 82–99.

[8] See the comments on More as a persecutor of heretics by Marius, *CW* 8, III, pp. 1346–8, which challenge recent attempts to exculpate him, and G. R. Elton's suggestion of a sexual obsession in 'The Real Thomas More?', in *Reformation Principle and Practice: Essays in Honour of Arthur Geoffrey Dickens,* ed. Peter Newman Brooks (London, 1980), pp. 23–31.

the vital material that connects them is so persistently overlooked.[9] The real Thomas More will inevitably remain an enigma until a comprehensive and coherent view of the man is derived from the tangible evidence of his own thought, expressed voluminously in his writings as it evolved.

A synoptic view of More's works reveals that the man was even more complex than has been commonly acknowledged. Everyone admits that he is elusive and subtle, but too often the impression is left either that the difficulties can be resolved simply by assuming a commitment in More to Catholic orthodoxy, or that they are ultimately undefinable and hence insoluble. Neither case is true. First, it is a mistake to read back into More's earlier writings the attitudes of his later ones, because history had not yet brought them fully into being. The More who was the bosom friend and soul mate of Erasmus in 1506 was not the same More who took up cudgels against Christopher St German's proposals for the reform of ecclesiastical abuse, as the Marian biographers well knew.[10] In any case, to equate More's later attitudes with a post-Tridentine doctrinal position is merely to beg the question. Second, to assume that More was an incomprehensible bundle of antitheses is to imply that he was a psychotic, which the evidence equally will not support.

Many of the common misconceptions arise from the tendency in scholars to concentrate either on More's earlier writings and activities, or else on those of the last phase of his life. This heightens the illusion that a radical hiatus exists between the two ends of his career. More, however, was a prolific writer, and the regularity with which his works appeared testifies to a steady progression in the evolution of his thought, not a disjunction. Indeed, the writings show precisely how More's death came about as the logical outcome of his response to his life.

That life was a turbulent one. It is wrong to assume that More was

[9] Chambers, for example, glided over the controversies in barely four pages; Bridgett's account of the works was too generalized and superficial to be useful; all subsequent biographies have shared the same faults. Judith P. Jones makes a gesture in the right direction in *Thomas More* (Boston, 1979), but her account is descriptive rather than analytic.

[10] For the attempts of Harpsfield, Stapleton and the later sixteenth-century biographers to discredit Erasmus and detach More from him, see James K. McConica, 'The Recusant Reputation of Thomas More', in *Essential Articles*, pp. 141–9.

born either a reactionary or a radical, for to his own discomfort he found himself born both. His earliest works reveal that he experienced acutely the tensions arising from an age in transition. On one hand he felt a calling towards the ascetic piety of medieval Catholicism, on the other he felt drawn towards the new learning and the possibilities it held out for the transformation of society; one moment he was convinced of the intrinsic corruption of the world and the flesh, the next he would seek to enjoy it. More found the experience of these rival impulses tribulatory and perturbing, and his first reaction was to withdraw from the world altogether, as being too satanically perverted and perverting to be safely approached. As the calling to an active (and married) life in the world became too persistent to be ignored, he sought to discover a *modus vivendi* and philosophy that would allow him legitimately to follow it. *Utopia* embodies the paradoxical synthesis that ensued, when More, refusing to choose arbitrarily between court and cloister, tried to find a way of uniting the virtues of both in a public career.

The Morean Christian–humanist synthesis, however, contained forces that were centrifugal as well as centripetal, and as his public life plunged him deeper into the realm of political practicalities, he found the synthesis difficult to sustain. Even before the Lutheran explosion shook his equilibrium, a *Treatise on the Four Last Things* had shown how easily the more conservative element could outweigh the rest. Once he had been drawn irrevocably into religious controversy, the nature of historical circumstances and of his own personal involvement threatened to destroy the synthesis altogether. By the close of his polemical campaign in late 1533 More was close to despair. Had his intellectual career ended there, posterity would have been left only with the tragic exemplum of a failed experiment.

It did not end there, however, for out of this potential despair grew a new synthesis, subsuming the old one within it, but infinitely more profound and secure. Paradoxically, the experience of failure had enlarged More's understanding of his own world view and confirmed him in his belief in its truth. His final sacrifice expressed his willingness to surrender to the ultimate implications of the view of things he had first depicted in *Utopia*, but which he had almost, unwittingly, repudiated during the period of the controversies. Having grasped confidently the nature of the divine drama at hand, he was prepared to enact the role he believed God required of him.

One intellectual preoccupation links all of More's writings: his attempt to discover the precise nature of the divine providence by which he believed the world must be ruled. In the course of his works one can trace the process by which he reconciled the diverse aspects of his own personality and life within a comprehensive view of the human situation. His interest did not stop only at explaining himself to himself; he sought also to understand the shape, meaning and purpose of history at large. Although More derived his belief from the commonplace Christian view that history shows the known march of God's providence, he developed his own personal sense of it, particularly of the way in which that providence works. Eventually, his whole doctrinal and intellectual position came to depend upon his view of universal history and the grand design of God. His peculiar angle of appraisal, in effect, imbued his writings, religious as well as secular, with a highly idiosyncratic character. In the final analysis, More stood for himself; he cannot easily be classified with any of his contemporaries, and that is partly what makes it both difficult to give an accurate account of him and also all the more necessary for an account to be given.

The formulation of More's view of providence and history provides the central theme of this book. It has determined the emphases and the principles by which material has been selected for discussion. This study in no way presumes to be definitive; it merely aims to offer a new perspective and to suggest some new directions – or (to adapt one of More's favourite metaphors) to present the induction to a new play.

PART ONE

Youth and Mid-Career

1

Contrary Impulses: English Poems, *Life of John Picus*, Translations of Lucian, *Epigrammata*

The character of the young More as inherited from Erasmus is so well rounded and humanistically coherent that until recently it has seemed hardly necessary to question it: More was a natural genius of a delightfully affable nature and quick wit, who delighted in writing farces and acting in them; his enthusiasm for the new preoccupations of humanism was discreetly conditioned by a gentle piety like that of Erasmus that allowed him to act in the world without being really of it, reluctantly the king's good servant, a Democritus in good humour, and a Socrates in wisdom.[1]

Close scrutiny of More's own writings from this period, however, raises doubts as to the completeness of Erasmus' portrait. Far from unruffled affability, the early works reflect a capacity for severe melancholy in More, and suggest that he may have been extremely perturbed by a tragic sense of the apparent futility, injustice and absurdity of the world, the victim of conflicts within his own personality, and highly unresolved as to whether he should laugh or cry at the world, repudiate or join it. From behind the discreet obscurity of the Latin language he gave vent to sentiments history has tended not to remember in him: bellicose, chauvinistic patriotism in the epigrams against Brixius, often vindictive, sometimes petty;[2] pornographic voyeurism;[3] and antifeminist cynicism.[4] The young More seems to have been unable to hold all the components of his personality in any kind of balance capable of satisfying him; his early

[1] Erasmus, Letter to Ulrich von Hutten, Allen, IV, no. 999.

[2] *The Latin Epigrams of Thomas More*, ed. and trans. L. Bradner and C. A. Lynch (Chicago, 1953), nos. 170, 171, 174, 177, 178, 179.

[3] ibid., nos. 98, 148. On the discreet purging of four sexually indelicate epigrams from the Louvain *Opera omnia* of 1565, see McConica, 'The Recusant Reputation of Thomas More', *Essential Articles*, p. 144.

[4] Bradner and Lynch, nos. 44, 66, 67, 68, 140, 147, 219.

works are by turns comic, satiric, optimistic and pessimistic, and contain no consistent philosophical viewpoint that can be identified with his later thought. One gains the impression that More had to forge his understanding of the world out of a chaos of contradictory impressions and impulses, and that the process was not a comfortable one. Fortunately, his writings, together with the known facts of his early career, furnish evidence of the stages by which his thinking developed. The English poems project a near-manichean view of things between 1500 and 1504; the *Life of John Picus* suggests the otherworldly spirituality into which he contemplated seeking escape in the period to 1505; the translations of Lucian indicate how his encounter with that author gave him his cue for responding without despair to the world as he saw it; the earlier Latin epigrams show how variegated and unstable the different aspects of More's personality nevertheless remained, and how quickly the pendulum could swing from one extreme attitude to another. At the end of this phase of his literary career, More had not definitively settled upon a coherent, comprehensive world view, but the stage had been clearly set up for him to do so.

In his mid-twenties, More appears to have been a man of extremes not held in any accommodating relation as they were to be later. On one hand he was furthering his legal career at Lincoln's Inn and Furnivall's Inn, avidly pursuing his study of Greek under Grocyn and Linacre, and proving himself (if Roper's account is to be trusted) in Parliament; on the other, he was giving himself to devotions in the Charterhouse of London, private asceticism, and study of the church fathers, which issued forth in his lectures on *De civitate Dei* in Grocyn's church. Commentators have argued that this combination of pursuits reflected the harmony of a Christian–humanist synthesis,[5] but More's English poems suggest otherwise. Three of the poems project a perplexed Augustinian sobriety; the other is a Chaucerian farce revealing a sensual mirth in his nature which he himself was reluctant to accept. The contrast between the first three and the fourth rests upon a sharp conflict between delight in the world and a pious impulse to repudiate it, and More could no more successfully resolve this conflict than Chaucer, for example, had been able to do in his

---

[5] See, for example, Sister Mary Edith Willow, *An Analysis of the English Poems of St Thomas More* (Nieuwkoop, 1974), pp. 24, 95.

'Retractions' to the *Tales of Caunterbury*.[6] If nurture pulled one way, nature nevertheless pulled in the other, and More was responsive to both.

The common theme of the *Nine Pageants*, *A Rueful Lamentation* and the *Verses for the Book of Fortune* is the vanity of all temporal things.[7] These poems variously express the commonplace topoi of *ubi sunt*, *memento mori* and *contemptus mundi*. What is not commonplace is the emotional force with which More invests them. It would be a grave mistake to dismiss any of his earlier works (or his later ones, for that matter) as mere 'convention', for a convention, after all, is used by all but the most mindless of writers for its inherent and inherited 'fitness to mean'.[8] More chose these ones because they were highly appropriate vehicles for the expression of his own anxiety and perturbation.

In the *Nine Pageants*, imitated from Petrarch's *Trionfi*,[9] but also drawing upon a long medieval iconographic tradition, More depicts the progression through all the stages of man's life from childhood to eternity. Each state embodies discomforting irony. The Child, shown in the first pageant playing with a top and whip, desires only to play, but is frustrated by the reality of school:

> would to god these hateful bookes all,
> Were in a fyre brent to pouder small.
> Than myght I lede my lyfe alwayes in play:
> Whiche lyfe god sende me to myne endyng day.[10]

As innocent as this image may appear, it reflects More's sense of the conflict between what men desire to do and what they are obliged to do.

---

[6] For More's continuing ambivalence at the end of his career, see his remarks in *A Dialogue of Comfort* (*CW* 12, p. 83/7ff.) and in 'A Godly Meditation' (*CW* 13, p. 227/ 11–14).

[7] I have simplified and modernized Rastell's periphrastic titles.

[8] I use the phrase of Charles Muscatine, *Chaucer and the French Tradition* (Berkeley, 1969), p. 2: 'The conventionalization of a style is usually described as a purely historical, associational phenomenon, the result of (mostly mindless) imitation; it is only partly so. The "meaning" of a conventional style is partly determined by the meanings of previous poems in that style, but also partly – and this too accounts for its conventionalization – by an inherent fitness-to-mean.'

[9] Willow, p. 81.

[10] *EW* 1557, sig. Ciii. More was later to return to this image in the *Confutation*, where he elaborated the idea of the child's inclination to truancy into a figure for the temptation to sinfulness which men must fight to resist (*CW* 8, I, pp. 497–8).

The 'goodly freshe yonge man' of the second pageant derides the child's belief that his state is sweetest, but finds his own pride subdued by Venus:

> Now thou which erst despysedst children small,
> Shall waxe and chylde agayne and be my thrall.[11]

The 'olde sage father' of the fourth pageant, believing himself immune from Cupid's dart, and filled with satisfaction at his wisdom and influence in the public weal, must in turn yield to Death; Death must yield to Fame; Fame must yield to Time:

> I shall in space destroy both see and lande.
> O simple fame, how darest thou man honowre,
> Promising of his name, an endlesse flowre,
> Who may in the world haue a name eternall,
> When I shall in proces distroy the world and all.[12]

But even Time must be trampled under the feet of Eternity; when the sun and moon leave their course, 'thou shalt be brought, / For all thy pride and bostyng into nought'.[13]

A final pageant depicts a poet sitting in a chair, and some concluding lines in Latin declare the moral:

> Gaudia laus et honor, celeri pede omnia cedunt,
>   Qui manet excepto semper amore dei?
> Ergo homines, leuibus iamiam diffidite rebus,
>   Nulla recessuro spes adhibenda bono,
> Qui dabit eternam nobis pro munere vitam,
>   In permansuro ponite vota deo

(Pleasures, praise, homage, all things quickly disappear. What remains except the love of God? Therefore, men, henceforth have no trust in trivial things, no hope in having transitory good. Offer your prayers to God everlasting, who will give us the reward of eternal life.)[14]

---

[11] *EW* 1557, sig. Ciii.
[12] ibid., sig. Ciii^v.
[13] ibid., sig. Civ.
[14] ibid., sig. Civ.

As conventional as this poem may be, aspects of its form reflect the degree of idiosyncrasy in More's approach to his theme. Each verse originally accompanied a tapestry emblem that depicted the figure in the preceding verse overthrown, lying under the feet of the next triumphant personification. These visual images capture the violence of the process without any sense of beneficent purpose. More would later conclude that mutability was purposeful, but here he regards it as depriving men of any chance of temporal happiness. Already implicit is More's conception of life as a play. The word 'pageant' could mean 'dumb show', 'stage', 'tableau'; More's allegorical per-sonifications also speak in the first person: these two facts together suggest that he had been influenced by the mode and connotations of the medieval English morality plays.[15] However, the kind of human drama acknowledged is not the dynamic, if unpredictable, affair it is in Lucian's *Menippus* (the source of More's later amplification of the stage metaphor), but a relentless process of systematized futility designed to frustrate all human endeavour, rather like the situation depicted in Shelley's *Triumph of Life*. More knew from his medieval religious heritage that men were supposed to accept this and turn their minds away from the world towards eternal life and a transcendent deity. As much as he tried to believe it and make himself do it, he could not.

A Rueful Lamentation, an elegy on the death of Queen Elizabeth in 1503, presents a variation on the same theme. Developing the motif of *ubi sunt*, More makes the queen use her own life as an exemplum to illustrate the folly of placing one's confidence 'In wordly ioy and frayle prosperite'.[16] His stress is not merely on the sad fact that death deprives one of all earthly possessions, but on the tragic misery of living at all. Everything in life seems to be paid for by twice its worth in pain:

> O bryttill welth, ay full of bitternesse,
> Thy single pleasure double is with payne.
> Account my sorow first and my distresse,
> In sondry wyse, and recken there agayne,
> The ioy that I haue had, and I dare sayn,
> For all my honour, endured yet haue I,
> More wo then welth, and lo now here I ly.[17]

[15] See Willow, pp. 78–9.
[16] *EW* 1557, sig. Civ.
[17] ibid., sig. Civ[v].

The pessimism of the poem is far more intense than the convention requires.[18] It springs from More's sense of the pity of it all, expressed poignantly in the queen's farewell to her family:

> Adew myne owne dere spouse my worthy lorde,
>
>   *   *   *   *   *
>
> Erst wer you father, and now must ye supply,
> The mothers part also, for lo now here I ly.
>
> Farewell my doughter lady Margarete.
> God wotte full oft it greued hath my mynde,
> That ye should go where we should seldome mete.
> Now am I gone, and haue left you behynde.
>
> Adew lord Henry my louyng sonne adew.
> Our lorde encrease your honour and estate,
> Adew my doughter Mary bright of hew.
> God make you vertuous wyse and fortunate.
> Adew swete hart my little doughter Kate,
> Thou shalt swete babe such is thy desteny,
> Thy mother neuer know, for lo now here I ly.[19]

In these lines More achieves a degree of pathos not seen in English poetry since Chaucer's *Clerk's Tale*, pathos that derives from an unusual depth of compassion for mortals suffering in a human situation loaded unjustly against them.

The entirely conventional moral is delivered near the end of the poem, but its delivery is so perfunctory as to accord uneasily with the tone of the rest of the piece:

> Lo here the ende of wordly vanitee.
> Now well are ye that earthly foly flee,
> And heuenly thynges loue and magnify,
> Farewell and pray for me, for lo now here I ly.[20]

Earthly folly is left undefined, but we can conjecture as to what More thought it consisted of by contemplating what he wondered if he

---

[18]For a similar conclusion, see Frederic B. Tromly, ' "A Rueful Lamentation" of Elizabeth: Thomas More's Transformation of Didactic Lament', *Moreana*, 53 (1977), pp. 45–56.

[19] *EW* 1557, sigs Civ^v–Cv; Margaret had married James IV of Scotland.

[20] ibid., sig. Cv.

should avoid: marriage, children, a secular career, merriment – in short, most of the realities of an ordinary human life that make a man, to adapt Bacon, 'a hostage to Fortune'.[21] More's later distress when his own daughter Margaret lay apparently dying of the sweating sickness showed that, at least as far as close familial ties were concerned, his humanity was too powerful to be effectively sedated by the pious commonplaces he tried to administer to it.[22] That was the root cause of his melancholy.

The *Verses for the Book of Fortune* are the most revealing of all. Rastell declares that More had these 42 stanzas printed to preface the English translation of *Le livre de passetemps de la fortune*, a kind of early renaissance horoscope guide.[23] More's scorn at superstition, an attitude he shared with Erasmus,[24] was the ostensible cause of these lines, but they express far more than that.

The main part of the work begins with 'The Wordes of Fortune to the People', a self-eulogy delivered by Lady Fortune extolling, in terms that anticipate Folly in *Moriae encomium*, her 'high estate power and auctoritie':

> enserche and ye shall spye,
> That richesse, worship, welth, and dignitie,
> Ioy, rest, and peace, and all thyng fynally,
> That any pleasure or profit may come by,
> To mannes comfort, ayde, and sustinaunce,
> Is all at my deuyse and ordinaunce.[25]

Some men, she scoffs, have written books to her dispraise, but that is only because she has withheld her smiles from them:

> Thus lyke the fox they fare that once forsoke,
> The pleasaunt grapes, and gan for to defy them,
> Because he lept and yet could not come by them.[26]

[21] *Essays*, ed. M. J. Hawkins (London, 1972), no. VIII: 'Of Marriage and Single Life', p. 22.
[22] William Roper, *The Lyfe of Sir Thomas More, Knighte*, ed. Elsie Vaughan Hitchcock (London, 1935), pp. 28–9.
[23] For full discussions, see A. W. Reed, *EW* 1931, I, p. 17; Willow, pp. 177–8.
[24] For Erasmus' attitude towards superstition, see Sister M. Geraldine Thompson, 'As Bones to the Body: The Scope of *Inventio* in the Colloquies of Erasmus', in *Essays on the Works of Erasmus*, ed. Richard L. DeMolen (New Haven, 1978), pp. 166–8.
[25] *EW* 1557, sig. Civ^v.
[26] ibid.

Was More fully aware of the irony he created by making Fortune level this charge against her own creator in the fiction? Continuing, Fortune tries to discredit her detractors further by appealing to the realistic findings of common sense, in terms that enigmatically prefigure *Utopia*:

> But let them write theyr labour is in vayne.
> For well ye wote, myrth, honour, and richesse,
> Much better is than penury and payne.
> The nedy wretch that lingereth in distresse,
> Without myne helpe is euer comfortlesse,
> A wery burden odious and loth,
> To all the world, and eke to him selfe both.[27]

After insinuating this possibility of wilful self-deception, Fortune, like Satan in *Paradise Regained*, offers the temptation of wordly power to him who is prepared to seek high office:

> O in how blist condicion standeth he:
> Him self in honour and felicite,
> And ouer that, may forther and encrease,
> A region hole in ioyfull rest and peace.[28]

Lady Fortune's whole performance is indeed a satanic temptation first to despair and then to repudiate wisdom: 'Better is to be fortunate than wyse.'[29]

More's counter-assertion of wisdom in the section entitled 'Thomas More to Them That Trust in Fortune' betrays an element of uncertainty in its very length. In *Paradise Regained* it is Satan who protests too much and allows his speeches to sprawl formlessly, Christ who is cryptic and brief. More was unwise to reverse the strategy, particularly since his assertions are merely time-worn commonplaces: Fortune is inconstant, she has many attendant troubles, there is no reason or justice in the bestowal of her gifts, and history is full of illustrious men who fell from high places.[30] The only remedy is a life of virtuous poverty:

[27] ibid.
[28] ibid.
[29] ibid.
[30] ibid., sigs Cvi–Cviii.

> yf thou in suretye lyst to stande,
> Take pouerties parte and let prowde fortune go,
> Receyue nothyng that commeth from her hande:
> Loue maner and vertue: they be onely tho.
> Whiche double fortune may not take the fro.
> Then mayst thou boldly defye her turnyng chaunce:
> She can the neyther hynder nor auaunce.[31]

At this climactic moment in the poem, the whole argument falters because its ground has shifted. Fortune began the poem by inviting those who aspire to wealth and power to put their trust in her. More has forgotten that it was this misplaced trust, solicited by the dice game in *The Book of Fortune*, that was originally the object of his attack; instead, he now offers means of insulation against the buffeting effects of misfortune, a different matter altogether. His remedy amounts to an exhortation to play dead in case you get killed.

The third section in the Rastell edition, 'Thomas More to Them That Seke Fortune', reveals cracks not successfully papered over by More's commonplaces. The argument changes yet again: Fortune is not merely variable and inconstant, but also deliberately malicious:

> she kepeth euer in store,
> From euery manne some parcell of his wyll,
> That he may pray therfore and serue her styll.[32]

More's advice is correspondingly qualified:

> Then for asmuch as it is fortunes guyse,
> To graunt no manne all thyng that he wyll axe,
> But as her selfe lyst order and deuyse,
> Dothe euery manne his parte diuide and tax,
> I counsayle you eche one trusse vp your packes,
> And take no thyng at all, *or be content,*
> *with suche rewarde as fortune hath you sent.*[33]

Manifestly ambiguous and indecisive, the *Verses for the Book of Fortune* are potentially self-destructive because they are insincere. More could

[31] ibid., sig. Cviii.
[32] ibid., sig. Cviii[v].
[33] ibid. My italics.

not bring himself to acknowledge openly the real source of his anxiety, which was a fear that human experience lacked any intrinsic providential purpose capable of justifying the participation in it to which he felt drawn by instinct and propelled by his family.

One could infer this from the poem as it stands in the black-letter edition of 1557, but it emerges more forcefully in two stanzas which Rastell suppressed. Rastell was not beyond tampering with More's text in order to tone down sentiments too violently expressed, or inappropriate for the purposes of the Marian propagandists, as when he altered the wording of More's condemnation of the Nun of Kent in his letter to Cromwell.[34] For whatever reasons, Rastell omitted from the *Verses for the Book of Fortune* two stanzas that have been preserved in a separate edition of the poem published in 1538 by Robert Wyer, who beat Rastell to the press by 15 years:[35]

> Fortune, O mighty and varyable
> What rule thou claymest, with thy cruel power
> Good folke thou stroyest, and louest reprouable
> Thou mayst not waraunt thy giftes for one houre
> Fortune unworthy men setteth in honoure
> Thorowe fortune thinnocent in wo and sorow shricheth
> The iust man she spoyleth, and the uniust enrycheth.
>
> Yonge men she kylleth, and letteth olde men lyue
> Onryghtuously deuydynge, tyme and season
> That good men leseth, to wycked doth she gyue
> She hath no difference, but iudgeth all good reason
> Inconstaunce, slypper, frayle, and full of treason
> Neyther for euer cherysshynge, whom she taketh
> Nor for eure oppressynge, whom she forsaketh.

Finis. q. T.M.[36]

Included with More's verses, Wyer printed two analogous stanzas in French:

---

[34] On Rastell's partiality as editor, see McConica, 'The Recusant Reputation of Thomas More', *Essential Articles*, pp. 139–41.

[35] *Boke of the fayre Gentylwoman, that no man shulde put his truste, or confydence in: that is to say, Lady Fortune: flaterynge euery man that coueyeth to haue all, and specyally, them that truste in her, she deceyueth them at laste* (London, 1538). STC² 18078.5.

[36] *EW* 1931, I, p. 226.

Fortune peruersse
Qui le monde versse
Toust a ton desyre
Jamais tu nas cesse
Plaine de finesse
Et y prens pleasire

Par toy vennent moulx
Et guerres mortaulx
Touls inconueniens
Par mons et par vaulx
Et aulx hospitaulx
Meurent tant de gens.[37]

(Perverse Fortune, you turn the world upside down entirely at your whim; full of subtle wiles, you never cease, but take pleasure in it. Through you come mortal wars and sickness. In mountains, valleys, and hospitals, so many men meet unlooked-for death.)

The editors of the 1931 edition of More's English works thought that these stanzas must have been the originals from which More translated. There is, however, no evidence that More ever knew French, and even if he did, it is hard to see how his verses could ever have derived from the French ones, for the similarity is only coincidental. More's stanzas are, in fact, a very close rendering of a pseudo-Virgilian epigram out of the *Anthologia latina,* printed by Sebastian Brant in 1502:

O Fortuna potens, ac nimium levis,
Tantum juris atrox quae tibi vindicas,
Evertisque bonos, erigis inprobos.
Nec servare potes muneribus fidem.
Fortuna immeritos auget honoribus.
Fortuna innocuos cladibus adficit.
Justos illa viros pauperie gravat.
Indignos eadem divitiis beat.
Haec aufert juvenes, et retinet senes,
Injusto arbitrio tempora dividens.

[37] ibid., pp. 224–7.

Quod dignis adimit, transit ad impios.
Nec discrimen habet, rectave judicat.
Inconstans, fragilis, perfida, lubrica.
Nec quos clarificat, perpetuo fovet:
Nec quos deseruit, perpetuo premit.[38]

Not knowing of this Latin original, but recognizing the common topos of More's stanzas, Wyer must have included the French analogue for the sake of edifying copiousness.

The striking thing revealed by a comparison of More's imitation with the Latin epigram is how much more deeply felt More's translation is than the original: his antitheses are more pointed, his verbs more active, and his diction more heightened, all of which serves to register a stronger sense of injustice and convey a deeper sense of outrage. The relatively bland 'Fortuna innocuos cladibus adficit', for example, becomes the much more powerfully affective 'Thorowe fortune thinnocent in wo and sorow shricheth', in which the doublet, the alliteration, and the onomatopoeia, underlined by a more potent rhythm, work together to paint a vivid image of human suffering not unlike that which More would later bestow on his souls suffering in purgatory in the *Supplication of Souls*. The adaptation is so loaded with tragic intensity that it grows, in effect, into a complaint against providence. If the *Nine Pageants* express frustration at the futility of earthy endeavour, the *Rueful Lamentation* pity at the human suffering enforced by mutability, the *Verses for the Book of Fortune* convey More's near-despair that the human situation should be so. He is at once indignant and dismayed. Fortuna was a convenient personification to level at, but the real, unacknowledged target was elsewhere.

The possibility that More may have undergone some severe spiritual crisis during the years when he wrote these English poems is supported by a letter he wrote to John Colet, his spiritual advisor, on 23 October 1504.[39] Describing how he had met Colet's servant, More declares his sadness that Colet himself has not yet returned to

---

[38] Printed by Hubertus Schulte Herbrüggen, 'Sir Thomas Mores Fortuna-Verse: Ein Beitrag zur Lösung einiger Probleme', in *Lebende Antike: Symposium für Rudolf Sühnel*, ed. Horst Meller and Hans-Joachim Zimmermann (n.p., 1967), p. 166. Herbrüggen demonstrates conclusively the relation between the Latin epigram and More's stanzas (ibid., pp. 155–72).

[39] Rogers, *Correspondence*, no. 3; on More as Colet's disciple, see James K. McConica, *English Humanists and Reformation Politics* (Oxford, 1963, pp. 46–51).

London, for his absence leaves him destitute: 'By following your footsteps I had escaped almost from the very gates of hell, and now, driven by some force and necessity, I am falling back again into gruesome darkness. I am like Eurydice, except that she was lost because Orpheus looked back at her, but I am sinking because you do not look back at me'[40] ('Et qui tua nuper vestigia sequutus iam pene ex ipsis orci faucibus emerseram, nunc rursum tamquam Euridice (contraria tamen lege; Euridice quidem quod illam respexit Orpheus, ego vero quia tu me non respicis) in obscuras retro caligines nescio qua vi ac necessitate relabor').[41]

These lines have not been adequately explained. It is not enough to account for them merely as excessive humanist flattery, or as alluding to Colet's advice that More should marry rather than enter the priesthood (that can hardly have been 'the very gates of hell' or 'gruesome darkness'·in More's mind).[42] From the rest of the letter it is clear that More thought the city was a dangerous place, with all its temptations devoted to the service of the world, the flesh and the devil; but what did he really think Colet's example had saved him from in the past, and might save him from again? Surrender to illicit voluptuous delights is possible, but hardly likely, given More's rigid self-discipline; Colet's influence was far more subtle and profound than that. Any attempt to find the answer is necessarily speculative, but several pieces of evidence provide a tangible cue.

One can retrace what it may have been by looking at Colet's neglected pamphlet, *A Ryght Fruitfull Monicion Concernynge the Order of a Good Christen Mannes Lyfe*, printed by Johan Byddell in March 1534.[43] This tract is so close to More's own later thought that it might have been made by him; possibly Colet wrote it for him, or at least with him in mind. How far More had diverged in 1503–4 from the order of life Colet urges can be seen in the contrast between Colet's piece and More's *Verses for the Book of Fortune*.

Colet begins by urging that a man know himself, purge himself of

[40] Rogers, *SL*, p. 4.

[41] Rogers, *Correspondence*, pp. 6/11–7/21.

[42] J. H. Lupton thought they were simply the product of excessive humanist flattery (*A Life of John Colet* (London, 1909), p. 145); Guy suggests that More is referring to his decision to marry (*The Public Career of Sir Thomas More*, pp. 4–5).

[43] The whole treatise is reprinted in Lupton, *A Life of John Colet*, Appendix D, pp. 303–10.

pride, and acknowledge the bountiful gifts he receives from God in this world:

> Remember fyrst of all, vertuous reder, that it is hygh wyse-
> dome and great perfection to knowe thy selfe, and than to dispise
> thyselfe; as, to know thou haste nothing that is good of thy selfe,
> but all together of God. For the gyftes of nature, and all other
> temporall gyftes of this worlde, which ben laufully and truely
> opteyned, well consydered, ben comen to the by the infinite
> goodness and grace of God.[44]

Here is a view of temporal things which More seems to have rejected in the English poems. Being concerned to avoid all temporal gifts as a means of standing in greater surety against the vicissitudes of fortune, More had urged repudiation of the lot in favour of a life of poverty. He thus missed Colet's central point: that temporal things are a gift from God to be used for good, so long as men do not presume to believe that they possess them of their own right. Lacking that first premise, More had no grasp on Colet's next, more important one: 'And most in especiall it is necessarye for the to knowe howe that God of his greatte grace hath made the lyke to his owne similitude or ymage, hauynge regarde to thy memory, vnderstandyng, and fre wyll.'[45] Because of this, Colet continues, human experience involves trial and assay, choice, and a most energetic commitment of all the faculties to an effort to shape the different facets of a man's life into right order and proportion:

> [it is necessary] to consyder and to knowe the goodly order
> which God of his infynyte wysdome hath ordeyned the to be
> ordred by, – as, to haue these temporall goodes for the necessytie
> of the bodye, the body and sensuall appetytes to be ordred by thy
> soule, thy soule to be ordred by reason and grace, by reason and
> grace to know thy duetie to God and to thy neighbour.[46]

More appears in 1503 to have been unable feelingly to know any of these, and in spite of his versified didactic exhortations, one senses

---

[44] ibid., p. 305.
[45] ibid.
[46] ibid., p. 306.

that he probably knew it. If, in earlier days, Colet had shown More how to avoid sensual intemperance, he now needed to teach him how to avoid the spiritual intemperance of excessive *contemptus mundi*. In his letter to Colet, More's use of the Eurydice figure almost suggests that there had been a degree of coolness and distance on Colet's side. Perhaps the older man had detected the manichean undertones in More's spirituality, and had withdrawn his assent from them. Certainly, he cannot have helped feeling disturbed by his young apostle's exaggerated fear of the world he wished to join.

This interpretation of More's letter of 23 October 1504 is supported by the evidence of the severe rebuke that he himself later administered to the hapless John Batmanson on the occasion of the latter's attack on Erasmus' edition of the Greek New Testament. In his *Letter to a Monk* of 1519–20 answering Batmanson's charges, More caustically asks Batmanson, perhaps with a degree of transference, to consider whether his motives for taking holy orders had been valid, 'or whether you only lightly examined your motives *and thought you were fleeing into a holy retreat and withdrawing from dangerous pleasures . . . to gain* the luxury of idleness and *a shelter from troubles*'.[47] The sting in More's fillip comes, as in the case of his later harping on Luther's marriage, in the controversies, from his resentment at the prospect of another enjoying the priesthood while indulging attitudes and inclinations that, in his own case, had barred him from it. One senses that he saw in the young monk what he himself might have been had not Colet and his own conscience turned him around to face into the world, rather than away from it.

Although there is a lot of the quintessential More in the three English poems already discussed, they contain nothing of the More most remember best; fortunately, *A Merry Jest, How a Sergeant Would Learn to Play the Friar* does. It expresses the mirthful side of More which, however much he may have mistrusted it, ultimately saved him from being a forgettable misanthrope.

A Merry Jest is an imitation Chaucerian fabliau describing the downfall of a sergeant-at-law who presumed to disguise himself as an Augustinian friar so as to arrest a bankrupt merchant miser. Like Chaucer's *Summoner's Tale*, it hinges on dramatic irony; the sick

[47] Rogers, *SL,* no. 26, p. 140. My italics.

merchant admits the disguised friar–sergeant out of greed for the
advantage he thinks the latter can bring him:

> Downe went the mayd,
> The marchaunt sayd,
>   Now say on gentle frere,
> Of thys tydyng,
> That ye me bryng,
>   I long full sore to here.[48]

Similarly, it is the fact of the sergeant's clerical disguise that makes
him liable to experience the fierce beating he receives. In typical
fabliau fashion the tale ends with a crescendo of fast-moving, noisy,
knockabout farce:

> And with his fist,
> Upon the lyst,
>   He gaue hym such a blow,
> That backward downe,
> Almost in sowne,
>   The frere is ouerthrow.
> Yet was this man,
> Well fearder than,
>   Lest he the frere had slayne,
> Tyll with good rappes
> And heuy clappes,
>   He dawde hym vp agayne.
> The frere toke harte,
> And vp he starte,
>   And well he layde about,
> And so there goth,
> Betwene them both,
>   Many a lusty cloute.
> They rent and tere,
> Eche others here,
>   And claue togyder fast,
> Tyll with luggyng,

---

48 *EW* 1557, sig. Cii G–H.

> And with tuggyng,
>   They fell downe bothe at last.
> Than on the grounde,
> Togyder rounde,
>   With many a sadde stroke,
> They roll and rumble,
> They turne and tumble,
>   As pygges do in a poke.[49]

Such passages as this appeal directly through the five senses to belly laughter for its own sake. As late as *A Dialogue of Comfort against Tribulation*, More could still, through the person of Antony, express discomfort at the existence of this penchant for comedy:

> my selfe am of nature euen halfe a gigglot and more. I would I could as easily mende my faulte as I well knowe it, but scante canne I restraine it as olde a foole as I am: howbeit so parcial wil I not be to my fault as to praise it.[50]

And three of the petitions he wrote in the margins of his prayerbook while in the Tower were:

> To abstaine from vaine confabulacions.
> To eschewe light foolishe mirthe and gladnes.
> Recreacions not necessary to cut of.[51]

Apparently the mirthful aspect of More's character was not entirely under his control; it is interesting, therefore, that both his mirth and his melancholy have the same object: *A Merry Jest* plays yet another variation on the theme of the other English poems – men should stick with what they already have, aspire to no more, otherwise they will 'Beshrewe themselfe at last.'[52] The sergeant's real fault is not the ostensible one, that he is meddling in a role outside his competence, but that he is a victim of pride. He changes roles out of exaggerated

[49] ibid., sig. Cii[v] A–C.
[50] ibid., p. 1171 C–D.
[51] ibid., p. 1417 B.
[52] ibid., sig. Ci F.

self-esteem and ambition to succeed in arresting the delinquent
merchant where others have failed:

> Yet in a glasse,
> Or he would passe,
>   He toted and he peered,
> His harte for pryde,
> Lepte in his syde,
>   To see how well he freered.[53]

This pride leads him to perpetrate a gross perversion of the spiritual
office of a friar; hence his chastisement is as befitting as it is severe.
   Part of the irony of *A Merry Jest* has almost been lost to us. That it
was an occasional poem is clear from the ending:

> In any wyse,
> I would auyse,
>   And counsayle euery man,
> His owne craft vse,
> All newe refuse,
>   And lyghtly let them gone:
> Play not the frere,
> Now make good chere,
>   And welcome euery chone.[54]

The poem was written to entertain guests and initiate a feast, but
which one? Reed and Chambers suggest the Sergeants' feast of
13 November 1503, but internal evidence suggests one of the feasts of
the 12 livery companies of London is more probable.[55] Alison
Hanham is surely right when she proposes that *A Merry Jest* was
written for, and delivered at, the occasion when More was made an
honorary mercer.[56] If that were so, the whole poem was conceived to
be ironically self-referential at both the public and private levels:

---

[53] ibid., sig. Cii A–B.
[54] ibid., sig. Cii^v G–H.
[55] See Willow, pp. 21–2.
[56] 'Fact of Fantasy: Thomas More as Historian', in *Thomas More: The Rhetoric of
Character*, ed. A. G. Fox and Peter Leech (Dunedin, 1979), p. 66.

A man of lawe
That neuer sawe,
  The wayes to bye and sell,
Wenyng to ryse,
By marchaundise,
  I pray god spede hym well.[57]

At the public level, More is comically mocking his own elevation as a mercer; at a deeper, private, symbolic level, he is subjecting his own inclinations to ironic scrutiny, just as he would later do in translating the *Life of John Picus*. The moral is the same as in the other poems: do not aspire through pride; but in his mood of levity, More invites his audience to laugh with him at his manifest unwillingness to take his own advice.

That unwillingness was precisely the cause of the underlying perturbation and uncertainty of the other English poems. In *A Merry Jest* More shows himself as capable of viewing things from a comic perspective as from a tragic one. This sprang partly from a different aspect of his personality, but also partly reflected the influence of an audience. The public More, as the historical record attests, always tended to project himself through a comic persona, in contrast with that of More in private meditation.[58] Young More seems to have had two images of himself and the world, a tragic and a comic one; only when he found a way of superimposing the one upon the other, without excluding or suppressing either, was he able to achieve a central, truly human point of view. That was not to be for a while yet.

Interpretation of More's *Life of John Picus, Erle of Myrandula*, a translation of the *Vita Pici* by his nephew, Giovanni Francesco, is one of the most vexed questions of More scholarship. Whichever way one looks at it, the work is a very ambiguous piece indeed, being rendered so not only by its intrinsic matter, but also by its context in More's life.

---

[57] *EW* 1557, sig. Ci C–D.

[58] Only the Elizabethan dramatists who wrote the play, *Sir Thomas More*, publicly acknowledged the melancholic aspect of More's personality, notably in the long speech beginning 'Now will I speak like More in melancholy. . . .' (*The Book of Sir Thomas More*, ed. W. W. Greg (London, 1911), Addition I. pp. 1ff.).

According to the family tradition recorded by Cresacre More, about the time of More's marriage he 'propounded to himself, as a pattern of life, a singular lay-man, John Picus, Earl of Mirandula', which would suggest that More translated the *Vita Pici* once he had decided not to become a priest.[59] Given that he was in the Charterhouse for four years from 1500–1 and married in late 1504 (his daughter Margaret was born in September 1505), the *Life of John Picus* was probably written sometime in 1504, soon after More had completed his *Rueful Lamentation* and *Verses for the Book of Fortune*. As the preface makes clear, it was presented subsequently as a New Year's gift to Joyce Lee, who had recently taken the veil in the convent of Poor Clares near London;[60] New Year 1505 would therefore seem the most feasible date.[61]

If this date is accepted, the *Life of John Picus* is surrounded by contextual ironies, being presented to a nun ostensibly in praise of the cloister by a man who had just decided to come out of it. Indeed, it has recently been asserted that More must have translated the work before 1504, on the grounds that its apparent praise of the religious life is not consistent with his decision not to join it.[62]

One should not, however, be distracted by problems of dating into the false assumption that the work's interpretation depends entirely on its date. Many of the ironies are intrinsic as well as extrinsic; for example, it holds up as an ideal model of 'temperance in prosperitie', 'pacience in aduersitie', and 'the dispising of wordly vanitie', a man depicted in purgatory 'all compassed in fire . . . punished for his negligence, and his vnkindenesse' is not heeding the 'priuey inspiracion' by which he was 'called of god vnto religion'.[63] As with Giovanni Francesco's original, More's *Life of John Picus* focuses upon the unresolved tensions and paradoxes in Pico's life rather than any supposed solution of them.

It is important to acknowledge from the outset that the *Life of John Picus* is a translation, and a close one at that.[64] This makes it difficult

[59] See Chambers, p. 92.

[60] *EW* 1557, p. 1 C–F.

[61] See Germain Marc'hadour, *L'Univers de Thomas More: Chronologie critique de More, Erasme, et leur époque, 1477–1536* (Paris, 1963), p. 135.

[62] Reynolds, *The Field is Won*, pp. 44–5.

[63] *EW* 1557, pp. 1 E–F, 9 E–10 D.

[64] The Latin and English texts are conveniently printed in parallel by Max Kullnick, 'Th. Morus, Picus Erle of Mirandula', *Archiv für das Studium der neueren Sprachen und Literaturen*, 121 (1908), pp. 47–75, 316–40, and 122 (1909), pp. 27–50.

to determine precisely the full extent of More's awareness of the ironies in his undertaking, but not impossible. His omissions and additions suggest a conscious intent to bring into highlight those aspects of Pico's character and career that could serve to turn his biography into an instrument for the investigation and critical analysis of his own personal dilemma. In many of the historical 'facts' of Pico's life, for example, such as the intricacies of his genealogy and the precise details of his learning, he shows little or no interest.[65] His concern is with Pico's 'connyng and vertue', as the preface implies,[66] in such a way as to juxtapose his *eruditio* and *pietas*, his worldliness and spirituality.[67] By foreshortening the *Vita*, he was able more forcefully to emphasize what had been already implicit in Giovanni Francesco's *Vita*: that Pico's embodiment of both had been fraught with problems.

It was precisely because he recognized this, one feels, that More became interested in the *Vita* in the first place. Some (like Joyce Lee) would, he knew, respond to the pious ideal intimated in the work, and he himself, no doubt, felt a powerful nostalgia for it; but he was equally aware of paradoxes in Pico's life that reflected his own dilemma in trying either to reconcile or choose between his conflicting aspirations. As his later works show, More was in the habit of counterpointing a superficial meaning with a second one not quite in harmony with the first. To such as himself, Pico's life was as much a cautionary exemplum as an edifying one. On one hand Pico exemplified the moral danger inherent in seeking success in the world of learning, as one of More's self-fabricated additions to the Latin text makes clear. At the point where he recounts Pico's narrow escape from charges of heresy when he presented his 900 questions at Rome More concludes:

Lo, this ende had Picus of his hye mynde and proud purpose: that where he thought to haue gotten perpetuall praise: there had he muche worke to kepe him self vpright: that he ranne not in perpetuall infamy and sclaundre.[68]

---

[65] For a full catalogue of More's omissions and additions, see Kullnick, pp. 51–2; see also Stanford E. Lehmberg, 'Sir Thomas More's Life of Pico della Mirandola', *Studies in the Renaissance*, 3 (1956), pp. 61–74.

[66] *EW* 1557, p. 1 E.

[67] See Heinz Holeczek, *Humanistiche Bibelphilologie als Reformproblem bei Erasmus von Rotterdam, Thomas More und William Tyndale* (Leiden, 1975), pp. 35–7.

[68] *EW* 1557, p. 4 C; cf. Kullnick, p. 62, and Holeczek, p. 36.

On the other hand Pico also exemplified the danger of falling into spiritual negligence in failing to fulfil the vocation to which he was called. Echoing Savonarola's critical judgement, More writes:

> he purposed oftentymes to obey this inspiracion, and folow his calling. How be it, not being kind enough for so great benefices of God: or called back by the tendrenes of his flesh (as he was a man of delicate complexion) he shrank from the labour.[69]

Rather than a comfortable synthesis of pious and worldly endeavours, religion and humanism, More saw in Pico the tribulatory conflicts to which, at the very time he was translating the *Vita*, he knew himself subject.

It is, in effect, easy to see what attracted More to Pico. The young Pico was an image of one side of himself: the humanist prodigy. Once Pico had begun to study the humanities, he was 'accompted amonge the chiefe oratours and poetes of that time, in lernyng merueilously swifte'.[70] Turning his attention to canon law, Pico, just as More had made the divines marvel at his precocity in lecturing on *De civitate Dei*, 'compiled a breuiary or a summe vpon all the decretals, in which as briefly as possible was, he comprised theffect of all that whole great volume, and made a boke, no sclender thyng to right conning and parfite doctours'.[71] Succumbing to the way of all flesh, however, Pico grew 'ful of pride, and desirous of glorie and mannes praise',[72] the very things More is so obsessively determined to denounce in his own English poems. This lust to gain 'perpetuall praise' took him to Rome, where he challenged all oncomers to defeat him in disputation over the infamous 900 arcane questions. Once he found that his 'hye mynde and proud purpose' had landed him merely a charge of heresy, even though he defended himself successfully against it, he was left filled with a sense of the error of his ways.[73]

Then came the spectacular conversion, after which Pico started to manifest the symptoms of More's own Charterhouse spirituality. Pico, we learn, had been 'kindled in vaine loue, and holden in voluptuouse use of women' before this, and, indeed, 'was somwhat fallen in to

[69] *EW* 1557, p. 9 G.
[70] ibid., p. 2 H.
[71] ibid., p. 3 B–C.
[72] ibid., p. 3 D.
[73] ibid., pp. 3 D–4 D.

wantonnesse', owing to 'the comelynes of his body, with the louely fauoure of his visage', among other, more cerebral attributes. Suddenly, seeing the mortal danger he was in, Pico burnt 'fyue bokes, that in his youth of wanton verses of loue, with other like fantasies he had made in his vulgare tonge', and applied himself instead 'most feruently to the studies of scripture'. 'Womens blandimentes he chaunged in to the desire of heauenly ioyes',[74] and, having rid himself of all the distraction of 'his patrimonie and dominions, that is to say: the third part of therldome of Mirandula, and of Concordia' (except that he still kept 'of the olde plentie in deintie viande and siluer vessell'), he secretly 'bet and scourged his own flesh . . . for clensing of his olde offences'.[75] Now, having 'gotten aboue fortune', Pico refused wordly promotion in the king's court so that he might 'the more quietly geue him self to studie, and the seruice of god'.[76] Needless to say, 'wedding and wordly busines, he fled almost alike'.[77]

Pico's life was clearly a mirror for More in which he saw both sides of himself: worldly ambition resulting from precocity, together with a proclivity towards 'wantonness', and an otherwordly recoil from it under the pressure of intense spirituality. As the same time as it intimated the ideal towards which More aspired, it also, however, revealed to him the reasons why he should *not* join the priesthood: to imitate Pico would in his case probably mean imitating his weakness also in failing to live up to the priestly ideal. The idea that More uncritically accepted Pico as the ideal pattern for his own life is far too simple. Giovanni Francesco was not uncritical of his uncle, and More chose to reproduce his criticisms:

> Liberalitee only in him passed measure: for so farre was he from the geuyng of any diligence to erthly thinges, that he semed somwhat besprent with the frekell of negligence. His frendes oftentimes admonished him, that he sholde not all vtterly despise richesse, shewing him, that it was his dishonestie and rebuke, when it was reported (were it trew or false) that his negligence, and setting nought by money, gaue his seruauntes occasion of disceit and robberie.[78]

---

[74] ibid., pp. 4 D, 4 H, 4 E.
[75] ibid., pp. 6 A–B, 6 B–C and 6 E.
[76] ibid., pp. 6 G–H, 6 H–7 A.
[77] ibid., p. 8 B.
[78] ibid., p. 7 E–F.

This passage implies gently that Pico was spiritually irresponsible in the extremity of his contempt for earthly goods (in a way that would have horrified Colet) and in his failure to take adequate care of those nearest to him: 'that mynde of his (which euer more on high cleued fast in contemplacion, and in thenserching of natures counseill) could neuer let down it selfe to the consideracion and ouerseyng of these base, abiecte, and vile erthly trifles'.[79] More had no occasion to explore this matter fully in his translation, but he revived it as an issue in book 1 of *Utopia*, where Raphael Hythlodaeus' Pico-esque irresponsibility concerning family ties and material possessions is certainly subjected to ironic scrutiny. The translation of the *Life of John Picus* is nevertheless seasoned with such a flavour as makes it susceptible to an ironic reading, and at least one of More's own notable descendants read it that way. Referring to More's *Life of John Picus* in his *Essays in Divinity*, John Donne saw Pico depicted in it as 'a man of an incontinent wit, and subject to the concupiscence of inaccessible knowledges and transcendencies'.[80] Donne turns a mere hint into an unequivocal statement, but not without some degree of assent from More's own silent ambiguity.

If it is impossible to read the *Life of John Picus* as More's uncritically accepted blueprint for his own life, it is equally impossible to see it as consistently, or even pervasively, undercut through irony. More admired Pico's spirituality, and wanted to be like Pico, even though he knew he would not be able to, and that Pico himself had not been able to. Even though Pico 'in the inward affectes of the mynde . . . cleued to god with very feruent loue, and deuocion', nevertheless 'sometime that meruelouse alacritee languished, and almost fell: and eft agayn with great strength rose vp in to god'.[81] In a fit of burning fervour, Pico confessed to his nephew his secret aspiration: 'fensyng my selfe with the crucifixe, bare fote walkyng about the worlde in euery town and castel, I purpose to preche of Christ'.[82] Afterwards, however, 'he chaunged that purpose', determining that he would 'professe him self in the order of freres prechours'.[83] But by the time of

---

[79] ibid., p. 7 F–G.

[80] *Essays in Divinity*, ed. Evelyn M. Simpson (Oxford, 1952), p. 13. Donne added parenthetically that Pico was 'happier in no one thing in this life, then in the Author which writ it to us' (ibid.).

[81] *EW* 1557, p. 8 D.

[82] ibid., p. 8 E.

[83] ibid.

his death, even though he had 'purposed oftentymes to obey this inspiracion, and folow his calling', nevertheless 'he shrank from the labour, or thinkyng happely that the religion had no neede of hym, differed it for a tyme'.[84] Pico, like More, really wanted to be a priest, but in spite of his most fervent aspirations, found that he remained a layman. More fully understood and sympathized with that tragic dilemma.

The *Life of John Picus* has two functions. As a present to Joyce Lee it celebrates the superiority of spirit over flesh, of being 'godly prosperous' over 'worldly fortunate',[85] and provides an exemplum of the supersession by spirituality of carnal vainglory and pride. As a private exercise, which, according to Stapleton, it essentially was,[86] it gave More an instrument through which he could simultaneously find a justification for himself, administer a reproof to himself, and depict the tensions, contradictions, ironies and paradoxes involved in the decisions he had recently made and the circumstances he was currently in. This second function signals the emergence of the quintessential More, although not yet fully formed or fledged. More would soon discover a mode of literary representation capable of capturing the full complexity of life, which his own experience was rapidly teaching him not to simplify or ignore. He would also discover in that complexity a meaning that was not dependent on the dualistic structures of thought upon which he had hitherto relied.

The material surrounding the actual *Life of John Picus*, Pico's three epistles, his exposition of Psalm 16, *Conserva me domine*, More's rhyme royal versifications of 'Twelve Rules of John Picus', 'The Twelve Weapons of Spiritual Battle', 'The Twelve Properties or Conditions of a Lover', and 'A Prayer of Picus Mirandula Unto God', show that More was nonetheless still dominated at this time by a rigidly dualistic cast of mind, in spite of his tacit acknowledgement of the ambiguities in his own personal situation. In his preface to Pico's letter of 15 October 1492 to Giovanni Francesco, More sounds a predictable manichean blast against 'the sensual affections of the flesh', which 'make vs dronke in the cuppes of Circes, and misshap vs in to the likenes and figure of brute bestes',[87] while he clearly approves

---

[84] ibid., p. 9 F–H.
[85] ibid., p. 1 D.
[86] See Willow, p. 216.
[87] *EW* 1557, pp. 10 G–11 B.

of Pico's own advice in the letter itself, which is to turn away from 'erthly thinges, slipper, vncertaine vile' to 'heuenly thinges, and godly'.[88] This spiritual withdrawal does not merely concern unlawful voluptuous pleasures: 'a perfite man shold abstain not only fro vnlawful pleasures, but also from lawful. To thend that he may altogether hole haue his mind into heauenward, and the more purely intend vnto the contemplacion of heauenly thynges.'[89] The effects of More's radical segregation of the physical and spiritual, the material world and the transcendent, can be seen in the three main sets of rhyme royal stanzas. 'The Twelve Properties or Conditions of a Lover' is a *contrafactum*, or divine parody, in which all the aspects of a carnal lover are translated into their sanctified, spiritualized alternatives; for example:

THE .X. PROPERTEE.

The louer is of colour dead and pale,
There will no slepe in to his eyes stalke,
He sauoureth neither meate, wine, nor ale,
He mindeth not, what menne about him talke,
But eate he, drinke he, sitte, lye downe or walke,
He burneth euer as it were with a fire
In the feruent heate of his desire.

Here shoulde the louer of god ensaumple take
To haue him continually in remembraunce,
With him in prayer and meditacion wake,
Whyle other playe, reuil, sing, and daunce,
None earthly ioye, disporte, or vayne pleasaunce
Should him delite, or any thyng remoue
His ardent minde from god his heauenly loue.[90]

More's assumption seems to be that flesh is flesh and spirit is spirit, and never the twain may meet. This governs his whole conception of what spiritual warfare involves in 'Twelve Rules of John Picus . . . Partly Exciting, Partly Directing a Man in Spiritual Battle'. These

---

[88] ibid., p. 11 G–H.
[89] ibid., p. 19 E: Pico's exposition of the words 'Non congregabo conventiculum eorum de sanguinibus, nec memorero nominum eorum' (Psalm 16).
[90] ibid., p. 31 B–C.

verses are written in such appalling doggerel that it is kinder not to quote them; suffice it to say that successful strife consists of a threefold strategy: 'the resistence of any sinfull mocion, / Against any of thy sensuall wittes fiue',[91] the fixing in one's mind of images of the crucified Christ,[92] and the eschewing of all occasions for sin, 'For he that loueth peril shall perishe therein.'[93] Nothing could be further removed from More's later understanding of what the imitation of Christ meant than the facile treatment of this poem. Because he had not yet grasped the concept that all things are not intrinsically bad, but yield themselves either to good use or abuse, he could not conceive of human experience as being dynamically militant. He still regarded the world as a place to be stoically endured, rather than as actively instrumental to regeneration through its very imperfections. Neither history nor providence had yet begun to have any significant meaning for him.

Critics have been perplexed by More's attraction to Lucian, 'the flippant critic of all religion'.[94] That More enjoyed 'the humor, shrewd wit, fancy, and plain common sense' in Lucian is true enough,[95] but the real reasons behind the translations of 1505–6 were far more complex. His encounter with Lucian was absolutely crucial to the development of his mature vision, and its literary and philosophical consequences were long lasting.

Occurring very soon after More left the Charterhouse, his involvement with Lucian was as opportune as it was natural. His expertise in Greek had just reached the point of enabling him to translate Lucian, his own sense of the comic drew him personally to him, and Erasmus paid his second visit to England in 1505, ready and willing to join in a venture to turn some of Lucian's dialogues into Latin[96] – a happy convergence of circumstances that coincided with More's decision to face back into the world instead of away from it. More was ripe for Lucian, who was the ideal author for providing him with new means for forging a *modus vivendi* less exclusive than the one he had been

---

[91] ibid., p. 21 D.
[92] ibid., pp. 21 D–22 D.
[93] ibid., p. 23 D.
[94] See Craig R. Thompson, *CW* 3, Part I, pp. xxii–xxiii.
[95] ibid., p. xxiii.
[96] ibid., pp. xxvii–xxviii.

contemplating; these means included a form of dialogue that dramatized ambiguity as a function of meaning, a demonstration that all
aspects of human experience could be comprehended within an ironic
view of life, and an active response that was non-despairing, even
though it originated in a view of things as sceptical as More's own.

The dedicatory letter to Thomas Ruthall furnishes the nearest thing
we have to More's apology for Lucian, but it is a deceptive document
which needs to be approached with caution. As a piece of literary
criticism it has received high praise.[97] Without wishing to lessen its
importance in the history of literary theory, I would nevertheless
suggest that it shows More to have been provocatively disingenuous.
A piece of propaganda pleading, it is aimed at securing Lucian
admission to pious society, if only through the didactic back door.
Lucian, More implies, was really a moral preacher: 'Refraining from
the arrogant pronouncements of the philosophers as well as from the
wanton wiles of the poets, he everywhere reprimands and censures,
with very honest and at the same time very entertaining wit, our
human frailties' ('Qui et superciliosis abstinens Philosophorum
praeceptis, et solutioribus Poetarum lusibus, honestissimis simul et
facetissimis salibus, uitia ubique notat atque insectatur mortalium').[98]
Because he was so clever, More continues, Lucian got away with
administering a stronger dose of moral reproof than is usually
achieved, and thus he 'fulfilled the Horatian maxim and combined
delight with instruction' ('Horatianum praeceptum impleuerit, uolup-
tatemque cum utilitate coniunxerit').[99]

Probably More was being sincere when he asserted that the function of Lucian's fiction was to sugar-coat a didactic pill, but he was
not telling the whole truth as to why he had become intrigued with it;
nor, in the contemporary context, could he, without causing offence or
being misunderstood. Just how deliberately elusive he was can be
judged by his comments on two of the three dialogues he chose for
translation: *Cynicus* and *Menippus siue Necromantia*.

He defended his choice of the *Cynicus* on the grounds that St John
Chrysostom had also approved it, having introduced a large part of it
into a homily on the Gospel of St John, and not without reason:

---

[97] H. A. Mason, *Humanism and Poetry in the Early Tudor Period* (London, 1959), p. 66ff.
[98] *CW* 3, I, pp. 3/7–10, 2/7–10.
[99] ibid., pp. 2/5–6, 3/5–6.

For what should have pleased that grave and truly Christian man more than this dialogue in which, while the severe life of Cynics, satisfied with little, is defended and the soft, enervating luxury of voluptuaries denounced, by the same token Christian simplicity, temperance, and frugality, and finally that strait and narrow path which leads to Life eternal, are praised?

(Quid enim placere magis uiro graui, uereque Christiano debuit, quam is dialogus, in quo dum aspera, paruoque contenta Cynicorum uita defenditur, mollis, atque eneruata delicatorum hominum luxuria reprehenditur? Nec non eadem opera, Christianae uitae simplicitas, temperantia, frugalitas, denique arcta illa atque angusta uia, quae ducit ad uitam, laudatur.)[100]

The *Cynicus* could indeed be read in this way, as a pagan version of the *Life of John Picus,* by pious Christian–humanist moralists seeking to find such reassurance in it, but More's own revival in *Utopia* of the main concern of the dialogue – whether it is better to live a life of self-denial or to enjoy the gifts of nature – proves that he knew Lucian's piece was infinitely more subtle in its working than that.

His comments on the next dialogue, *Menippus,* are even more obviously a red herring: 'felicitous in content – how wittily it rebukes the jugglery of magicians or the silly fictions of poets or the fruitless contentions of philosophers among themselves on any question whatever' ('materia . . . felicissima, quam salse taxat, uel Magorum praestigias, uel inania Poetarum figmenta, uel incertas quauis de re philosophorum inter se digladiationes').[101] This remark so violently distracts the reader from the real matter of the dialogue – the apparent absurdity of the human situation and human pretensions, and how one is to act in the face of them – that the attention of anyone who had actually read the work is redirected back towards the central issues. More had his tongue in cheek when he addressed Ruthall, for one of the inane figments of the poetic imagination he purloined from *Menippus* was the idea that life is like a play – the very keystone of More's subsequent philosophy and *modus vivendi.* As with the *Life of John Picus,* More seems to have been aware of two separate, not necessarily complementary, functions in the material he was present-

---

[100] ibid., pp. 3/33–5/6, 3/29–4/6.
[101] ibid., pp. 5/8–11, 4/7–10.

ing: one public, the other predominantly private and personal. The private function of the Lucianic translations can be inferred by examining their intrinsic matter and manner in the context of More's evolving career.

In the period of the English poems, or when he was in the Charterhouse, More would have read the *Cynicus* simply as a praise of temperance and the avoidance of worldly pleasures. Such is the entirely harmless interpretation he invites the reader to accept in the Letter to Ruthall. But More himself had just come *out* of the Charterhouse, having decided to reject the life of a cynic, and to wed instead. There is thus a degree of contextual irony surrounding his translation of the *Cynicus*, just as there was surrounding the *Life of John Picus*. Christianize the Cynic and he easily resembles the later Pico; Christianize the questioner, Lycinus, and he suggests the post-Charterhouse More. The dialogue becomes a subtle instrument of self-assessment and analysis of alternative lifestyles. While More had a genuine admiration for the ascetic life, and never rid himself of a yearning for it, he could see that it was not the only, nor necessarily the best, path through life, as strait and heaven-bent as it might indubitably be. He chose the *Cynicus* to translate because he saw that it dramatized the very difficulty involved in deciding whether to be holy or wise: his own personal dilemma.

The fact a simple didactic interpretation must necessarily ignore is Lucian's irony, which is far more subtle than most critics have allowed,[102] comprising 'the irony of complexity' as well as mere verbal dexterity.[103] The conditioning central irony of the *Cynicus* is that although Lucian allows the Cynic to appear to win his case, the fiction works to discredit him, even if it does not justify Lycinus, his critic. The Cynic is rationally right, but wrong nonetheless, for our sympathy is manipulated to remain with the perplexed Lycinus. This is brought about largely through the deflatingly comic characterization of the Cynic. His appearance creates an absurd visual image: 'Cultus ergo meus huiusmodi est, squalidum esse, hirsutum esse, tritum pallium indui, comam producere, ac sine calceis ingredi' ('my dress is, as you see, a dirty shaggy skin, a worn cloak, long hair and bare

---

[102] For example, Leonard Dean, 'Literary Problems in More's Richard III', *Essential Articles*, p. 318.
[103] I use Leonard Dean's definition, ibid., pp. 319–20.

feet').[104] This picture, which provoked Lycinus' sceptical query in the first place, is made more comic by the entirely facetious ending, where the Cynic invites his interlocutor to peruse statues of the gods for proof that his impoverished state is best: 'And I'd have you know that my style of dress becomes not only good men but also gods, though you go on to mock it; and so consider the statues of the gods. Do you think they are like you or me?' ('At ut cultum hunc intelligas, non bonos modo uiros, sed ipsos etiam deos decere, atque eum deinde, si libet, irrideas deorum statuas consydera, utri uideantur uobis ne, an mihi similiores').[105] Humour also derives from the sophistical nature of the Cynic's argument; his logic is not refuted, but it remains wilfully tangential to the real issue. He misses the point, that what he is arguing for is not temperance, as he claims, but abstinence, as when he proves that physically he is no worse off than other men by using the example of his bare feet:

CYNIC: What is the function of feet?
LYCINUS: To walk.
CYNIC: Then, do you think my feet walk worse than the feet of the average man?
LYCINUS: In this case perhaps the answer is no.
CYNIC: Then neither are they in worse condition, if they fulfil their function no worse.
LYCINUS: Perhaps so.
CYNIC: Then, as far as feet are concerned, I seem to be in no worse condition than the average man?
LYCINUS: So it seems.[106]

The tone of this exchange moves the reader to smile at the Cynic's success in getting away with more than a more experienced opponent than the young Lycinus might ordinarily let him. Rather than approving uncritically the Cynic's viewpoint, Lucian has created a

---

[104] *CW* 3, I, pp. 21/16–18, 116. More later invoked the cynic as an object of ridicule in *De Tristitia Christi*, in declaring that John the Evangelist could not have been the young man who ran away naked at the capture of Christ: 'Christi enim fuit non cynicae sectae discipulus' – 'for he was a disciple of Christ, not of the cynic sect' (*CW* 14, p. 573/2).
[105] *CW* 3, I, pp. 168, 23/26–9.
[106] ibid., p. 161.

self-characterizing dramatic character whose mode of justification
emanates from his wilful determination to be justified. Ironically, the
Cynic grows increasingly intemperate as he argues for temperance,
progressively losing self-control until he has silenced Lycinus altogether with his invective and monopolizes the stage – rather like his
later Portuguese descendant in book 1 of *Utopia*. Although Lucian
seems to have allowed the Cynic to win the argument, the latter's
manner of arguing shakes our confidence in the truth of the argument.
With our knowledge of More's biographical circumstances, we can
infer that he must have had a deep sympathy for the defeated Lycinus,
whose doubts and questions reflected his own at this time:

> CYNIC: How then, tell me, when all this is so, can you denounce
> and pour scorn on my way of life, and call it miserable?
> LYCINUS: Because, in heaven's name, although Nature, whom
> you hold in such honour, and the gods have given the earth for
> all to enjoy, and from it have provided us with many good
> things, so that we have abundance of everything to meet not
> only our needs but also our pleasures, nevertheless you share
> in few if any of all these things, and enjoy none of them any
> more than do the beasts. You drink water just as they do, you
> eat anything you find, as do the dogs, and your bed is no
> better than theirs. For straw is good enough for you just as it is
> for them. Moreover the coat you wear is no more respectable
> than that of a pauper. However, if you who are quite content
> with all this turn out to be of sound mind, god was wrong in
> the first place in making sheep to have fleeces, in the second
> place in making the vines to produce the sweetness of wine,
> and yet again in giving such wonderful variety to all else with
> which we are provided, our olive-oil, honey and the rest, so
> that we have foods of all sorts, and pleasant wine, money, a
> soft bed, beautiful houses, and everything else admirably set
> in order. For the products of the arts too are gifts of the gods,
> and to live deprived of all these is miserable.[107]

Between the two of them, the Cynic and Lycinus voice the two
contradictory impulses More himself felt. What he appreciated in
Lucian's dialogue was its lack of a simplified, definitive, arbitrary

[107] ibid., pp. 162–3.

norm. The Cynic wins the battle, but the war remains to be fought and won. The dialogue has worked to make one experience the rational and emotional tension involved in trying to ascertain the truth.

Even at this early stage in his career, certainly later when he wished *Utopia* and *Moriae encomium* could be burnt,[108] More probably realized that this kind of mimetic fiction could be potentially subversive; that is why in the Letter to Ruthall he offered a harmless didactic alternative reading. But there is one piece of evidence that suggests he wished to signpost the way to a more complex reading for anyone desiring to follow it: he changed the name of the Cynic's questioner from 'Lycinus' in the 1496 and 1503 Greek texts to 'Lucianus' – Lucian.[109] The effect is to reinforce our inclination to sympathize with the defeated questioner, because we associate his perplexity with that of the author himself – a strategy More would later adopt himself in his own *Utopia*. It is very hard, perhaps impossible, to define the norm of this work; its meaning exists in what it does as much as what it says, and what it does is to make the reader experience feelingly the problematic nature of the question. More saw an ironic structure of meaning in the *Cynicus* very like that into which he had placed the *Life of John Picus*, with the difference that in the dialogue it was intrinsically figured forth in the dramatization, whereas in the biography it had been largely extrinsic. His discovery of the intrinsic ironic mode was a breakthrough for More, because it reflected a recognition that contradictory impulses can be experienced simultaneously, and that such ambivalent experience is not necessarily a cause for dismay or despair. To experience the reality of both possibilities is better than to be bound narrowly or simple-mindedly within the confines of any single definitive alternative: that produces a cynicus on one hand, or a voluptuary on the other. Lucian taught More the need to allow himself a more inclusive human viewpoint, and to trust his own inclination not to try and unravel human experience into simplified absolutes.

Menippus siue Necromantia is placed strategically after the *Cynicus*, as if to provide a corrective comment on it, in case anyone had read it in the way More pretended to invite them to do. Menippus, another Cynic, is disillusioned with the inability of anyone to show him 'uitae

---

[108] *The Confutation of Tyndale's Answer*, *CW* 8, I, p. 179/8–17.
[109] *CW* 3, I, p. 141n.

. . . uiam aliquam simplicem ac certam' ('a plain, solid path in life').[110] At first he had been attracted to the gods, with their amours, assaults, lawsuits and incest, but was perplexed upon coming to age to find that 'hic leges rursus iubentes audio poetis apprime contraria, neque uidelicet adulteria committere, neque seditiones mouere, neque rapinas exercere' ('the laws contradicted the poets and forbade adultery, quarrelling, and theft').[111] He then resolved to go to the philosophers, but was again disillusioned: 'Apud enim hos maxime diligenter obseruans summam repperi ignorantiam, omniaque magis incerta' ('For I found in the course of my investigation that among these men in particular the ignorance and the perlexity was greater than elsewhere').[112] The ensuing lines, as well as anticipating some of the ethical problems of the Utopians, recall the dialectic and context of the *Cynicus*; Menippus finds nothing but contradiction among the philosophers:

> One of them would recommend me to take my pleasure always and to pursue that under all circumstances, because that was happiness; but another, on the contrary, would recommend me to toil and moil always and to subdue my body, going dirty and unkempt, irritating everybody and calling names; and to clinch his argument he was perpetually reciting those trite lines of Hesiod's about virtue, and talking of 'sweat', and the 'climb to the summit'. Another would urge me to despise money and think it a matter of indifference whether one has it or not, while someone else, on the contrary, would demonstrate that even wealth was good. . . . And the strangest thing was that when they expressed the most contradictory of opinions, each of them would produce very effective and plausible arguments, so that when the selfsame thing was called hot by one and cold by another, it was impossible for me to controvert either of them.[113]

Filled with disappointment ('frustratus'), Menippus therefore decided to go to the underworld to enquire from Teiresias what was the best life a man of sense could choose. Having observed in Hades how the

[110] ibid., pp. 27/35, 171.
[111] ibid., pp. 27/26–8, 171.
[112] ibid., pp. 27/38–9, 171.
[113] ibid., pp. 171–2.

proud are stripped of all their former splendour after death, Menippus comes to a startling realization:

> as I looked at them it seemed to me that human life is like a long pageant, and that all its trappings are supplied and distributed by Fortune, who arrays the participants in various costumes of many colours . . . often, in the very middle of the pageant, she exchanges the costumes of several players; instead of allowing them to finish the pageant in the parts that had been assigned to them, she re-apparels them, forcing Croesus to assume the dress of a slave and a captive, and shifting Maeandrius, who formerly paraded among the servants, into the imperial habit of Polycrates. For a brief space she lets them use their costumes, but when the time of the pageant is over, each gives back the properties and lays off the costume along with his body, becoming what he was before his birth, no different from his neighbour.[114]

In the course of this intellectual quest, Menippus has attained several perceptions pertinent to More's current state of mind: that human life is irreducibly problematical so that even the wisest of men are likely to be thoroughly confused, perplexed and perturbed by it; that there is no one simple path of life capable of resolving its difficulties; and that life's trappings, because they are distributed by Fortune and stripped away by death, are essentially a deception. No one can fail to notice how similar in implication is Lucian's elaboration of the life-as-a-play simile to More's own sense of Fortune as expressed in his *Verses for the Book of Fortune*: both imply that earthly endeavour is futile and the disposition of its goods and advantages meaningless. There is a major difference, however. More's perception left him vulnerable to despair, and motivated his yearning for escapist spiritual withdrawal; Lucian's, in contrast, issues forth in a light-hearted, practical, worldly proposal to take life as it comes, without undue worry. More learnt from this how easily the other side of his tragic coin could bear a comic face with only a slight shift of perspective, and how much more comfortable it was to laugh at absurdity rather than feel laughed at by it. As the dialogue nears its close, Menippus finally manages to coax a reluctant Teiresias to

---

[114] ibid., p. 176.

advise him as to the best sort of life a man can adopt. Furtively, out of the hearing of others, Teiresias whispers the Lucianic answer:

> The life of the common sort is best, and you will act more wisely if you stop speculating about heavenly bodies and discussing final causes and first causes, spit your scorn at those clever syllogisms, and counting all that sort of thing nonsense, make it always your sole object to put the present to good use and to hasten on your way, laughing a great deal of taking nothing seriously.

> (Optima est, inquit, idiotarum priuatorumque uita, ac prudentissima. Quamobrem ab hac uanissima sublimium consyderatione desistens, mitte principia semper ac fines inquirere, et uafros hosce syllogismos despuens, atque id genus omnia nugas aestimans, hoc solum in tota uita persequere, ut praesentibus bene compositis minime curiosus, nulla re sollicitus, quam plurimum potes hilaris uitam ridensque traducas.)[115]

As much as this exhortation to frivolous practicality appealed to the sunny side of More's personality, he also realized that it was not sufficient in itself, for he felt impelled to modify and develop the Menippean pose in *Utopia*. A full discussion of that elaboration will be reserved for a later chapter; suffice it to suggest here that, however frivolously it was presented, Menippus' view of a world governed by meaningless Fortune was latently agnostic, and prompted More to recognize the spiritual danger in his own earlier effusions on that topic. Lucian's version of the life-as-play figure excited him into modifying it in a way that rendered both Menippus' view of Fortune and his own equally obsolete. *Utopia*, the result, gives the first public intimation that he had developed an idiosyncratic sense of providence. Lucian had given him the means of accurate perception; he then had to find a more positive meaning for what he perceived.

The third Lucianic dialogue, *Philopseudes*, or 'The Lover of Lies', and Lucian's *Tyrannicida*, together with More's hubristic declamation in reply, are not immediately relevant to an understanding of More's intellectual development, so I shall pass on to a group of poems that was.

---

[115] ibid., pp. 179, 41/34–43/1.

Apart from their enormous range of subject matter, which includes merchants, lawyers, courtiers, harlots, cuckolds, wordly priests, step-mothers, actors, sailors, peasants, physicians, drunkards, illiterate bishops, and wives of various unsavoury sorts, More's *Epigrammata*, written between 1509 and 1519, are chiefly interesting to the student of his intellectual career for the five poems celebrating the accession of Henry VIII.

The naïve optimism expressed in them is disconcerting because it is so unexpected after the pessimism of the English poems and the sophisticated ambivalence surrounding the translations of Pico's life and Lucian's dialogues. Everyone else in England was intoxicated at the prospect of an ideal philosopher prince to succeed his unprepossessing father, but one would not have expected More to have been so unequivocally swept along by the popular tide. That he was suggests a degree of post-Charterhouse euphoria at finding himself free to participate competitively in the world.

The poems addressed to Henry VIII show him doing just that. Even allowing for the clichés of ritual humanist praise, the flattery they contain is fulsome indeed:

> O si animi praestans una cum corpore uirtus
>   Cerni, natura non prohibente, queat!
> Imo etiam uultu uirtus pellucet ab ipso,
>   Est facies animi nuncia aperta boni.
> Quam matura graui sedeat prudentia mente,
>   Quam non solliciti pectoris alta quies,
> Quoque modo sortem ferat, et moderetur utranque,
>   Quanta uerecundae cura pudicitiae,
> Quam tranquilla fouet placidum clementia pectus,
>   Quam procul ex illo fastus abest animo,
> Principis egregius nostri (quas fingere non est)
>   Prae se fert certas uultus et ipse notas.

(If only nature would permit that, like his body, the outstanding excellence of his mind be visible. But, even so, his moral perfection does shine forth from his very countenance. His frank face reveals his noble heart. How ripe the wisdom in his judicious mind, how profound the calm of his untroubled breast! With what restraint he would endure his lot and be master of his fortune, good or bad! How great his

care to honour modesty! How serene the mercy which
warms his gentle heart! How far removed from arrogance
his mind! Yes, of all these gifts, the very countenance of our
prince, extraordinary as it is, wears upon itself sure
evidence which cannot be falsified.)[116]

This, together with the succeeding four poems, was bound into an
ornamented presentation copy (British Museum MS Cotton Titus
D IV) for the king.[117] However sincere More may have been in his
praise, his act was an attempt to gain favour and attention. It is not
hard to see why. Humanists everywhere were in an ecstasy of
optimistic expectation. Mountjoy, declaring that heaven was laughing
and the earth rejoicing, wrote to entice Erasmus back to England from
Rome: 'You will come to a Prince who will say, "Accept our wealth
and be our greatest sage."'[118] More appears to have been momentarily seduced by the same fervour, and wished to be in the vanguard
of the enlightened band who would guide England into a new golden
age. Gone was his medieval manichean gloom, and, perhaps more
regrettably, his Lucianic ambivalence. They were replaced by a
combination of humanist commonplaces concerning the movement
and meaning of history.

In the third epigram, entitled in the MS 'de aureo seclo per eum
redeunte epigramma', More invokes a cyclical view of history com-
pounding the notions of the four ages of man and that of the Platonic
magnus annus, or great year:[119]

> Cuncta Plato cecinit tempus quae proferat ullum
>   Saepe fuisse olim, saepe aliquando fore.
> Ver fugit ut celeri, celerique reuertitur anno,
>   Bruma pari ut spacio quae fuit ante redit,
> Sic, inquit, rapidi post longa uolumina coeli
>   Cuncta per innumeras sunt reditura uices.
> Aurea prima sata est aetas, argentea post hanc.
>   Aerea post illam, ferrea nuper erat.
> Aurea te, princeps, redierunt principe secla.
>   O possit uates hactenus esse Plato.

[116] Bradner and Lynch, pp. 18, 140.
[117] Chambers, p. 100.
[118] Allen, I, no. 215; quoted by Chambers, p. 100.
[119] See Bradner and Lynch, p. 144n.

(Plato foretold that everything which any particular time can produce had often existed and would often sometime in the future exist again. 'As spring is banished and returns with the swift passage of the year, as familiar winter after an unchanging interval returns, just so,' he said, 'after many revolutions of the speeding sky all things in their countless turn will be again.' The golden age came first, then the silver; after that the bronze, and recently the iron age. In your reign, Sire, the golden age has returned. May Plato be to this extent a true prophet.)[120]

Apart from the qualifying final sentence, there is nothing in this poem to suggest that More did not heartily mean what he wrote. Henry, in his eyes, seemed to be rectifying all the injustices that had sent him scuttling for the shelter of *contemptus mundi* in the *Verses for the Book of Fortune*:

> Ille magistratus et munera publica, uendi
>   Quae sueuere malis, donat habenda bonis.
> Et uersis rerum uicibus feliciter, ante
>   Quae tulit indoctus praemia, doctus habet.

(He now gives to good men the honors and public offices which used to be sold to evil men. By a happy reversal of circumstances, learned men now have the prerogatives which ignoramuses carried off in the past.)[121]

Because Henry seemed to be frustrating the malevolence of Fortune, More embraced, momentarily at least, Erasmus' pedagogical optimism:

> . . . quid enim non principe fiat ab illo
>   Cui cultum ingenuis artibus ingenium est,
> Castalio quem fonte nouem lauere sorores,
>   Imbuit et monitis philosophia suis?

(What could lie beyond the powers of a prince whose natural gifts have been enhanced by a liberal education, a

[120] ibid., pp. 23, 144.
[121] ibid., pp. 19, 141.

prince bathed by the nine sisters in the Castalian font and
steeped in philosophy's own precepts?)[122]

All of More's tumescent optimism rises to the near-blasphemous
statement that here is a king 'qui cunctis lachrymas detergat ocellis, /
Gaudia pro longo substituat gemitu' ('as will wipe the tears from
every eye and put joy in the place of our long distress').[123] As
H. A. Mason has pointed out, these lines are meant to evoke
Revelation 21:

> And I saw a new heaven and a new earth: for the first heaven
> and the first earth were passed away; and there was no more sea.
> And I John saw the holy city, new Jerusalem, coming down from
> God out of heaven, prepared as a bride adorned for her husband.
> And I heard a great voice out of heaven saying, Behold, the
> tabernacle of God is with men, and he will dwell with them, and
> they shall be his people, and God himself shall be with them, and
> be their God. And God shall wipe away all tears from their eyes;
> and there shall be no more death, neither sorrow, nor crying,
> neither shall there be any more pain: for the former things are
> passed away.[124]

Henry, the ideal prince, is to descend like the saviour of his own
dynasty's myth, to make the heavenly city earthly and visible in
England's green and pleasant land, bringing with him the *gaudia* of the
beatific vision itself. More's enthusiasm must have been extreme for
him to have uttered a view of history so radically repugnant to
anything he affirmed before or after. Later in his career, it must have
struck him with keener than usual irony that he had got almost
everything wrong that he possibly could have, not least his prophecy
that

> regina tibi sexu foecunda uirili
> Vndique firmatam perpetuamque dabit

> (your fruitful queen will present you with a male heir, a
> protection in unbroken line, who shall be supported on
> every side)[125]

---

[122] ibid., pp. 19, 141.
[123] ibid., pp. 16, 138.
[124] See also Mason, p. 50.
[125] Bradner and Lynch, pp. 21, 143.

and his belief that

> Connubium ut superi hoc sicut fecere, secundent,
> Vt data coelesti sceptra regantur ope
> Vtque ipsis gestata diu haec diademata tandem
> Et natus nati gestet, et inde nepos

(Heaven, as it has brought about this marriage, will also foster it, that the gift of power will be wielded with divine aid, and that, when these crowns have been long worn by our present king and queen, their grandson and their great-grandson will still be king.)[126]

His experience soon purged him of this facile sense of the action of providence and the way that history was shaped. The Henrician epigrams affirm a grand design effected deterministically by God alone; its great flaw was that it required the king to remain a humanist fiction rather than the man of red blood and iron will he was soon to prove himself.

I have suggested that there was, to speak metaphorically, a pendulum swinging throughout More's life. In the course of these early works we see it swing from one extreme point to the other: from manichean pessimism to undiluted optimism. It is only when the pendulum swings back to its mid-position that More was able to constrain all the aspects of his personality, his intellect and his impulses into an inclusive synthesis. That is when he wrote *Utopia*, the high point of the humanist renaissance in England.

The subsequent epigrams trace the movement by which More recovered towards his central position. They include ones that reaffirm the power and fickleness of Fortune (numbers 29, 30, 50, 51 and 54), ones that figure forth the comic absurdity of human perversity, stupidity and folly (numbers 42, 43, 45, 81, 99 and 126), some that muse on the tragic inevitability of death and decay (numbers 22, 27, 28, 52, 57, 101 and 243), some, usually antifeminist, recognizing that life allows for sex as well as saintliness (numbers 66, 98, 105, 140, 147, 149, 169 and 219), and some that administer a salutary reminder that as well as good kings there are also tyrants (numbers 91, 92, 96, 97, 102, 103, 124, 144, 182, 211, 222 and 227). All these later epigrams attest to the variegated mind and experience from which emerged the genuine Morean synthesis.

[126] ibid., pp. 21, 143.

2

The Morean Synthesis: *Utopia*

Commentators have numbered the streaks on *Utopia* so often that one hesitates to treat it yet again. They have identified variously its function as a paradigm,[1] its reformist practicality,[2] its medievalism,[3] its modernity,[4] its desirability,[5] its detestability,[6] its seriousness,[7] its frivolity as a *jeu d'esprit*,[8] its modified Platonism,[9] its Aristotelianism,[10] and its Augustinianism.[11] And yet somehow *Utopia* escapes from all attempts to contain its meaning within reductive rational formulas.

Many of the interpretative disagreements the work has provoked have arisen from partial responses to the various possibilities and philosophies More contemplated in it. While it is unlikely that the book's elusiveness will ever be completely dispelled, one can at least go a fair way towards identifying its general character and concerns by approaching it from the direction of More's earlier works. When this is done, *Utopia* emerges as the next, logical step in More's

[1] H. Schulte Herbrüggen, 'More's *Utopia* as Paradigm', *Essential Articles*, pp. 251–62.

[2] Karl Kautsky, *Thomas More and His Utopia* (New York, 1959).

[3] Chambers, p. 136 *et passim*; P. Albert Duhamel, 'Medievalism of More's *Utopia*', *Essential Articles*, pp. 234–50.

[4] J. H. Hexter, *CW* 4, p. xlvff.

[5] Edward Surtz, *The Praise of Pleasure* (Chicago, 1957); *The Praise of Wisdom* (Chicago, 1957).

[6] T. S. Dorsch, 'Sir Thomas More and Lucian: An Interpretation of *Utopia*', *Archiv für das Studium der neueren Sprachen und Literaturen*, 203 (1966–67), pp. 345–63.

[7] Robbin S. Johnson, *More's Utopia: Ideal and Illusion* (New Haven, 1969).

[8] Lewis, *Essential Articles*, p. 391.

[9] John A. Guegen, 'Reading More's *Utopia* as a Criticism of Plato', in *Quincentennial Essays on St Thomas More*, ed. Michael J. Moore (Boone, North Carolina, 1978), pp. 42–54.

[10] Thomas I. White, 'Aristotle and *Utopia*', *Renaissance Quarterly*, 29 (1976), pp. 635–75.

[11] Martin N. Raitiere, 'More's *Utopia* and *The City of God*', *Studies in the Renaissance*, 20 (1973), pp. 144–68.

continuing effort to resolve the contradictions in his own divided impulses; having decided to pursue the vocation of layman rather than priest, he was concerned to explore the possibilities of secular life for all men as well as himself. To this end he envisioned a polity embodying the virtues of the cloister at the same time as it acknowledged the social and political hopes of contemporary humanists.[12] No one who has read the enthusiastic epigrams addressed to Henry VIII in 1509 need doubt that More was sincere in speculating upon the best state of a commonwealth in 1515 when almost all things still seemed possible under the mirror of Christian kings.

Yet the sentiments of the English poems, with their deep sense of the mutability of things and conviction in the sinfulness of man's fallen nature, had been far from effaced; More's realism was ultimately too strong for that. It comes as no surprise, therefore, to find in *Utopia* that, at the same time as More created an image of the happiest world in which men might live, he subjected it to a penetrating critique, in which he contemplated the frustration of his own utopianism. Even if Utopian polity could be instituted in the real world (over which he remained agnostic), the fundamental realities of human experience would remain unchanged. The vision being paradoxical, the book could not fail to be equally so, especially since More's encounter with Lucian had taught him how to dramatize ambiguity as an integral function of meaning. In the light of philosophical maturity he proceeded to investigate what the recurrent frustrations, tensions and paradoxes of the human condition might mean in terms of a larger providential purpose underlying them. Just as much as the *Life of John Picus*, *Utopia* was an instrument of analysis rather than a definitive statement. The work does attain a genuine Morean synthesis, but it is not where we, like More, would like to be able to find it – in the rationalized polity described in book 2 – but in the effect the whole fiction is designed to induce in the reader, and in the religious significance More ascribed to that response.

Utopia, as I have suggested, comprises an extremely complex fictional structure, and any sound understanding of the work depends upon a grasp on it. The ambivalence of the *Life of John Picus* was generated

[12] See D. B. Fenlon, 'England and Europe: *Utopia* and its Aftermath', *Transactions of the Royal Historical Society*, 25 (1975), pp. 115–35; also Quentin Skinner, *The Foundations of Modern Political Thought* (Cambridge, 1978), I, p. 255ff.

partly by the ironic relation between its substance and the context in which it was written and presented to its dedicatee. An even more ironic relation between substance and context was engendered by *A Merry Jest, How a Sergeant Would Learn to Play the Friar* if it was indeed delivered at the feast when More was made a freeman of the Mercers' Company in 1509.[13] *Utopia* exploits the same procedure by depicting a possibility on book 2 which its context, both literal and philosophical, ironically subverts, the difference being that the context is explicitly presented in the fiction of *Utopia,* in the dialogue of book 1, instead of being left merely implicit. The work is complicated still further by More's adoption of the ironic strategy he observed in Lucian's *Cynicus*: the use of a 'foolish' interlocutor whose philosophical defeat merely intensifies the reader's unwillingness to believe entirely in the victory of his opponent because of a discrepancy depicted between the findings of emotion as against reason. Given this general complexity of *Utopia,* perhaps the most effective way of perceiving how it works is to retrace the order in which it was composed, since Erasmus records that book 2 was written first while More was in the Netherlands, book 1 being written after his return to England.[14] If the work is read in this sequence, one can see more clearly how More began by fabricating the 'eutopia', or 'happy land', mentioned by Anemolius in his prefatory Hexastichon,[15] which, from the outset, contained the possibility of being a nowhere and an everywhere as the puns in its title suggest.[16] Having seen that, one can then see how he dramatized two alternative responses to the state of human affairs he had discovered. The first response is that of Hythlodaeus, the stoical idealist whose encounter with the mixed nature of reality leads him to imitate the early More in oscillating between two opposed extreme impulses: to withdraw from the world on one hand, and to become thrall to the phantasmal possibility of the temporal perfecting of the world on the other. The second response is that of Morus, the Lucianic doubting Thomas who feels the presence in life of a calling to achieve rather more by aspiring to less. In conclusion, one can see how, through the process of writing *Utopia,* More discovered most of the rudiments of his later beliefs and actions.

[13] See above, p. 26.
[14] Letter to Ulrich von Hutten, Allen, IV, no. 999.
[15] *CW* 4, p. 20/9.
[16] ibid, pp. 10/2 and 385 (note to p. 112/1–2). Henceforth I use the words 'eutopia' and 'eutopian' with this specific signification.

The circumstances were right for More to entertain his eutopian fantasy when he sat down to write *Utopia* in 1515. His imagination had been excited by the discoveries of Cabot and Vespucci in the New World and the explorations of the Portuguese around the Cape of Good Hope to the East; his legal career in the City was advancing as well as he could wish; the momentum of Erasmian reform was approaching its height; and he had the stimulating company on the Flanders mission of Cuthbert Tunstal, Busleiden and Peter Giles, humanists with interests and ambitions similar to his own.[17] The eutopian quality of the book can be seen in the extent to which More created the Utopians in his own image. They share his contempt for material ostentation, as attested by their simple monastic garb[18] and their debasing use of gold for chamber pots and slaves' fetters, and of jewels for children's toys.[19] They, too, believe that the secret of a happy life consists in the cultivation of the mind ('animi libertatem cultumque')[20] and achieve the same kind of communal domestic order for which More strove in his own household.[21] Specifically, he projected into the Utopians his own fondness for gardens ('eoque nullius rei, quam huiusmodi hortorum, maiorem habuisse curam uidetur is qui condidit'),[22] his liking for music,[23] his delight in fools ('Moriones in delitijs habentur'),[24] and his receptivity towards foreign guests.[25] Even the monkey to be seen in Holbein's sketch of the family group finds his way into the action, having ripped up Hythlodaeus' copy of Theophrastus during the voyage.[26]

Once the degree of whimsy in this self-projection is grasped, some of the book's thematic problems become more comprehensible, particularly those which arise from the Utopians' epicurean philosophy. This derives in part from Vespucci's description in *Mundus novus* of people who 'live according to nature, and may be called Epicureans rather

---

[17] Chambers, p. 120.
[18] *CW* 4, p. 132/29ff.
[19] ibid., pp. 152–9.
[20] ibid., p. 134/19–20.
[21] ibid., p. 144/5.
[22] ibid., p. 120/21–3.
[23] ibid., p. 144/16–17.
[24] ibid., p. 192/7. The Latin contains the pun on More's name recently made famous by Erasmus in *Moriae encomium*.
[25] ibid., p. 184/3ff.
[26] ibid., p. 180/29ff. Erasmus mentions More's monkey in his Letter to von Hutten.

than Stoics',[27] but also from More's own engagement with the problem that had interested him in Lucian's *Cynicus*: whether the enjoyment of temporal things is compatible with virtue, a thing indifferent, or repugnant, the ascetic way being better. Observing (like Menippus) the inconsistency in even the sternest ascetics who, while imposing a life of labour, vigils and general discomfort on one nevertheless exhort that same person to relieve the privations of others,[28] the Utopians focus the issue into a combined proposition–question:

> either a joyous life, that is, a pleasurable life, is evil, in which case not only ought you to help no one to it but, as far as you can, should take it away from everyone as being harmful and deadly, or else, if you not only are permitted but are obliged to win it for others as being good, why should you not do so first of all for yourself, to whom you should show no less favour than to others?[29]

More then allows them a privilege he would never have allowed himself in real life: to explore the implications of an assumption that virtue and pleasure *are* compatible. After having Hythlodaeus utter a discreet disclaimer against it ('At hac in re propensiores aequo uidentur in factionem uoluptatis assertricem, ut qua uel totam, uel potissimam felicitatis humanae partem definiant')[30] he gives a serious and coherent praise of pleasure.[31]

Utopian hedonism is founded on much the same religious beliefs as those More was still asserting as the basis of salvation at the end of his career: 'Those principles are as follows: that the soul is immortal and born for happiness through the beneficence of God, and that our virtues and good deeds are destined to be rewarded after this life, and

---

[27] Quoted by Paul Turner in his edition of *Utopia* (Harmondsworth, 1965), p. 141, n. 11.

[28] *CW* 4, p. 162/28–35.

[29] 'Aut mala est uita iucunda, id est, uoluptaria, quod si est, non solum neminem ad eam debes adiutare, sed omnibus utpote noxiam ac mortiferam, quantum potes adimere, aut si conciliare alijs eam, ut bonam non licet modo, sed etiam debes, cur non tibi in primis ipsi? cui non minus propitium esse te quam alijs decet' (ibid., pp. 164/2–8, 165/3–11).

[30] ibid., p. 160/20–3.

[31] I echo the title of Surtz's study, *The Praise of Pleasure*.

our misdeeds punished.'[32] These beliefs make the Utopians Christians *de facto*, if not in name, because, as More asserted later, pagans who accepted the end of salvation implicitly professed Christ, who was the means.[33] One should not, therefore, make too much of their paganism to explain away More's excursus into theoretical hedonism. It cannot be seriously argued that the Utopians' view embodies merely the findings of blind reason unilluminated by faith,[34] for the Utopians themselves, acknowledging that reason alone is inadequate for the investigation of happiness, realize that the very legitimacy of their ethic depends upon religious principles ('ab religione . . . sententiae'), and accept the necessary co-operation of reason and faith just as fervently as More did later in *A Dialogue Concerning Heresies*.[35] As far as their morality was concerned, More allowed the Utopians to live as he would have liked to have been able to live, but could not. Nothing would have pleased him more than to have been able to be a married priest, or to have gratified his five senses with the harmless pleasures that grace, for example, Utopian meals;[36] but although desire inclined him towards them, other forces in his personality caused him to withhold the assent of his will to them.

Much the same is true of the common ownership upon which Utopian polity rests. More could have it both ways: he could explore the implications of a communal way of living without necessarily proposing it, however much he may have felt emotionally or intellectually inclined towards it, as one suspects he was. Hythlodaeus' summation of the general advantage of the Utopian way of life betrays the reason for its attractiveness to More; although no man owns anything, all are rich: 'For what can be richer than to live with a happy and tranquil mind, free from anxiety?') ('Nam quid ditius esse potest, quam adempta prorsus omni solicitudine, laeto ac tranquillo animo uiuere?').[37] In effect, the Utopians' repudiation of private property is a remedy against the same Fortuna against whom More

---

[32] 'Ea principia sunt huiusmodi. Animam esse immortalem, ac dei beneficentia ad felicitatem natam, uirtutibus ac bene factis nostris praemia post hanc uitam, flagitijs destinata supplicia' (*CW* 4, pp. 160/30–162/2).

[33] *A Treatise upon the Passion*, *CW* 13, p. 43.

[34] See W. E. Campbell, *Erasmus, Tyndale and More* (London, 1949), pp. 85, 124; Reynolds, *Saint Thomas More*, p. 88; and Surtz, *The Praise of Wisdom*, pp. 7–13.

[35] *CW* 4, pp. 160/26–30, 24–5, 162/3–6; cf. *CW* 6, p. 131/19–32.

[36] *CW* 4, p. 144/16–23; cf. the description of natural gifts, p. 176/24ff.

[37] ibid., p. 238/11–12.

had railed in the *Verses for the Book of Fortune*.[38] Once again, he allows them to live according to a synthesis he could only imagine: a fusion of the religious and secular lives. As Budé and Beatus Rhenanus recognized, and Giles indicated in his marginal glosses, the Utopians have adopted 'the customs and true wisdom of Christianity for public and private life' ('Christianos uero ritus ac germanam ipsam sapientiam publice priuatimque'), consisting of 1) the equality of all things among citizens, 2) love of peace and quiet, and 3) contempt for gold and silver.[39] In short, they import all the virtues of monastic life into political and social affairs, and when More in a famous daydream indulged the fantasy that he was their king, it was in a 'Franciscan frock' that he saw himself, 'crowned with a diadem of wheat . . . carrying a handful of wheat as my sacred scepter'.[40] The complex collocation of associations in these images suggests that More enviously viewed the Utopians as successful Carthusian (Franciscan if you like) mercers, the governing of whom would allow him to bring the cloister into the court, where he already knew he might be headed.[41]

A large part of book 2, then, describes the happy place of More's dream; but that reflects only one aspect of the titular paradox. As happy as eutopia is, it is also 'nusquama', nowhere, and 'udepotia', a land that will never be.[42] To complicate the matter further, Utopia was conceived from the outset as being in an ambiguous relation with England: the more the two countries appear to be opposed, the more they turn out to be similar – the obvious differences paradoxically serve to underline the more significant parallels.

At one level, particularly with respect to geographical details, Utopia and England share a shadowy identity. Utopia is an island separated from the continent by a channel,[43] Amaurotum, its capital city, together with the tidal river Anydrus, and the magnificently arched stone bridge across it, resemble London and the Thames, as the marginal glosses make clear,[44] and the houses reflect those evolved

---

[38] See, in particular, the phrasing of *CW* 4, p. 156/25–6.

[39] ibid., pp. 10/3–8, 11/6–13; cf. Rhenanus' letter to Pirckheimer (*CW* 4, p. 253).

[40] Rogers, *SL*, no. 11, p. 85.

[41] See G. R. Elton, 'Thomas More, Councillor', in *St Thomas More: Action and Contemplation*, ed. R. S. Sylvester (New Haven, 1972), pp. 87–122.

[42] See William Budé's letter to Thomas Lupset, *CW* 4, p. 10/2. In his letters More referred to the work first as 'Nusquama'; see, for example, the letters to Erasmus of 21 June 1516 and 16 September 1516 (Allen, II, nos. 424, 465).

[43] *CW* 4, p. 112/5ff.

[44] ibid., pp. 116/28–118/23.

in England in their disposition, their handsome flint facings, and their glass windows (even if their flat roofs and occasional oil-smeared linen window-screens are calculated to blur the image slightly).[45] The stage is thus set up for the Utopian illusion to dissolve into the reality of England and Europe, as it does – at the very point where Hythlodaeus asserts the most extreme degree of contrast between the two.

This occurs in the description of the Utopians' mistrust of treaties, and of their military affairs. They never make treaties with any nation, Hythlodaeus says, 'because in those parts of the world treaties and alliances between kings are not observed with much good faith' ('quod in illis terrarum plagis, foedera pactaque principum solent parum bona fide seruari').[46] He then draws a savagely satiric contrast with Europe, meaning the exact opposite of what he says:

> In Europe, however, and especially in those parts where the faith and religion of Christ prevails, the majesty of treaties is every-where holy and inviolable, partly through the justice and good-ness of kings, partly through the reverence and fear of the Sovereign Pontiffs.[47]

This ironic inversion is not simply rhetorical, but serves to focus the reader's attention on the presence in the antipodean world of some-thing that makes the rationally ideal polity of the Utopians somewhat of a lie, if not an irrelevancy – the ineradicable sinfulness of human nature.

Utopia gradually turns out to be no more and no less removed from Europe in a social and moral sense than it is in a geographical one. As an island it resembles England, but it also differs in that its tapering ends give it the appearance of a 'renascent' moon: 'insulam totam in lunae speciem renascentis effigiant'.[48] The emblem suggests at one level that Utopia figures forth the renovated polity that an optimistic humanist might envision for England in the context of the con-temporary historical 'Renaissance'. But beneath the seductive ap-

---

[45] ibid., pp. 120/1–122/7.
[46] ibid., pp. 196/19–20, 197/24–6.
[47] 'Etenim in Europa idque his potissimum partibus quas CHRISTI fides et religio possidet, sancta est et inuiolabilis ubique maiestas foederum, partim ipsa iustitia et bonitate principum, partim summorum reuerentia metuque pontificum' (ibid., pp. 196/21–4, 197/26–30).
[48] ibid., p. 110/12.

pearance of the Utopians' simplified, rationalized laws and mores is
the human perversity that makes their existence necessary: the lust
that wrecks their ideal of the inviolability and permanence of marriage
and leads them to permit an extremely liberal policy of divorce,[49] the
recalcitrance of hardened criminals which forces them to slaughter
repeated offenders with a savagery equal to that in Europe ('tum
demum uelut indomitae beluae . . . trucidantur'),[50] and the anger
which, in their warfare, induces them to duplicate some of the most
fiendish practices devised by human nature: vengeful reprisals,
rewards for assassination, the hiring of mercenaries, the fostering of
treason, discord, and rival claims to the throne of the enemy, and the
surrounding of soldiers on the battlefield by their wives and children.[51] The Utopians even have their own heretics, notably after the
introduction of Christianity.[52]

As well as being frustrated in their reformist idealism by the sinfulness of human nature, the Utopians also experience a paradox in the
nature of things: that rational action can give rise to unreasonable
consequences. Their most determined efforts to fulfil the most laud-
able of intentions often meet with failure.

The most striking example of this is the war they fight on behalf of
the Nephelogetes against the Alaopolitans. Ironically, this grew out of
their willingness to fulfil what More would later describe as God's
behest, in which 'he byndeth euery man to the helpe and defence of his
good and harmles neyghbour / agaynst the malyce and cruelty of the
wronge doer', according to the text of Ecclesiastes 17: 'vnicuique dedit
deus curam de proximo suo'.[53] On these grounds, the Utopians went
to the assistance of the Nephelogetes, who claimed that they had
suffered injustice at the hands of the Alaopolitans under the pretext of
law. The outcome was catastrophically tragic:

> whether right or wrong, it was avenged by a fierce war. Into this
> war the neighboring nations brought their energies and re-
> sources to assist the power and to intensify the rancor of both
> sides. Most flourishing nations were either shaken to their
> foundations or grievously afflicted. The troubles upon troubles

[49] ibid., p. 190/1ff.
[50] ibid., p. 190/25–7.
[51] ibid., p. 202/8ff.
[52] ibid., p. 218/20–30.
[53] *A Dialogue Concerning Heresies*, *CW* 6, pp. 4–8.

that arose were ended only by the enslavement and surrender of the Alaopolitans. Since the Utopians were not fighting in their own interest, they yielded them into the power of the Nephelo-getes, a people who, when the Alaopolitans were prosperous, were not in the least comparable to them.[54]

More recognized, just as acutely as he had in the English poems, that what men experience is often very different from anything they intend, desire, seek or foresee.

Utopia is full of comparable instances of tragic paradox; for example, the suffocating constraints on individual liberty required to effectuate the Utopians' attempt to secure more liberty and leisure for all,[55] or the moral injustice of the rational justice by which they regulate numbers in their families and colonies.[56] Through imagin-atively registering this vitiation of Utopian reformist aspirations, the reader is eventually brought to the same recognition that More had expressed in his earlier English poems: that in this temporal world men are always deprived of some portion of their will, however rationally or virtuously they try to act. *Utopia* thus contains an inbuilt ambiguity; it represents to a large extent what More wished for, even while he saw that if it could be, which it never would, the human situation would remain essentially unchanged in its character and function.

Once More had finished describing his imaginary commonwealth, he could have left the work as it was – a self-contained speaking picture; instead, he chose to surround it with an elaborately developed dialogue concerning the question of whether or not a wise man should enter a king's service.

By late 1516 More was about to join Henry VIII's Court himself. Book 1 was contrived to dramatize the nature of the choice before him

[54] 'siue illud ius, siue ea iniuria fuit, bello tam atroci est uindicata, quum ad proprias utriusque partis uires, odiaque circumiectarum etiam gentium studia atque opes adiungerentur, ut florentissimis populorum alijs concussis, alijs uehementer afflictis, orientia ex malis mala, Alaopolitarum seruitus demum, ac deditio finierit, qua in Nephelogetarum (neque enim sibi certabant Vtopienses) potestatem concessere, gentis, florentibus Alaopolitarum rebus, haud quaquam cum illis conferendae' (*CW* 4, pp. 200/20–8, 201/24–33).

[55] ibid., p. 144/28ff.

[56] ibid., p. 136/17ff.

(or, possibly, already recently behind him) in terms that anticipate the frustration of Utopian eutopianism in book 2. Both books lead the reader into experiencing parallel cruces bearing closely upon what More might expect to achieve, or not achieve, in office, and what he was doing in accepting it. To gain this end, he created a dispute between two new characters: Raphael Hythlodaeus, the embittered idealistic reformer, and Morus, a fictional version of himself.

The precise relation between Hythlodaeus and Morus to More has been the subject of much inconclusive scholarly debate. Opinions range from assumptions that More is Hythlodaeus,[57] through Chambers' belief that More is Morus,[58] to Hexter's gymnastic argument that More was Hythlodaeus when he wrote book 2, but Morus by the time he wrote book 1.[59] Viewing *Utopia* in the context of More's earlier works enables one to see that Hythlodaeus and Morus are both More, but in a far more complicated way than has been suggested of late.[60]

There are, in fact, two Hythlodaeuses, who resemble the two Mores reflected in the English and Latin poems. The Hythlodaeus who enthusiastically extols the example of the Utopian commonwealth might have written the epigrams on the accession of Henry VIII; the Hythlodaeus who lacerates European perversity and declares his willingness to abandon it to its own satanic devices, in book 1, could easily have written the *Verses for the Book of Fortune*. Hythlodaeus' reformist impulse and his pessimism are both sides of the same Morean coin, and in him More contemplated the meaning of the conflict within his earlier self. Both impulses, he saw, were inadequate. Hythlodaeus' attitude towards reform is flawed because he believes in the necessity for absolute, radical change; he cannot comprehend the possibility of allowing to remain in existence a state that contains good and bad together; hence he is not satisfied merely with applying remedies that relieve symptoms of disease, but looks for the means of a complete cure ('ut sanentur uero').[61] This attitude leads him wilfully to misread the meaning of his own exemplum by

---

[57] For a resumé of the respective positions, see Jones, pp. 65–8.

[58] Chambers, p. 155.

[59] Hexter, pp. 99–155.

[60] As by David M. Bevington, 'The Dialogue in *Utopia*: Two Sides to the Question', *Studies in Philology*, 58 (1961), pp. 496–509; and W. J. Barnes, 'Irony and the English Apprehension of Renewal', *Queen's Quarterly*, 73 (1966), pp. 357–76.

[61] *CW* 4, p. 104/31.

overestimating the extent to which Utopian communism has eliminated Pride, 'omnium princeps parensque pestium'.[62] His peroration, which Hexter has convincingly argued was written at the same time as book 1,[63] commits, metaphorically speaking, a form of euthanasia in the way it desperately frees Utopian polity from the human ills More had taken pains to depict in it – just as the Utopians themselves free their incurably sick from the ills of the body. His summation is full of images of deracination and pruning whose very forcefulness serves to beg the question:

> In Utopia all greed for money was entirely removed with the use of money. What a mass of troubles was then cut away! What a crop of crimes was then pulled up by the roots! Who does not know that fraud, theft, rapine, quarrels, disorders, brawls, seditions, murders, treasons, poisonings, which are avenged rather than restrained by daily executions, die out with the destruction of money? Who does not know that fear, anxiety, worries, toils, and sleepless nights will also perish at the same time as money?[64]

Hythlodaeus cannot imagine that his questions are anything more than rhetorical, whereas the whole exemplum has served to emphasize that they are. He distorts the truth by reading into Utopia what he needs to be able to do in order to save himself from despair, but More has made it impossible for the reader to do likewise, even while inviting him to do so.

Just as Hythlodaeus' expectations are unrealistic, his reaction to their imagined frustration by European reality is out of all proportion in the degree of its pessimism. When Peter Giles suggests that his wide experience would make him an invaluable royal councillor if he were to enter some king's sevice, he denounces such a course of action as 'servitude'. The distinction Giles tries to draw between 'servitude' and

---

[62] ibid., p. 242/25.

[63] ibid., pp. 240/31–243/7.

[64] 'e qua cum ipso usu sublata penitus omni auiditate pecuniae, quanta moles molestiarum recisa, quanta scelerum seges radicitus euulsa est? Quis enim nescit fraudes, furta, rapinas, rixas, tumultus, iurgia, seditiones, caedes, proditiones, ueneficia, cotidianis uindicata potius quam refrenata supplicijs, interempta pecunia commori, ad haec metum sollicitudinem, curas, labores, uigilias, eodem momento quo pecunia perituras' (ibid., pp. 241/39–243/7, 240/31ff.).

'service' ('mihi uisum est non ut seruias regibus, sed ut inseruias') has no meaning for him: 'Hoc est inquit ille, una syllaba plusquam seruias.'[65] In the same way that he wanted to see Utopian polity as more perfected than it really was, he wants to see European polity as more hopelessly vitiated than it really is. The most striking example of this occurs when he recounts his experience in the household of Cardinal Morton.

This inset story anticipates the mode and meaning of the larger Utopian exemplum by subverting the view it is ostensibly meant to illustrate. Hythlodaeus recounts the episode to prove his contention that people are so jealous of everyone else's ideas, so self-opinionated, and so full of proud, absurd and obstinate prejudices that he would not be listened to in a king's council if he were to suggest any wise policy.[66] He was once sitting at Morton's table, he says, when an English lawyer's boasting over the stern measures taken to punish thieves provoked him into anatomizing the social and economic causes of thievery and proposing remedies for them.[67] When Morton asked him to declare why he objected to capital punishment for theft, Hythlodaeus proposed as an alternative the example of the Polylerites, who punish crime more conveniently and humanely with slavery.[68] He then describes the array of different reactions his proposal received: the lawyer patronizingly dismissed it out of hand; a jester treated it facetiously by using the occasion to propose a mock remedy for friars; and a friar aborts the whole proceeding by becoming indignantly outraged at the fool's affront to his vanity, eventually forcing the Cardinal to direct the conversation another way and then wind up the party.[69] Hythlodaeus thinks the occasion justifies his determination to remain out of public service; however, he failed to appreciate the most important response he elicited – that of Morton himself.

Morton, significantly, is already *in* public office, and that the highest in the land under the king: Lord Chancellor of England.[70] Without seeming to acknowledge that fact, Hythlodaeus praises him in the highest terms as '[vir] non autoritate magis, quam prudentia ac

---

[65] ibid., p. 54/27–9.
[66] ibid., p. 56/33ff.
[67] ibid., pp. 60–70.
[68] ibid., p. 74/19ff.
[69] ibid., p. 78/32ff.
[70] ibid., p. 58/20.

uirtute uenerabili' ('a man who deserved respect as much for his prudence and virtue as for his authority'),[71] and as being 'greatly experienced in the law' ('iuris magna peritia').[72] Morton has developed extraordinary natural gifts of remarkable intellect and a phenomenal memory further by 'learning and practice',[73] with the result that 'the king placed the greatest confidence in his advice, and the commonwealth seemed much to depend upon him'.[74] Although Hythlodaeus conceals any recognition of it, Morton is thus an example of a man with his own kind of talents who has decided to follow the advice of Morus and Giles, and his reaction to Hythlodaeus will inevitably be more crucial to the ultimate significance of the exemplum than that of any of the other characters present.

Hythlodaeus was so paranoically indignant at the behaviour of the lawyer, jester and friar that he fails to see that Morton's response confutes him. Morton was genuinely interested in his anatomy of England's ills, and was keen to hear his objection to capital punishment for theft.[75] When Hythlodaeus proposed the Polylerite system of penal servitude, far from dismissing it out of hand, Morton not only suggests an accommodation of the system to English circumstances, but contemplates its possible extension to cover vagrants as well.[76] In short, he reacts with exactly the same kind of judicious receptivity that the Utopians themselves show towards any new possibility.

Not surprisingly, Morus sees a meaning in the exemplum directly opposite to that which Hythlodaeus intends, and urges his own viewpoint even more strongly:

> Even now, nevertheless, I cannot change my mind but must needs think that, if you could persuade yourself not to shun the courts of kings, you could do the greatest good to the common weal by your advice. The latter is the most important part of your duty as it is the duty of every good man.[77]

[71] ibid., pp. 58/21–2, 59/25–7.
[72] ibid., p. 58/28–9.
[73] ibid., p. 59/35–8.
[74] ibid., pp. 58/31–60, 59/39–61/1.
[75] ibid., p. 70/28ff.
[76] ibid., p. 80/7ff.
[77] 'Caeterum non possum adhuc ullo pacto meam demutare sententiam, quin te plane putem, si animum inducas tuum, uti ne ab aulis principum abhorreas, in publicum posse te tuis consilijs plurimum boni conferre. quare nihil magis incumbit tuo, hoc est boni uiri, officio' (ibid., pp. 86/6–10, 87/7–11).

Such service is no longer described merely as being 'convenient', but as a positive responsibility ('hoc est boni uiri, officio');[78] however, Morus' refusal to acclaim spontaneously the self-evident rightness of Hythlodaeus' conclusion drives the latter to deny even more vehemently any possible merit in the alternative course being suggested to him.

The most perturbing irony in book 1 is that however wrong Hythlodaeus is in some respects, he is nonetheless ultimately right. At the very moment More seems unequivocally to have destroyed Hythlodaeus' credibility by putting his objectivity in doubt, he permits Hythlodaeus' main point to challenge all that has been established against it. This occurs in the climactic clash of views after Hythlodaeus has imagined himself proposing the laws of the Achorians and Macarians in the French king's council. When he suggests that his advice would fall on deaf ears, Morus voices the objection that might occur to anyone moved by pragmatic common sense: ' "Deaf indeed, without doubt", I agreed, "and, by heaven, I am not surprised. Neither, to tell the truth, do I think that such ideas should be thrust on people, or such advice given, as you are positive will never be listened to." '[79] Developing Menippus' sceptical conclusion in Lucian's *Necromantia*, More goes on to assert, with a blend of idealistic cynicism, that there is another kind of practical philosophy ('alia philosophia ciuilior'), which amounts to acting one's part in the play at hand, observing the decorum of the piece so as not to turn it into a tragi-comedy. This saves one from having to abandon the ship in a storm when one cannot control the winds, and allows that which cannot be turned to good to be made as little bad as possible: ' "For it is impossible that all should be well unless all men were good, a situation which I do not expect for a great many years to

---

[78] More is drawing upon a long tradition here; cf. Chaucer, *The Parlement of Foules*:
> Than prayde him Scipioun to telle him al
> The wey to come un-to that hevene blisse;
> And he seyde, 'know thy-self first immortal,
> And loke ay besily thou werke and wisse
> To comun profit, and thou shalt nat misse
> To comen swiftly to that place dere,
> That ful of blisse is and of soules clere.

(*The Complete Works of Geoffrey Chaucer,* ed. Walter W. Skeat (London, 1912), p. 102.)
[79] 'Surdissimis inquam, haud dubie. neque hercule miror, neque mihi uidentur (ut uere dicam) huiusmodi sermones ingerendi, aut talia danda consilia, quae certus sis nunquam admissum iri' (*CW* 4, pp. 96/31–98/3, 97/39–99/3).

come"' ('Nam ut omnia bene sint, fieri non potest, nisi omnes boni sint, quod ad aliquot abhinc annos adhuc non expecto').[80] Since More chose to act according to this pragmatic philosophy for the next 16 years, it comes as a shock to find that Hythlodaeus' repudiation of it is not refuted. If this advice were to be followed, he replies, almost everything Christ himself taught would need to be dissembled, when he forbad such dissembling ' "to the extent that what He had whispered in the ears of His disciples He commanded to be preached openly from the housetops"'.[81] To do otherwise is to accommodate Christ's teaching to men's morals like a rule of soft lead ('uelut regulam plumbeam'), which is merely to allow men to be bad in greater comfort.[82] All that the indirect approach achieves, he continues, is to force one openly to 'approve the worst counsels and subscribe to the most ruinous decrees' ('approbanda sunt aperte pessima consilia, et decretis pestilentissimis subscribendum est'), since at Court one cannot keep one's opinion to oneself without being considered a traitor.[83] The result is either a loss of personal integrity, or else a willing connivance in the wickedness and folly of others ('alienae malitiae, stultitiaeque').[84] Although More chose to follow Morus' advice for the time being, he foresaw the truth of Hythlodaeus' claims as much as his own future experience would tragically confirm them.

Book 1, by forcing the reader to recognize this moral crux, anticipates the frustration of his idealism that he will experience in book 2, and thus serves to make his sense of the absolute insolubility of the human dilemma more complete; there is, More shows, no way of escaping the experience of it. The problem is far larger than either Hythlodaeus or Morus thinks. Hythlodaeus' response is inadequate because it renders him impotent in a way that perverts the public responsibility that every man is enjoined to fulfil. His insights are just, but his actions are not justified. To be right he has to be wrong, and as his name implies, he is a faithless angel whose pessimism amounts to an indictment of the human situation which God, in his wisdom, has instituted. Morus' response, on the other hand, is vitiated because it

---

[80] ibid., pp. 98/11–100/3, 101/2–4.

[81] ibid., p. 101/26–8.

[82] ibid., pp. 100/26–8, 101/33–6. More uses the image of the Lesbian rule again in *A Dialogue Concerning Heresies* (*CW* 6, pp. 129/10–14, 135/33), and in the *Letter to Dorp* (Rogers, *Correspondence*, p. 43).

[83] *CW* 4, pp. 102/5–8, 103/6–7.

[84] ibid., p. 102/12.

requires a man to compromise himself by winking at tainted deeds.

Once the presence of this crux has been felt, the function of book 1 becomes clear. It has been constructed to force its readers into a state of intellectual helplessness so as to make them all the more eager for Hythlodaeus to make good his claim that communal living can yet put all things right. When the Utopian *exemplum* fails to justify the full extent of Hythlodaeus' confidence in communal living as a radical cure-all, the reader's perplexity is compounded because book 1 has made desperately necessary the proof of its success. The two books taken together drive the reader into the same corner, from which he cannot move without either choosing some form of self-deception, or else acknowledging his helplessness as a human being to determine the shape and condition of his existence entirely according to his own wishes. But at the very point where book 2 seems about to deprive the reader of any sure support, it presents evidence of a true remedy, of which Hythlodaeus' eutopian remedy turns out to have been a parody: the religious response of the Utopians.

The essential feature of Utopian religion is that it is not definitive, and resides in a responsive condition of mind rather than an elaborate and arbitrary dogma. Its main principles were instituted by Utopus, the founder of Utopia, who allowed for a range of beliefs and provided for the possibility of wise doubting: 'On religion he did not venture rashly to dogmatize. He was uncertain whether God did not desire a varied and manifold worship and therefore did not inspire different people with different views' ('[religio] ... de qua nihil est ausus temere definire, uelut incertum habens, an uarium ac multiplicem expetens cultum deus, aliud inspiret alij').[85] The Utopians must, however, accept two fundamental tenets: that the world is governed by providence, not chance, and that the soul is immortal and will receive rewards and punishments after this life. To believe otherwise is to degenerate from the dignity of human nature.[86] In practice, they let their faith instruct their reason, so that they are capable of modifying the rational rigour of their hedonistic philosophy to allow for the justified existence of their ascetic religious order as well as that whose members prefer to marry and enjoy honest pleasures:

> The Utopians regard these men as the saner but the first-named
> as the holier. If the latter based upon arguments from reason

[85] ibid., pp. 220/10–12, 221/13–16.
[86] ibid., p. 220/22–5.

their preference of celibacy to matrimony and of a hard life to a
comfortable one, they would laugh them to scorn. Now, however, since they say they are prompted by religion, they look up
to and reverence them. For there is nothing about which they are
more careful than not lightly to dogmatize on any point of
religion.[87]

At the level of their religious response to life, as against their strictly
rational one, the Utopians are prepared, as here, to accept the
experience of paradox. Correspondingly, they become far more
flexible and responsive to the leadings of the providence they believe
in. Even more crucially, in their common prayers, the account of
which is strategically placed by More at the climactic point of the
whole work, they profess willingness to contemplate the possibility
that all their assumptions may, after all, be false. After acknowledging
God as the author of all blessings and returning him thanks,
particularly for having been placed in the happiest commonwealth
and given the truest form of religion, each individual reaffirms his
readiness to follow wherever God might lead him:

> If he errs in these matters or if there is anything better and more
> approved by God than that commonwealth or that religion, he
> prays that He will, of His goodness, bring him to the knowledge
> of it, for he is ready to follow in whatever path He may lead him.
> But if this form of a commonwealth be the best and his religion
> the truest, he prays that then He may give him steadfastness and
> bring all other mortals to the same way of living and the same
> opinion of God – unless there be something in this variety of
> religions which delights His inscrutable will.[88]

[87] 'Hos Vtopiani prudentiores, at illos sanctiores reputant. Quos quod caelibatum
anteferunt matrimonio, asperamque uitam placidae anteponunt, si rationibus
niterentur irriderent, nunc uero quum se fateantur religione duci suspiciunt ac
reuerentur. Nihil enim sollicitius obseruant, quam ne temere quicquam ulla de
religione pronuncient' (ibid., pp. 226/11–17, 227/16–23).

[88] 'Qua in re, si quid erret, aut si quid sit alterutra melius, et quod deus magis
approbet, orare se eius bonitas efficiat, hoc ut ipse cognoscat. paratum enim sequi se
quaqua uersus ab eo ducatur, sin et haec Reipublicae forma sit optima, et sua religio
rectissima, tum uti et ipsi constantiam tribuat, et caeteros mortales omneis ad eadem
instituta uiuendi, in eandem de deo opinionem perducat, nisi inscrutabilem eius
uoluntatem etiam sit, quod in hac religionum uarietate delectet' (ibid., pp. 236/16–
24, 237/17–26).

Their prayers manifest immediate faith and hope arising out of mediate doubt, as reflected in the accumulation of conditional clauses and qualifications. In repudiating absolute certitude, the Utopians show themselves prepared to respond to the providence of each emergent occasion, without presuming to fix a form and limit to the purpose of the Almighty, and in so doing, they diverge from Hythlodaeus, whose inability to accept the providential nature of actual human experience amounts to a form of despair.

By choosing to opt for the political role of Morus, More must have believed he was affirming the same faith as the Utopians. His trust in providence was revealed in his readiness to commit himself to action, not in any confidence that his chosen course was definitively the best. On the contrary, he knew from the outset that his political career was fraught with moral dangers, but he knew equally that Hythlodaeus' way was even more perilous because it ended in a negation of human responsibility, both temporal and spiritual. More chose action because he realized that there was no solution in trying to escape from the continuous experience of the human dilemma: a frightened withdrawal from one peril could merely land one in another. But as he was later to declare in *A Dialogue of Comfort against Tribulation*, the danger of falling into a further peril should not prevent one from escaping from the immediate, Hythlodaean one:

> if the ship were in perell to fall into Scilla / the fere of fallyng into Charibdis on the tother side / shall neuer let any wise master thereof to draw him from Scilla toward Charibdis first in all that euer he maye / But when he hath hym ones so far away fro Scilla, that he seeth hym safe out of that dainger / than will he begyn to take good hede to kepe hym well fro the tother.[89]

More's career after *Utopia* shows his efforts to know when to avoid Hythlodaeus' Scylla, by being Morus, and to realize the time when, to save himself from falling into Morus' Charybdis, he had to choose to be Hythlodaeus. Rather than being the helpless victim of his contrary impulses, More, by 1516, had concluded that to avoid the dangers of either one, he needed to be prepared to enact both as the time required. He believed that one must be in a perpetual state of responsiveness, just as he had shown the Utopians ultimately pre-

---

[89] *CW* 12, p. 148/3–8.

pared to be. As he advised John Batmanson in his *Letter to a Monk* of 1519–20, one should

> live in trembling, and, though hopeful, still [be] very fearful not only of the possibility of falling in the future, according to the saying 'He who stands, let him take heed lest he fall,' but also of the possibility of having fallen in the past, yes, even at the very moment you thought you were advancing the most.[90]

Through the process of composing *Utopia*, More discovered the rudiments of his mature philosophy. Such a penetrating consideration of the meaning of things was bound to be tied inseparably to a sense of history; it is not surprising, therefore, to read in Stapleton's *Life of More* that 'he studied with avidity all the historical works he could find'.[91] Few commentators have noticed that *Utopia* presents his first tentative conclusions concerning the process and pattern of history.

The Utopians preserve their historical records in annals ('diligenter et religiose perscriptos'), spanning 1,760 years from the original conquest of the peninsula by Utopus.[92] He began the process whereby a rude and rustic rabble ('rudem atque agrestem turbam') was eventually transformed into the most humane and cultured people in the world ('id quo nunc caeteros prope mortales antecellit cultus, humanitatisque').[93] Utopus did not attempt to institute a perfected state, but left Utopia in a condition to be embellished and developed through the course of future history, like the gardens of which he was so fond.[94] The Utopians have always made the most of their open options by being willing to exploit historical 'accidents' and take the best from other races and civilizations, as when some Romans and Egyptians survived shipwreck on the Utopian coast in AD 315: 'Now mark what good advantage their industry took of this one opportunity. The Roman empire possessed no art capable of any use which they did not either learn from the shipwrecked strangers or discover

---

[90] Rogers, *SL*, no. 26, p. 140.
[91] *The Life and Illustrious Martyrdom of Sir Thomas More*, trans. P. Hallett (London, 1929), p. 15.
[92] *CW* 4, p. 120/26ff.
[93] ibid., p. 112/4–5.
[94] ibid., p. 120/18ff.

for themselves after receiving the hints for investigation.'[95] Likewise, when Hythlodaeus tells them about Greek literature and philosophy, they reacted with the same eager responsiveness. They quickly mastered the language, and when shown some of Aldus' books, they shrewdly guessed how it was done: 'Though previously they wrote only on parchment, bark, and papyrus, from this time they tried to manufacture paper and print letters. Their first attempts were not very successful, but by frequent experiment they soon mastered both.'[96] Thus, by remaining open to its possibilities, the Utopians discover that history becomes the medium of various kinds of revelation: both of the potentiality for scientific development and good use of nature's gifts, also of the nature of truth, which emerges, they believe, through the process of time by its own natural force.[97] This is partly why they are so receptive to Christianity when it is preached to them, and why they allow for the possibility that further truths inherent in it may be revealed by its adaptation to their own situation, as when they fall into discussion concerning the necessity or otherwise of the apostolic succession.[98]

Because of their responsiveness to it, the Utopians find in their history the known march of God's providence. Yet their annals also attest to another manifestation of that providence: the tribulations that prevent men from perfecting an earthly paradise at the same time as they induce in them the wish to attempt to do so. Violent epidemics of pestilence have ravaged the population at least twice in their history, requiring the Utopians to replenish their lost numbers by recalling citizens from their colonies.[99] This in turn forces them into immoral and inequitable action, however rational: 'They would rather that the colonies should perish than that any of the cities of the island should be enfeebled' ('Perire enim colonias potius patiuntur,

[95] 'Hanc unam occasionem, uide quam commodam illis sua fecit industria. Nihil artis erat intra Romanum imperium, unde possit aliquis esse usus, quod non illi aut ab expositis hospitibus didicerint, aut acceptis quaerendi seminibus adinuenerint' (ibid., pp. 108/6–10, 109/6–10).

[96] 'et quum ante pellibus, corticibus, ac papyro tantum scriberent, iam chartam ilico facere, et literas imprimere tentarunt: quae quum primo non satis procederent, eadem saepius experiendo, breui sunt utrumque consecuti' (ibid., pp. 182/30–3, 183/34–7).

[97] ibid., p. 220/16–17.

[98] ibid., p. 218/14–16.

[99] ibid., p. 136/19ff.

quam ullam ex insulanis urbibus imminui').[100] As well, they have to confront a climate that is not particularly wholesome and a soil not naturally fertile.[101]

The way that the Utopians respond to these deficiencies symbolically suggests the providential purpose behind them, and of tribulation at large. They improve the barrenness of their soil through art and industry ('arte atque opera'), while they protect themselves against the atmosphere by a life of temperance.[102] *Utopia* as a whole figures forth More's belief, which he was later to expound fully in the Tower works, that the tribulatory imperfection of human nature itself similarly induces – or should induce – creative effort, social as well as individual, to mitigate its effects. Utopian history, particularly, shows what might be achieved, in the context of what cannot.

It is important to recognize the nature of More's embryonic sense of history, because it significantly foreshadows the view of the church he later argued in the controversial works, and helps explain the basis of some of the positions he assumed.

An analogy exists between the relation of Utopus to his posterity and that of Christ to his church. Both leave their followers fundamental beliefs whose implications will be worked out through the course of future history, and both establish institutions to be cultivated responsibly and developed. Even at the mundane level of their scientific advances, the Utopians learn the same truth about the nature of revelation that More would invoke against the reformers in arguing for the validity of the unwritten traditions of the church: 'in dyuerse times there may be mo thinges farther and farther reveled, and other then were desclosed at the fyrst'.[103] To try and bypass 1,000 years of the church's experience by returning to the scriptural fount was not only to misread the nature of that experience in the way Hythlodaeus misreads Utopia, but also faithlessly to deny the providence in it. In more ways than one, More, in *Utopia*, had learnt the foundations of all his future beliefs and actions.

Through retracing the steps of its composition, one has been able to see that *Utopia*, although begun as a rather whimsical hypothesis, soon turned into much more: the instrument for More's resolved understanding

---

[100] ibid., pp. 136/21–2, 137/28–9.
[101] ibid., p. 178/20–1.
[102] ibid., p. 178/21–2, 26.
[103] *The Confutation of Tyndale's Answer, CW* 8, II, p. 923/16–18.

of the world and himself. A fascinating sequence of letters at this time suggests that the final product elicited a characteristically ambivalent response from him; on one hand he was so excited by it (and satisfied with it) that he ardently desired to have it published, on the other he felt a strong inclination to keep it cloistered unto himself. The letters show him swinging violently from first one attitude to the other. In a letter of 3 September 1516, presumably soon after he had completed book 1, he wrote to Erasmus to inform him that he was sending his 'Nusquamam' and to express confidence in Erasmus' ability to pay proper attention to 'everything else';[104] on 20 September he wrote again to impress upon Erasmus that he was anxious to have it published soon, and also that 'it be handsomely set off with the highest of recommendations, if possible, from . . . both intellectuals and distinguished statesmen';[105] on 31 October he was still very 'anxious' that *Utopia* should gain the approval of Tunstal, Busleiden and John le Sauvage, but feared that it might not, 'since they are so fortunate as to be top-ranking officials in their own governments';[106] on 4 December he described to Erasmus the expansive vision in which he imagined himself to be the Utopians' chosen leader;[107] and on 15 December he was eagerly awaiting the arrival of his *Utopia* 'with the feelings of a mother waiting for her son to return from abroad'.[108] Suddenly, soon after the time when he must have received some copies of the printed book, there is an abrupt change. In a letter of January 1517 to William Warham, former Archbishop of Canterbury, More, begging Warham to accept a copy, now protests that Peter Giles 'allowed his affection to outweigh his judgement, though it worthy of publication, and without my knowledge had it printed'.[109] He reiterates this notion in another letter of January 1517, to an unnamed member of Court, asserting that, without his knowledge ('me . . . insciente'), Giles had ravished *Utopia* of the first flower of her maidenhead.[110] There are various possible explanations for this about-face: More could have been being disingenuously modest, or he might have been annoyed that the text had been printed before he had

[104] Rogers, *SL,* no. 6, p. 73.
[105] ibid., no. 7, p. 76.
[106] ibid., no. 10, p. 80.
[107] ibid., no. 11, p. 85.
[108] ibid., no. 12, p. 87
[109] ibid., no. 13, p. 89.
[110] Rogers, *Correspondence,* no. 32, p. 87; *SL,* no. 14, p. 90.

had a chance of seeing any editorial emendations,[111] or he may have been embarrassed by the printer's errors and the general shoddiness of the 1516 volume. Another letter of the same month, however, suggests a far deeper reason. It is written to Antonio (?Bonvisi), and in it More declares that Bonvisi's esteem for him is the result of love's having spread darkness over his thinking, as witnessed by his approval of *Utopia*, 'a book which I think clearly deserves to hide itself away forever in its own island'.[112] This sentiment implies far more than mere dissatisfaction at defects in the book's presentation; it suggests that More had had second thoughts about the wisdom of publishing it at all. He perhaps came nearest to revealing the real truth of the matter in his choice of the profoundly suggestive metaphors of another statement in his letter to the unnamed courtier; More wonders whether he should have kept *Utopia* with him 'ever unwed', or perhaps have consecrated her to Vesta and initiated her into Vesta's sacred fires ('caelibem perpetuo apud me seruarem aut Vestae forsan consecrarem; sacrisque eius initiarem ignibus').[113] These images invoke one of the forms of sanctity More most revered: chastity; they also associatively recall his yearning for the spiritual devotion of the cloister. *Utopia* is associated with both, which attests to the real importance that the book had for him, and also the deeply private and personal nature of its meaning. More must have realized, as he certainly did later,[114] that few readers were likely to derive the same meaning from *Utopia* that he had, let alone want to. (History proves that indeed they have not!) For that reason, More regretted having published *Utopia* as soon as its publication was irrevocable – a familiar and understandable human reaction.

Utopia was the last occasion on which More succumbed to the temptation of airing the innermost complexities of his private thought in public. This book was the culmination of a strategy that had begun

---

[111] See the suggestions of Arthur E. Barker, '*Clavis Moreana:* The Yale Edition of Thomas More', *Essential Articles*, pp. 215–28, esp. pp. 219–23.

[112] Rogers, *SL*, no. 15, p. 90.

[113] Rogers, *Correspondence*, no. 32, p. 87; *SL*, no. 14, p. 90.

[114] See *The Confutation of Tyndale's Answers*, *CW* 8, I, p. 179/8ff.: 'I saye therfore in these dayes in whyche men by theyr owne defaute mysseconstre and take harme of the very scrypture of god, vntyll menne better amend, yf any man wolde now translate Moria in to Englyshe, or some workes eyther that I haue my selfe wryten ere this, all be yt there be none harme therin / folke yet beynge (as they be) geuen to take harme of that that is good / I wolde not onely my derlynges bokes but myne owne also, helpe to burne them both wyth myne owne handes.'

with the tacit contextual ironies of the earlier works, but which, after *Utopia*, was exhausted in its possibilities, dangerous for the misconceptions it could arouse, and unnecessary in any case. Thenceforth, More's works were cast in a different mould, being unambiguous, heuristic, and, with the exception of *De Tristitia Christi*, written primarily for others. More could afford to let them be so, because after *Utopia* he no longer had to struggle to find out what he understood about life and himself.

3

Archetype and Antitype: *The History of King Richard III, The Four Last Things*

In his 1557 edition of More's English works, William Rastell prefaced *The History of King Richard III* with the remark that it was written 'about the yeare of our Lorde. 1513' while More was 'than one of the vndersheriffs of London'.[1] Not only is this assertion inaccurate, but it has also distracted commentators from perceiving how central the *History* was in More's intellectual career.

Recent research has shown that he was certainly at work on the manuscript after 1 February 1514, when Henry Howard was made Earl of Surrey, and that he could have been working on it as late as 1527, when Elizabeth (alias Jane) Shore – referred to as still alive in the English text[2] and as 'nunc septuagenaria vetula' in the Arundel MS[3] – died. The *History* must thus be considered as the frame in which *Utopia* is set, having been begun before *Utopia* was written and resumed after its completion. The two works are parallel and complementary in ways that have not been recognized, rather than antithetical and divergent.

An important statement in More's letter to Oxford University of 29 March 1518, precisely the time when he was likely to have been most actively engaged with the *History*, suggests how this might be so. Defending the advantages of a secular liberal education, More asserts that the foundation of the study of theology is knowledge of human nature and the human situation ('Noscenda est et rerum humanarum prudentia') which, apart from the poets and orators, can best be learnt from historians ('quae peritia haud scio an alicunde vberius, quam e poetis, oratoribus, atque historicis hauriatur').[4] Given More's

---

[1] *CW* 2, p. 2.

[2] ibid., p. 55/27.

[3] See Sylvester's discussion, ibid., p. lxiv, and Alison Hanham, *Richard III and His Early Historians, 1483–1535* (Oxford, 1975), pp. 217–19.

[4] Rogers, *Correspondence*, no. 60, p. 116/132–6.

belief in the necessity of a prudent consideration of human behaviour as preparation for any effort to grasp the meaning of things, we can see why he should have been pursuing his own investigation of recent English history so near the time when he was formulating the philosophical conclusions of *Utopia*; we can also infer that his decision to enter the king's service was made in the light of the knowledge of political affairs which the usurpation of Richard III provided. We must look, therefore, for a meaning in the *History* that confirms rather than confutes that of *Utopia*.

What, then, did More see in the events of 1483 capable of inducing him to write about them so elaborately? More than anything else, the period furnished a mirror of the perpetual situation of men in temporal history, intensified in degree, and therefore more visible, but not different in kind. It reflected the vulnerability of human nature to the temptations of the devil, in this instance typified in the evil of Richard of Gloucester, the antitype of the true Christian man, and the power of the devil to pervert political institutions to the hurt of a whole society; it demonstrated the failure of free will and responsibility which allows such lapses to happen, and which engender their own chastising consequences; and it also revealed the kind of action required of men of good will in a political situation to prevent the triumph of the devil. At this level, More was contemplating the likely implications of his own entry into Tudor politics and, as in *Utopia*, he saw in John Morton the pattern of action he was inclined to imitate (as indeed he did, particularly as Chancellor between 1529 and 1532).[5] More's writing of *The History of King Richard III* was not just a diverting humanistic aside, but had a significant bearing on his own political career.

It was also important for his intellectual career. As the English poems reveal, More in his youth had been extremely perturbed by the tragic realities he observed in human affairs, such things as he would describe in *The Four Last Things* as

the bodily paines of deth, the troubles and vexacions spiritual, that come therewith by thy gostly enemy the deuil, the vnrestfull cumbrance of thy fleshly frendes, the vncertentie of thy self, howe soone this dreadfull time shal come, that thou art euer sick of

---

[5] See Elton, 'Sir Thomas More and the Opposition to Henry VIII', *Essential Articles*, pp. 79–91; Guy, pp. 95ff.

that incurable sicknes, by whiche if none other come, thou shalt
yet in fewe yeres vndoutedly die[6]

as well as a host of more immediate tribulations. In 1503 he had been
unable to find any meaning in them sufficient to prevent him from
seeking to withdraw into the shelter and comfort of the cloister; in
1504 he had decided to commit himself to an active life in the world,
but the *Life of John Picus* shows how ambiguous he nonetheless felt
about having done so; thereafter, his greatest need was to find an
explanation of the nature of things which could allay the perturbations of the mind at the same time as it justified the experience of
them. The reign of Richard III, for More, was the most apocalyp-
tically perturbing episode in English history; if he could discover a
divine purpose in it, then he could accommodate all the rest of human
experience, and his own, within a secure understanding. Both *Utopia*
and the *History* confirm that he did. More turned the reign of Richard
III into an archetypal image of the series of recurrent 'passions' which
he saw had constituted history at large and always would do until the
end of time. Although such disastrous lapses were entirely the product
of human free will, they were nonetheless comprised within God's
eternal providence; their tributatory consequences were not only the
means for divine chastisement of human sinfulness, but also the very
instrument by which God brought good out of evil through the
renovation and amendment they induced in men of good will. By
affirming this, the *History* both reinforced the conclusions of *Utopia* and
also anticipated all that More would later say in the controversial
writings. His opposition to the drift of future proposals for reform,
constitutional and legal as well as ecclesiological, sprang in part from
his interpretation of Richard's reign. If the Great Turk in More's last
English work, symbolically encompassing the heretics and Antichrist,
were to be the expected recurrence of all that Richard III had
archetypally prefigured, More's own later actions were to be the
unwritten continuation of his English *History*, and *A Dialogue of Comfort
against Tribulation* his conclusive exegesis of it.

Like Utopia, the *History* is representational and dramatic in its nature
rather than simply expositional.[7] For this reason its meaning must be

---

[6] *EW* 1557, p. 82 F–G.

[7] See A. F. Pollard, 'The Making of Sir Thomas More's *Richard III*', *Essential Articles*,
pp. 421–31; Arthur Noel Kincaid, 'The Dramatic Structure of Sir Thomas More's
History of King Richard III', ibid., pp. 375–87; and Hanham, *Richard III and His Early
Historians*, pp. 174–85.

inferred, since it is not directly stated; any attempt to do so presents the critic with a daunting array of 'literary problems' arising from More's pervasive use of irony,[8] whose function is to intimate an underlying reality in events that belies their superficial appearance.

The first striking example of this is More's depiction of Edward IV's reign, with which the *History* opens. At first sight, it appears as if More's thematic strategy will be to show a descent from ideal order, typified in the condition of England under Edward, into disorder wrought by Richard's usurping tyranny, and followed by the restoration of order under Henry VII in accordance with nature and religious law.[9] Such was the didactic pattern imposed upon events by Polydore Vergil according to his rationalizing humanist norm.[10] To Vergil, Edward IV, 'after all intestine dyvision appeasyd, . . . left a most welthy realme abownding in all thinges, which by reason of cyvill warres he had receavyd almost utterly voyd as well of hable men as money'.[11] Richard, having destroyed this order through the cruelty of his nature and ferocity of his ambition, 'had suddaynly suche end as wont ys to happen to them that have right and law of God and man in lyke estimation, as will, impyetie, and wickedness',[12] and was succeeded by Henry VII, the true type of the faithful Christian prince.[13] In Vergil's view, 'the reign of Richard III had been just an unfortunate incident that preceded, and paved the way for, the triumphant establishment of a new dynasty',[14] a temporary disturbance in the ordinary course of nature. The neat moral and aesthetic symmetry of Vergil's design was to be reproduced in John Hardyng's *Chronicle* and Edward Halle's *Union of the Two Noble Families*, and hence was to form the basis of an orthodox Tudor view of the period. More had no such illusions about the ideal nature of either Edward's reign or that of Henry VII.[15] Since the first draft of Vergil's manuscript can be dated

---

[8] Dean, 'Literary Problems in More's Richard III', *Essential Articles*, pp. 315–25.

[9] See Sylvester, *CW* 2, p. lxxxii; Hanham, *Richard III and His Early Historians*, p. 175; and Kincaid, p. 379.

[10] Probably in imitation of Tacitus' account of the contrast between Augustus' reign and that of Tiberius (see Sylvester, *CW* 2, p. xciii).

[11] Henry Ellis (ed.), *Three Books of Polydore Vergil's English History*, Camden Society (London, 1844), p. 172.

[12] ibid., p. 226.

[13] ibid.

[14] Hanham, *Richard III and His Early Historians,* p. 127.

[15] See the satiric portrayal of Henry VII's reign in More's epigram addressed to Henry VIII (Bradner and Lynch, no. 1).

to 1513 or 1514, More could have conceivably seen it, and almost certainly knew about it.[16] In his usual fashion, he subjected the didactic simplifications of the humanist view to ironic scrutiny. Just as *Utopia* contains an ironic discrepancy between Hythlodaeus' moralization of Utopian polity and its real character, so in the *History* does a second perspective obtrude to undermine the first, ostensible one.

The dual perspective appears in the description of Edward IV himself. More couches the description in the idealistic commonplaces of ritual humanist praise:

> He was a goodly parsonage, and very Princely to behold, of hearte couragious, politique in counsaile, in aduersitie nothynge abashed, in prosperitie, rather ioyfull then prowde, in peace iuste and mercifull, in warre, sharp and fyerce, in the fielde, bolde and hardye, and nathelesse no farther then wysedome woulde, aduenturouse.[17]

Almost immediately some disconcordant notes are sounded: 'howe bee it in his latter dayes wyth ouer liberall dyet, sommewhat corpulente and boorelye, and natheless not vncomelye, hee was of youthe greatelye geuen to fleshlye wantonnesse'.[18] The ideal prince, it appears, is infected with the sins of lust and gluttony, and as More adds one flashback to another, it becomes clear that to these must be added other sins more heinous. Along with Richard and Clarence, Edward was 'greate and statelye of stomacke, gredye and ambicious of authoritie, and impacient of parteners',[19] which led him first to seek revenge on Henry VI for the death of his father,[20] and then to procure the death of his brother Clarence, as More declares with caustic irony: 'whose death kynge Edwarde (albeit he commaunded it) when he wist it was done, pitiously bewailed and sorowfully repented'.[21] In the account of Edward's marriage to Elizabeth Grey, More shows him wilfully disregarding all politic council, taking instead 'counsaile of his desyre' to enter into a marriage which was 'an vnsitting thing, and a

---

[16] See Sylvester, *CW* 2, p. lxxvi, and Hanham, *Richard III and His Early Historians*, p. 147.
[17] *CW* 2, p. 4/9–14.
[18] ibid., p. 4/18–20.
[19] ibid., p. 6/26–8.
[20] ibid., pp. 6/28–7/1.
[21] ibid., p. 7/13–15.

veri blemish, and highe disparagement, to the sacre magesty of a prince, that ought as nigh to approche priesthode in clenes as he doth in dignitie, to be defouled with bigamy in his first mariage',[22] besides being the root cause for all the ensuing troubles because of the factionism it eventually brought into being.

The same ambivalence is established concerning Edward's reign. It is initially characterized as ideal: 'thys Realm was in quyet and prosperous estate: no feare of outewarde enemyes, no warre in hande, nor none towarde, but such as no manne looked for: the people towarde the Prynce, not in a constrayned feare, but in a wyllynge and louyng obedyence: amonge them selfe, the commons in good peace.'[23] Yet, as with the portrait of the king, a more ambiguous substructure is revealed behind the outward appearance. There is a precise reason for the harmony of the realm which makes us suspicious as to the game Edward has been playing: 'He hadde lefte all gatherynge of money', which, the narrator satirically adds, 'is the onelye thynge that withdraweth the heartes of Englyshmenne fro the Prynce'.[24] It becomes increasingly clear that Edward has been cynically bribing his subjects in a fashion Richard will soon try to emulate; in the last summer of his life, Edward sent for the Mayor and Aldermen of London to join him at Windsor:

> For none other eraunde, but too haue them hunte and bee mery with hym, where hee made them not so statelye, but so frendely and so familier chere, and sente Venson from thence so frelye into the Citye, that no one thing in manye dayes before, gate hym eyther moe heartes or more heartie fauoure amonge the common people, which oftentymes more esteme and take for greatter kindenesse, a lyttle courtesye, then a greate benefyte.[25]

The reality underlying Edward's reign, More shows, is that it is not essentially different in kind from that which Richard will try to erect; the main difference is that Edward gets away with it whereas Richard does not. Edward gives him all his leads, in his ambition, his wilfulness, his dissimulation, his violent affront against natural bonds

[22] ibid., p. 62/26–9; that we mistrust the motives of the Duchess of York who voices this reproach does not lessen its truth.
[23] ibid., p. 4/26–30.
[24] ibid., p. 5/1–2.
[25] ibid., p. 5/15–21.

of kinship, and his ruthless elimination of opponents. It is therefore a pathetic self-deception for Edward to hope that his posterity will be able to succeed him as if recent history did not exist, and his deathbed oration contains hints that he does not really expect that they will. He regrets too late the process by which he has achieved his own quiet, which has left the kingdom in a condition ripe for rivalry and dissension: 'Whiche thinges yf I coulde as well haue foresene, as I haue with my more payne then pleasure proued, . . . I woulde neuer haue won the courtesye of mennes knees, with the losse of soo many heades.'[26] It is not surprising that Buckingham is able to paint a very different picture of the previous reign in his address to the Londoners at the Guildhall, when he resuscitates Edward's crimes to plague his memory and deprive his son of the succession.[27]

In exposing the 'ideal' condition of Edward's reign as a contrived illusion, More was seeking to prepare his readers for the real import of the *History*: a realization that Richard's reign merely manifests in extreme form circumstances that pertain in all political situations. That fact was the real problem with which men had to come to terms in grappling with the meaning of history, and More's ironic exposure of the humanist utopianized version of the period reflected his awareness of how understandably eager men are to find ways of evading the issue. The undermined picture of a contrast between Edward's ideal reign and Richard's corrupt one is that which Raphael Hythlodaeus would have postulated, but More shows that the two reigns were no more and no less divergent than he had shown Europe to have been from Utopia.

The larger relevance of the *History* is communicated indirectly through its allusions, images and structure. These all serve to underline the archetypal nature of events.

Typical of More's literary procedure is the association and conflation of diverse literary allusions bearing a weight of symbolic suggestiveness.[28] In the *History* the significance of Richard in More's imagination is revealed through the archetypes adumbrated within his character. At one level, verbal allusions associate him with the

---

[26] ibid., p. 13/3–6.

[27] ibid., pp. 70–4.

[28] For a demonstration of this procedure in a specific instance, see Alistair Fox, 'Thomas More's *Dialogue* and the *Book of the Tales of Caunterbury*: "Good Mother Wit" and Creative Imitation', in *Familiar Colloquy: Essays Presented to Arthur Edward Barker*, ed. Patricia Brückmann (Ottawa, 1978), pp. 15–19.

long succession of tyrants described by the classical historians.[29] He overgoes Sallust's Jugurtha by being not merely 'homo omnium quos terra sustinet sceleratissimus', but 'virum omnium quos sustineret terra clarissimum' – 'a Sallustian villain masquerading as the most praiseworthy of heroes', as Sylvester aptly says.[30] Like Suetonius' Tiberius, who is 'asper et immitis', Richard is 'crudelis atque immitis', or, as the English version puts it, 'dispitious and cruell'.[31] Most of all, Richard reproduces the tyrannical characteristics of Tacitus' Tiberius in the depth of his dissimulation ('Hee was close and secrete, a deepe dissimuler . . . outwardly coumpinable where he inwardely hated'),[32] and the terrors he inflicts: 'a series of savage mandates, of perpetual accusations, of traitorous friendships, of ruined innocents'.[33] And like Tiberius, he suffers 'the out and inward troubles of tyrauntes'.[34] He is thus the symbolic apotheosis of all there is in human nature and political circumstances that produces the recurrence in history of the tyranny that More so intensely loathed.

This is not all that Richard represents, however. In the Council scene within the Tower, when Richard orders the summary execution of Hastings, he swears an oath which embodies a resonant allusion to scripture: 'by saynt Poule (quod he) I wil not to dinner til I se thy head of'.[35] This recombines associatively the details of Acts 23:12, which describes the Jews who 'banded together, and bound themselves under a curse, saying that they would neither eat nor drink till they had killed Paul'.[36] By likening Richard to the Jews and underlining the similarity between the two occasions, this allusion emphasizes the antichristian nature of Richard's malice; he is more than he knows he is. Another scriptural allusion deepens the implications still further. Richard is described in his dissimulation as 'not letting to kisse whome hee thoughte to kyll'[37] – a reference to Judas at the betrayal of Christ. As More made clear in his later writings, he

[29] Demonstrated definitively by Sylvester, *CW* 2, pp. lxxxvi–xcix.
[30] See *CW* 2, p. lxxxvii.
[31] ibid., p. xciii, n. 2, and p. 8/10.
[32] ibid., p. 8/7–9; see Sylvester, p. xciv.
[33] *Annals* 4, p. 34, quoted by Sylvester, *CW* 2, p. xcv.
[34] *CW* 2, p. 87/12ff. and marginal gloss; cf. *Annals* 6, p. 6.
[35] *CW* 2, p. 49/12–13.
[36] For further analysis of this allusion, see Alistair Fox, 'Richard III's Pauline Oath: Shakespeare's Response to Thomas More', *Moreana*, 57 (1978), pp. 13–23.
[37] *CW* 2, p. 8/9.

regarded Judas as the type of those who 'by defaute of good wyll . . . [wax] in conclusyon gracelesse',[38] so becoming 'the chyldren of darkenes' who 'be more polytyke in theyr kynde then are the chyldren of lyght in theyr kynde'.[39] The Judas reference thus paints Richard as representing something far more sinister than the mere tyranny of the Roman emperors, since Judas, in the nature of his treason, was 'worse also then the very worst in al the world beside'.[40] In More's mind Richard was a manifestation of the working of the devil, and he gave him an emblematic physical description to match. Richard's outward appearance reflects his inner distortion: 'little of stature, ill fetured of limmes, croke backed, his left shoulder much higher then his right, hard fauoured of visage'.[41] Even the circumstances of his birth (the account of which More warns us to read as fancy rather than fact) are contrived to suggest his unnaturalness, 'whiche in the course of his lyfe many thinges vnnaturallye committed'.[42]

We perceive as the *History* unfolds that the action is as metaphorical as it is literal, a representation of the perpetual subversion attempted by the devil in human affairs. A further sign of this function of the work resides in another strategically placed allusion. When the queen delivers up her son to be taken out of sanctuary, she utters words that echo Griselda's farewell to her child in Chaucer's *Clerk's Tale*:

> And therewithall she said vnto the child: farewel my own swete sonne, god send you good keping, let me kis you ones yet ere you goe, for God knoweth when we shal kis togither agayne. And therewith she kissed him, and blessed him, turned her back and wept and went her way, leauing the childe weping as fast.[43]

This echoes verbally and contextually both occasions when Griselda gives up her children to the 'ugly sergeant':

> And in her barm this litel child she leyde
> With ful sad face, and gan the child to kisse
> And lulled it, and after gan it blisse.

[38] *CW* 8: *The Confutation of Tyndale's Answer*, I, p. 514/28–9.
[39] ibid., p. 36/29–31.
[40] *The Apology*, *EW* 1557, p. 877 G.
[41] *CW* 2, p. 7/19–21.
[42] ibid., p. 7/29–30.
[43] ibid., p. 42/8–12.

And thus she seyde in hir benigne voys,
'Far weel, my child; I shal thee never see;
But, sith I thee have marked with the croys,
Of thilke fader blessed mote thou be,
That for us deyde up-on a croys of tree.
Thy soule, litel child, I him bitake,
For this night shaltow dyen for my sake,'[44]

This ugly sergeant, in the same wyse
That he hir doghter caughte, right so he,
Or worse, if men worse can devyse,
Hath hent hir sone, that ful was of beautee.
And ever in oon so pacient was she,
That she no chere made of hevinesse,
But kiste hir sone, and after gan it blesse.[45]

It is easy to see why the parallel between Queen Elizabeth and
Griselda occurred to More. Both suffer adversity brought about by the
tyranny of 'dispitious' rulers who deprive them of their children. In
the *History* it is Richard; in *The Clerk's Tale* it is Walter, who arouses a
murmur in the common people similar to that which Richard will
soon arouse: 'That of a cruel herte he wikkedly, / Hath mordred
bothe his children prively.'[46] The double parallel must also have
prompted More to realize how close the figurative meaning of
Chaucer's tale was to his own historical sense. At the figurative level
in *The Clerk's Tale*, Walter is not only a type of Satan, but also, from a
different perspective, a type of God in the way he tests men through
tribulation:

He preveth folk al day, it is no drede,
And suffreth us, as for our excercyse,
With sharpe scourges of adversitee
Ful ofte to be bete in sondry wyse;
Nat for to knowe our wil, for certes he,
Er we were born, knew al our freletee;
And for our beste is al his governaunce;
Lat us than live in vertuous suffraunce.[47]

---

[44] Chaucer, *Complete Works*, E 551–60.
[45] ibid., E 673–9.
[46] ibid., E 723–5.
[47] ibid., E 1155–62.

These lines could almost serve as a precise gloss on More's sense of the ambivalence of the historical experience he is depicting: from one perspective it manifests the rampaging of the devil; from another it is a manifestation of God's wise providence.

Richard is both a cause and a consequence of tribulation. The full relevance of the historical episode involves more than him alone. The nearest More comes to stating it explicitly is when he is moved to exclaim on the death of Hastings and the young princes. He observes of Hastings as the latter makes his fateful way to the meeting in the Tower that 'he was neuer merier nor neuer so full of good hope in his life', and is struck most forcibly by 'the vain sureti of mans mind so nere his deth'.[48] A page later he expresses even more powerfully the relevance of Hastings' fate: 'O good god, the blindnes of our mortall nature, when he most feared, he was in good suerty: when he rekened him self surest, he lost his life, and that within two howres after.'[49] The same moral is drawn concerning the pitiful fate of the two princes, raised royally and destined for rule, but traitorously ruined through 'the cruel ambicion of their vnnaturall vncle and his dispiteous tormentors': 'which thinges on euery part wel pondered: god neuer gaue this world a more notable example, in what vnsuretie standeth this worldly wel'.[50] Uppermost in More's mind is a sense that the tragic outcome of Richard's ambition is merely symptomatic of the human situation generally. In the short term its tribulation may be explicable as a result of human sinfulness exploited by the devil, but ultimately it is something that God allows men purposefully to suffer.

By emphasizing this idea, More was subjecting the influence of the classical historians to that of his own native English religious and historiographical tradition. To see this, one need look no further than the chronicles of his immediate English predecessors.

John Rous, for example, in his *Historia de regibus Anglie,* detected a typological analogy between Richard's reign and that of Antichrist, and was alert to the same cosmic irony of events in terms of the divine perspective: 'This King Richard, who was excessively cruel in his days, reigned for three years and a little more, in the way that Antichrist is to reign. And like Antichrist to come, he was confounded

---

[48] *CW* 2, p. 51/11–14.
[49] ibid., p. 52/13–16.
[50] ibid., p. 86/19–22.

at his moment of greatest pride.'[51] Rous also gives a ballad pur-
portedly written by Lord Rivers during his imprisonment at Ponte-
fract, in which Rivers reads in his fate the same lesson that More saw
in that of Hastings:

> Sumwhat musyng
> And more mornyng
> In remembryng
> The unstydfastnes
>
> Thy world beyng
> Of such whelyng
> Me contrarieng
> What may I gesse?
>
> I fere dowtles
> Remediles
> Is now to sese
> My wofull chaunce.
>
> Lo in thys traunce
> Now in substaunce
> Such is my dawnce
> Wyllyngly to dye
>
> Me thynkys truly
> Bowndyn am I
> And that gretly
> To be content.
>
> Seyng playnly
> That fortune doth wry
> All contrary
> From myn entent.[52]

For Rivers (or, more probably, Rous) the world's mutability mocks
the complacency of human expectations, and makes a vanity of
human wishes.

Such sentiments were universal in the chronicles and poetry of the
fifteenth century and earlier, and More's own English verse showed

[51] I quote Alison Hanham's translation (*Richard III and His Early Historians*, p. 123).
[52] ibid., p. 119.

how responsive he was to them from an early age. Unlike later humanist optimists, the native chroniclers did not look for a liberally educated prince to remedy the irremediable; rather, the typical response was like that of the author of the *Historiae Croylandensis continuatio*,[53] who drew his moral in some concluding Latin verses:

> Qui legis haec hominum tot mutatoria rerum
> Magnorum, cur non mundi mutabilitatem
> Totam contemnis? cur vanae gloria pompae
> To mentemve tuam tangit?[54]

More, too, knew that his *History* was dealing as much with the right and wrong responses that human experience induces as literal historical facts.

At the deepest level, then, *The History of King Richard III*, like *Utopia*, is a metaphor for the human situation itself. Yet although More was concerned to show that the nature of that situation is ultimately beyond men's power to control, he was also concerned to show the extent of human responsibility in bringing it into being and the extent to which it could be mitigated.

The prime reason was men's readiness to succumb to the temptations of their spiritual enemy, the devil, through the promptings of Pride. In the events of 1483 pride manifests itself as a pervasive, universal ambition in all the participants, as Edward IV recognizes when, in his deathbed oration, he voices a time-honoured commonplace: 'Suche a pestilente serpente is ambicion and desyre of vaine-glorye and soueraintye, whiche amonge states where he once entreth crepeth foorth so farre, tyll with deuision and variaunce hee turneth all to mischiefe.'[55] The image of ambition as a serpent evokes the temptation of Adam and Eve in the Garden which wrought the first fall of mankind. By doing so, it also suggests the presence of Satan in the events of the *History*, seeking to tempt men to repeat that first accursed fall, as indeed they do. Almost everyone proves to be infected

---

[53] Probably John Russell, Lord Chancellor under Richard III, whom More may conceivably have met; see Sylvester, *CW* 2, p. lxxii.

[54] *Rerum Anglicarum scriptorum veterum* (Oxford, 1684), I, p. 577. ('You who read of these innumerable changes in the lives of great men, why do you not despise the entire mutability of the world? Why does the glory of empty pomp touch your mind?')

[55] *CW* 2, p. 12/21–5.

with ambition, envy and pride, and these words resound through the text like a dominant chord. All three sons of Richard, Duke of York, are 'gredye and ambicious of authoritie';[56] Clarence was 'a goodly noble Prince' who would have been 'at all pointes fortunate, if either his owne ambicion had not set him against his brother, or the enuie of his enemies, his brother agaynste hym',[57] Richard is 'dispitious and cruell, not for euill will alway, but ofter for ambicion';[58] Catesby betrays Hastings because 'he trusted by his deth to obtaine much of the rule that the lorde Hastinges bare in his countrey';[59] Edmond Shaa, the Mayor of London, connives at events 'vpon trust of his own aduauncement, whereof he was of a proud hart highly desirouse';[60] Sir James Tyrell contrives the murder of the princes because he had 'an high heart, and sore longed vpwarde, not rising yet so fast as he had hoped, being hindered and kept vnder by the meanes of sir Richarde Ratclife and sir William Catesby, which longing for no moo parteners of the princes fauour, and namely not for hym, whose pride thei wist would beare no pere, kept him by secrete driftes oute of all secrete trust';[61] and Morton is able eventually to tempt Buckingham into rebellion because 'the duke was an high minded man, and euyll could beare the glory of an other'.[62] All these men are blind to the world's inherent unsurety, and so unwittingly help to bring it into being at the same time as ironically suffer its effects.

The catastrophe depicted in the *History* becomes as bad as it does not only because individuals succumb to their sinful motions, but also because of a massive failure of free will throughout the body politic. More believed that the good use of institutional customs and provisions could mitigate the worse effects of sinfulness; conversely, failure to use them or the perversion of their right use would accelerate the innate human tendency towards degeneration. In Richard's England he saw that this had happened.

The first instance is the failure of nerve of the then Chancellor, the Archbishop of York, in seeing through his resolve to keep the machinery of government in the hands of the queen. When news

---

[56] ibid., p. 6/27.
[57] ibid., p. 7/2–5.
[58] ibid., p. 8/10.
[59] ibid., p. 46/23–4.
[60] ibid., p. 58/17–18.
[61] ibid., p. 84/3–9.
[62] ibid., p. 90/9–10.

reaches him from Hastings that the Dukes have arrested Rivers, Gray and Vaughan at Stony Stratford and have seized custody of the young king, he at once sees the sinister implications: 'I assure him [i.e. Hastings] quod the Archebishoppe bee it as well as it will, it will neuer bee soo well as we haue seene it.'[63] Thereupon he arms his household and takes the great seal with him to the queen as a provision against usurpation. This action could have prevented the mischief from proceeding any further, had he seen it through:

> Madame quod he, be ye of good chere. For I assure you if thei crowne any other kinge then your sonne, whome they nowe haue with them, we shal on the morowe crowne his brother whome you haue here with you. And here is the greate Seale, whiche in likewise as that noble prince your housebande deliuered it vnto me, so here I deliuer it vnto you, to the vse and behoofe of youre sonne.[64]

When, however, he sees the Thames full of boats manned by Richard's retainers and sundry companies armed in the streets, the Archbishop's courage deserts him: 'fearing that it wold be ascribed (as it was in dede) to his ouermuch lightnesse, that he so sodainly had yelded vp the great seale to the Quene, to whome the custodye thereof nothing partained without especial commaundement, of the kynge, secretely sent for the Seale againe'.[65] Given that the Archbishop already foresees what might happen, his about-face amounts to a self-regarding preference for his own safety over that of the realm, justified by a disingenuous (and belated) scruple of conscience.[66]

The other most serious dereliction of responsibility also concerns the clergy, when they fail to sustain the privilege of sanctuary. When the Protector first proposes that the Duke of York be taken from sanctuary, the clergy at first agree to it only on condition that it should be by the queen's assent: 'it were not in anye wyse to be attempted to take him oute agaynste her wil. For it would bee a thynge that shoulde

---

[63] ibid., p. 21/13–15.
[64] ibid., p. 22/5–11.
[65] ibid., p. 22/28–32.
[66] Hastings, the Lord Chamberlain, similarly lets his actions be governed by his desire to remain in favour with the more powerful party. Commenting on the arguments Hastings used to allay the Lords' fears, More observes 'parte hym selfe belieued, of parte he wist the contrarye' (ibid., p. 23/25–6).

tourne to the greate grudge of all menne, and hyghe dyspleasure of Godde, yf the priueledge of that holye place should now bee broken.'[67] Just as he realized that the customary use of the great seal provided a potential safeguard against constitutional abuse, so does the Archbishop, acting as spokesman, recognize the true purpose of sanctuary: 'Godde forbydde that anye manne shoulde for anye thynge earthlye enterpryse to breake the immunitee, and libertye of that sacred Sainctuary, that hath bene the safegarde of so many a good mannes life.'[68] It is all the more ironic that the clergy give way and betray this privilege when events prove with an unparalleled tragic force how necessary it had been for them to have defended it. The clergy's submission is made reprehensible enough by the queen's ability to perceive the real aim of Richard's 'painted processe',[69] but it is made still worse by a suggestion that they may have acceded even while knowing the truth. More intimates this in his account of the climactic exchange between the queen and Cardinal Bourchier: 'she began to kindle and chafe, and speke sore biting wordes against the protectour, and such as he neither beleued, *and was also loth to here*'.[70] The Cardinal believes only what he wants to, and is reluctant to be reminded of anything, however true, that might threaten the comfort of the conscience he has framed for himself. More's exposure of this failure of responsibility in the clergy is in itself significant, for as he was to say in *A Dialogue Concerning Heresies*, quoting Colet, 'it can be no lye that our sauyor saythe hym selfe / whiche sayth of them that they be salt of the erthe. And yf the salte ones apalle / the worlde must nedys waxe vnsauery.'[71]

The nerveless collapse of the clergy is thrown into highlight by the contrast between them and those to whom they should have given a lead: the London citizens. When Buckingham at the Guildhall invites the Londoners, on behalf of Richard, to ensure their bodies and goods by expressing themselves 'prone and beneuolently minded toward his eleccion',[72] they forestall this attempt to bribe them into loyalty by invoking their customary procedure of being spoken to only by the

---

[67] ibid., p. 27/29–32.
[68] ibid., p. 28/9–12.
[69] ibid., p. 38/9–10.
[70] ibid., p. 40/9–11; my italics.
[71] *CW* 6, p. 298/5–8.
[72] *CW* 2, p. 74/32–3.

Recorder, 'whiche is the mouth of the citie'.[73] Hence they are able to spoil the effect Buckingham has been aiming for and reduce the situation into one of bathetic farce:

> When the duke had saied, and looked that the people whome he hoped that the Mayer [the collusive Edmond Shaa] had framed before, shoulde after this proposicion made, haue cried king Richarde, king Richard: all was husht and mute, and not one wod aunswered therunto. Wherewith the duke was meruailously abashed.[74]

When the Recorder is eventually forced to rehearse to the Commons what the Duke had twice rehearsed before, he is still able to 'temper' the matter in such a way that it elicits the same silence as before. Buckingham is thus foiled in his desire to dress Richard's usurpation in the trappings of popular acclaim, and the fake acclamation procured from his bought claque serves only to expose more nakedly the travesty of the 'mockishe ('ludicram') eleccion' taking place.[75]

The whole event is strangely prophetic of More's action as Speaker in the Parliament of 1523, when, if Roper can be believed,[76] he frustrated Wolsey's attempt to bully the Commons in proving 'by manye probable argumentes that for them to make awneswer was it neyther expedient nor agreable with the auncient libertie of the house'. The correspondence between the two episodes confirms More's belief in the power of custom and procedure to retard, at least, the onslaughts of tyranny. The tragedy in 1483 was that those in a position to exploit such provisions failed, through cowardice, to do so.

Human evil, although inherent and irremediable, is made worse when men wane in their determination to restrain its effects. Irresponsibility in men of good will is thus punished by the success of men of ill will which it promotes. But their apparent success, More shows, is never more than transitory and hollow; evil not only destroys, but is also self-detructive, working the means for its own chastisement.

Richard, with 'his restles herte continually tossed and tumbled

---

[73] ibid., p. 75/18–22.
[74] ibid., pp. 74/34–75/5.
[75] ibid., pp. 82/9, 5.
[76] Roper, pp. 18–19; Halle, however, does not mention the incident.

with the tedious impression and stormy remembrance of his abomin-able dede', and his reign, marked by dissension and conspiracy, provide the most striking exemplum of the consequences of infringing divine, natural and human law,[77] but his example is not the only one.

It is the queen's own ambition that is responsible for her commit-ting the fatal errors of judgement that ruin her party and deprive her children of life and the succession. More emphasizes that she had politicly placed her kin around the Prince of Wales 'whereby her bloode mighte of youth be rooted in the princes fauor'.[78] This taints both her and her kindred, as is suggested by the punning collocation of the name Rivers with a reference several lines earlier to the 'robbers and *riuers*' in Wales, a country which, 'being far of from the law and recourse to iustice, was begon to be farre oute of good wyll'.[79] Symbolically, Wales is the country that the queen and her party are aspiring to inhabit by their attempt to gather the advantages of sovereignty to themselves. Ironically, it is this very 'drift' that 'the Duke of Gloucester turned vnto their destruccion, and vpon that grounde set the foundacion of all his vnhappy building',[80] for he is able to play upon the queen's guilty awareness of it to persuade her not to have the prince brought to London attended by a large body of her party in case it is misconstrued.[81] Her fatal overcompensation allows Richard to gain possession of the prince and to replace her ambition with his own.

If there is a central moral design in the *History*, it revolves around the motif of 'the biter bit', according to which those who prey on others become victims of their own devices. Rivers, Gray and Vaughan fall because Richard is able to accuse them of having 'coumpassed to rule the kinge and the realme';[82] the irony of their ruin is not so much that the trumped-up charge is true, as that they are brought down by someone who has precisely the same ambition. Hastings, too, becomes a victim of a strategy that mirrors his own: 'he was of the taking of her kynred, and of their putting to death, which were by his assent before, deuised to bee byhedded at Pountfreit, this selfe same day, in which he was not ware that it was by other deuised,

[77] *CW* 2, p. 87/4–24.
[78] ibid., p. 14/16–17.
[79] ibid., p. 14/3–11; my italics.
[80] ibid., p. 14/17–19.
[81] ibid., p. 16/11ff.
[82] ibid., p. 19/10–11.

that himself should the same day be behedded at London'.[83] All these instances of retributive poetic justice show that although in history the innocent cannot escape the affliction of evil, the guilty do not prosper long in it, which intimates that the play at hand may be far more complicated than any of the participants in the action think.

Everyone these days acknowledges that the *History* is dramatic in nature, and there have been several fine studies of aspects of its dramatic construction, [84] but the full implications of the central play metaphor remain incompletely assessed.

Richard's usurpation is clearly presented as a play, stage-managed by Richard and Buckingham, in which the 'sowter' turns himself into the 'sowdayne' – or, metaphorically speaking, the Great Turk Antichrist.[85] It is a king's 'game', a comedy (in the medieval sense) consisting of Richard's rise to high degree and prosperity in his attainment of the crown. Yet More's reworking of the Lucianic conceit also makes it clear that Richard's comedy is simultaneously England's tragedy, as the stage becomes literally a scaffold, and the common man is forced increasingly into the role of a helpless onlooker, lest 'one of his tormentors might hap to breake his head . . . for marring of the play'.[86] The human drama is inevitably a tragi-comedy, depending upon whose perspective it is viewed from. Few of the protagonists realize that both the comic and tragic elements are contained within a larger divine comedy, in which God is frustrating the devil by turning human actions to his own end.

Herein lay the quintessential paradox of human experience for More. Men are entirely free to choose to act, or not to act, as they please, yet they create circumstances as a result of their free choices which limit the scope of their freedom. Surrounding this paradox was an even larger one: no matter what actions, good or bad, men chose to perform, they could not fail to become instrumental in God's encompassing design. His justice could not be mocked, nor could his creative purpose be frustrated.

This is depicted not only in the cleansing of evil by evil, but also in the response that the tragic intensity of events begins to induce in the

---

[83] ibid., p. 48/2–6.
[84] Kincaid detects the influence of the medieval morality plays (*Essential Articles*, pp. 375–87); Hanham stresses the influence of Terentian comedy and Lucian (*Richard III and His Early Historians*, pp. 177–8); see also Dean, p. 324.
[85] Cf. *CW* 2, p. 81/1ff.
[86] ibid.

course of the *History*. A kind of counterpointing of thematic and dramatic opposites is engendered in the action. Richard's rise to the summit of his 'comic' success precipitates a descent of the body politic towards a tragic nadir; yet the extremity of England's plight is in itself responsible for inducing a countermovement that will eventually procure his fall. In the *History* this countermovement is focused in the character and actions of John Morton, Bishop of Ely.[87]

The presence of Morton in the *History* forges its closest link with *Utopia*. In both works he is praised in unequivocal terms as a man who 'by the long and often alternate proofe, as wel of prosperitie as aduers fortune, hadde gotten by great experience the verye mother and maistres of wisdom, a depe insighte in politike wordli driftes'.[88] Morton has learnt through personal experience that life ordinarily involves men in adversity and shifts in fortune, and so he is able to view the usurpation in its true light: as merely an extreme manifestation of the tribulation brought about by the world's inherent mutability. He has also observed the workings of human nature. Because he recognizes the true nature of what is taking place, he is also able to grasp how he, as a man of good will, is required to act in the circumstances. To act like Hythlodaeus, by denouncing the imposter 'whyle he standeth in his magestie', would do no good and merely disorder the play; instead, Morton adopts the course of action advocated by Morus: he acts his part in the play at hand so as to make as little bad as possible that which cannot be made entirely good. His eventual success demonstrates the truth More asserted later in *The Confutation of Tyndale's Answer*: 'yf we be not only symple as douys, but also prudent and wyse as serpentes / his [God's] inwarde vnccyon wyll worke wyth our dylygence'.[89] Morton is careful to appear 'simple', as with Richard at the meeting in the Tower, or with Buckingham at Brecknock Castle, but he is as wily as the serpent that proverbially lies under the strawberries he is prepared to fetch for Richard.[90] By acting in this paradoxical way, he is outwitting the devil at his own game, and shows himself to be the true type of responsible

---

[87] For a similar view, see Kincaid, p. 379.

[88] *CW* 2, p. 91/18–21; cf. *Utopia*, *CW* 4, p. 58/19–30, where Morton is also praised for the wisdom ('prudentia') he has derived from experience.

[89] *CW* 8, II, p. 890/3–5.

[90] For variants of the serpent under the flower, see B. J. Whiting, *Proverbs* (Cambridge, Mass., 1968), S153, pp. 508–9.

Christian man of which Richard is the mere parody. Their mode of action is the same, but the difference in their motives lends substance to the one and hollowness to the other.

Morton's awareness of the larger divine context of historical events allows him to maintain a degree of detachment which enables him to be creatively involved in them. He was at first 'fast vpon the part of king Henry', and wished to see Henry's son succeed to the throne; however, 'after that god had ordered hym to lese it', Morton was content in conscience to serve Edward IV with equal faith and wisdom, and would have been glad if his son had succeeded him;[91] yet as he says to Buckingham: 'if the secrete iudgement of god haue otherwyse prouided: I purpose not to spurne againste a prick, nor labor to set vp that god pulleth down'.[92] Morton is at every point prepared to acknowledge a divine purpose in the happenings and consequently to be responsive to any providential calling he detects in them. His words to Buckingham conceal a double irony, since Buckingham does not realize the extent to which the 'prick' Morton feels involves the abuse of his own pride to Morton's deliverance, his destruction, and the establishment of a new royal dynasty.

More did not need to complete the *History*, because his own age was still in the process of enacting its continuation. Possibly he also foresaw that, like Morton, he would soon have to respond to yet another shift in England's stormy fortunes.

Altogether, the *History* demonstrates that history is continuously dynamic. Men cannot perfect the situation from which it derives, yet if they wane in their determination to try, evil will grow so rampant as to induce them back into the effort. Richard's usurpation is not merely a temporary disturbance in the natural course of history; it exemplifies the militant nature of the human condition.

More did not find this sense of history in his pagan models, nor in the didacticism of the humanist historians. I have already suggested that it was deeply ingrained in strands of the native English literary tradition, but to find a more precise source we have to look back to his study of *De civitate Dei*.

Stapleton tells us that in his lectures on *De civitate Dei* of about 1501, More discussed the work 'not from a theological point of view, but

---

[91] *CW* 2, pp. 90/24–92/11.
[92] ibid., p. 92/12–14.

from the standpoint of history and philosophy'.[93] It is hard to see how More could have separated history from theology in that work, and we need not follow Stapleton in the rigidity of his distinction. What he probably meant was that More concentrated on the original cause of Augustine's writing: the historical meaning of the fall of Rome in the context of the progress of the church militant through temporal history.

Augustine's task was to refute those who asserted that the sack of Rome by Alaric and his Goths in 410 was caused by the Romans' desertion of their pagan gods for Christianity. One can easily see how More might have sensed a typological relation between that apocalyptic assault and all the subsequent historical tribulations his investigation of history had revealed to him. The fall of the eternal city, associated with reason, law and order, was a symbol for all that has power to perturb the human mind; allegorically, it furnished an image of the apparent triumph of Antichrist in this world. As More's English poems attest, at the time of his lectures on *De civitate Dei* he was both perturbed by, and preoccupied with, the inescapable evidence of mutability, irrationality and injustice in human affairs. Augustine's attempt to justify God's ways to men in the first five books of his massive work must have impressed him with the intellectual consolation it sought to offer. As one contemplates More's own treatment of an English 'fall of Rome' in the recent history of his own country, it is as well to consider Augustine's view, upon which we know More commented in the church of St Lawrence Jewry.

Men should not, Augustine asserted, impute Rome's calamities unto Christ: 'if they had any judgment, they would rather attribute these calamities and miseries of mortality, all unto the providence of God, which useth to reform the corruption of men's manners, by war and oppressions, and laudably to exercise the righteous in such afflictions'.[94] Good and bad suffer tribulation together in this world, 'for as in one fire, gold shineth and chaff smoketh . . . so likewise one and the same violence of affliction, proveth, purifieth, and melteth the good, and condemneth, wasteth, and casteth out the bad'.[95] These same beliefs were absolutely central in More's thought. In his Preface to *The Confutation of Tyndale's Answer* he declared what, in his *History*, he had already shown:

[93] *Life of More*, p. 9.
[94] *The City of God*, trans. John Healey, with an Introduction by Ernest Barker (London, 1931), bk. 1 chap. 1, p. 5.
[95] ibid., chap. 18, p. 16.

our lorde of his especyall prouydence, vseth temporally to punyshe the hole people for the synnys of some parte, to compell the good folke to forbere and abhorre the noughty. . . . And yet bysyde thys somewhere he sendeth warre, sykenesse, and mortalyte / to punyshe in the fleshe that odyouse and hatefull synne of the soule, that spoyleth the frute from all manner of vertues. . . .[96]

As *A Dialogue of Comfort against Tribulation* more amply confirms, it was in terms of this same sense of providence that More understood the meaning of the Great Turk – symbolically encompassing the heretics, the Ottoman Turks and Antichrist in one.[97] Since More had encountered Augustine's exposition of this fundamental tenet as early as 1501, it is not likely that he temporarily abrogated it when dealing with the equally obvious manifestation of evil in the person of Richard III (or, for that matter, when contemplating the historical experience of his antipodeans in *Utopia*).

One consequence of the Augustinian view is that history is never likely to produce the ideal exemplary condition that humanist philosphers would have liked to construct. More's exposure of the parallels between the worlds of Edward IV and Richard III underlying the apparent contrasts showed that he had grasped this point full well.

Another of Augustine's assertions is equally relevant to Richard's reign. He declares that 'if the devils have any power or can do anything at all in these affairs, it is no more than what they are permitted to do by the secret providence of the Almighty'.[98] Furthermore, 'God, that only and true author of felicity, He giveth kingdoms to good and to bad; not rashly, nor casually, but as the time is appointed, which is well known to Him, though hidden for us. . . .'[99] This idea, too, predominates in the *History,* and underlies the belief and actions of Morton in particular. Events could have been otherwise, had God so willed, but for some secret cause he provided for them to be as they were. Edward IV himself realizes that even though he is trying to ensure the prosperous continuance of peace and

---

[96] *CW* 8, I, p. 3/11–26.
[97] *CW* 12, p. 17/12 *et passim.*
[98] *City of God,* bk. 2, chap. 23, p. 89.
[99] ibid., bk. 4, chap. 33, p. 212.

harmony, the fulfilment of his intent is dependent on God's will. In a subjunctive clause he prays that 'Godde as well forgeate as wee well remember' the civil dissension that had 'within these fewe yeares growen in this realme'.[100] He then expressed a further condition: 'Nowe be those griefes passed, and all is (Godde bee thanked) quiete, and likelie righte wel to prosper in wealthfull peace vnder youre coseyns my children, if Godde sende them life and you loue.'[101] Edward himself, however, undermines his own hope by half-expressing an expectation that events might be led to a different conclusion: 'Of whyche twoo thinges, the lesse losse wer they by whome thoughe Godde dydde hys pleasure, yet shoulde the Realme alway finde kinges and paraduenture as good kinges.'[102] Edward knows, as Shakespeare later made his citizens say, that 'All may be well; but, if God sort it so, / 'Tis more than we deserve or I expect.'[103] As More makes subsequent events show, God did not forget the ills of earlier years, nor did his pleasure confer life upon the princes and love between the nobles; the greatest challenge to men was to see how that was providentially so.

For both Augustine and More, to affirm this conception of God's often tribulatory ways was not to deny the freedom of human will, even though the two might seem irreconcilably opposed. Augustine declared that necessity and God's foresight do not hinder men's wills in anything; a man does not sin because God foreknew that he would sin: 'nay, . . . it is doubtless that he sins, when he does sin, because that God, whose knowledge cannot be mistaken, foresaw that neither fate nor fortune, nor anything else, but the man himself would sin, who if he had not been willing, he had not sinned'.[104] In his *Answer to Frith's Letter*, More similarly denied that God's providential foresight took away from men the ability to make their own free choices:

> Such blinde reasons of repugnaunce induceth many men into great errour, some ascribing all thyng to destyny without any power of mannes free wyll at all, and some gyuing al to mans

---

[100] *CW* 2, p. 13/1–2.

[101] ibid., p. 13/9–12.

[102] ibid., p. 13/12–14. The sense seems garbled, but the Latin makes it clear that Edward means that civil war would be even more catastrophic than the death of the princes (*CW* 2, p. 175, note to p. 13/12–13).

[103] *Richard III*, II. iii. 36–7.

[104] *City of God*, bk. 5, chap. 1, p. 217.

owne wyll, and no forsyght at all vnto the prouidence of God, and al because the pore blind reason of man cannot se so farre, as to perceiue howe goddes prescience and mannes free wyll can stande and agree togyther.[105]

The compatibility in More's mind between God's prescience and human free will meant that his *History* was devoid of the mechanistic conception of arbitrary providential retribution found in Polydore Vergil and of the larger predestinarian scheme imposed on fifteenth-century history by the later Tudor chroniclers.[106] In Vergil's *Anglica historia*, for example, destiny positively intervenes to prevent Richard from doing anything to save himself from escaping from the punishment he deserves. After having beacons prepared on the coast to warn of any invasion, Richard succumbs to a false sense of security:

And thus king Richerd, soomwhat easyd of his griefe, began to be more careles, least otherwise he might by dylygence have avoyded the desteny that hang over his head; for such is the force of divine justice, that a man lesse seath, lesse provydeth, and lesse hede taketh when he ys nighe the yealding of punishement for his haynous offences.[107]

Likewise, Hastings dies because 'He was one of the smyters of prince Edward, king Henry the vj[ths]. soon, who was fynally quyt with the like maner of death',[108] and the princes are murdered because 'suche matters often happen for thoffences of our ancestors, whose faults redownd to the posterytie'.[109] More's sense of providential retribution was far more complex than this. What happens in history is not because destiny determines that it should, but because the free choices of men are such that it inevitably will. Nevertheless, although historical events are not performed by God, they represent the outcome of his wise provision, since 'his wisdom better seeth what is

[105] *EW* 1557, p. 839 H.

[106] The predestinarian elaborations of historians such as Holinshed and Foxe are appraised by William Haller, *Foxe's Book of Martyrs and the Elect Nation* (London, 1963), pp. 140–86; and H. A. Kelly, *Divine Providence in the England of Shakespeare's Histories* (Cambridge, Mass., 1970).

[107] *Three Books of Polydore Vergil's English History*, p. 214.

[108] ibid., p. 151.

[109] ibid., pp. 189–90.

good for us than we do ourselves'.[110] More, with as much conviction as his Utopians, believed with Augustine that 'it is no way credible, that He would leave the kingdoms of men, and their bondages and freedoms loose and uncomprised in the laws of His eternal providence'.[111]

The probable date of composition of *The History of King Richard III*, sometime between 1513 and 1522, with the main part being written around 1518, makes its relevance to More's own political situation clear. Whereas *Utopia* had established the reasons for his decision to enter politics, the *History* explored the 'civil philosophy' in action in circumstances More knew he would probably have to confront. No one has yet acknowledged, however, that it has equally close relations with *The Four Last Things*.

These consist of verbal and thematic correspondences which, in the nature of the relationship they establish, may help to explain why More broke off the *History*, and also further illuminate his sense of the full implications of his decision to enter the king's service.

The correspondences are seen in small instances, such as the statement that 'the heart of a wicked wretch is like a stormy sea that cannot rest',[112] which recalls the reference to Richard's 'restles herte continually tossed and tumbled with the tedious impression and stormy remembrance of his abominable dede',[113] and also in larger thematic reduplications, as when More again reworks the Lucianic stage metaphor (with a significant shift from the third to the second person) to argue that worldly worship is no cause for a man to be puffed up with pride:

> If thou sholdest perceue that one wer ernestly proud of the wering of a gay golden gown, while the lorel playth the lord in a stage playe, woldest thou not laugh at his foly, considering that thou art very sure, that whan the play is done, he shal go walke a knaue in his old cote? Now thou thinkest thy selfe wyse ynough whyle thou art proude in thy players garment, and forgettest that whan thy play is done, thou shalt go forth as pore as he. Nor thou

[110] Letter of 3 September 1529 to Dame Alice More on the occasion of the burning of his barns (Rogers, *SL*, no. 42, p. 170).
[111] *City of God*, bk. 5, chap. 2, p. 218.
[112] *EW* 1557, p. 73 H.
[113] *CW* 2, p. 87/19–21.

remembrest not that thy pageant may happen to be done as sone as hys.[114]

Such parallels are close enough to suggest a proximity in composition. Yet the similarities offset the differences between the two works. In 1518 More was fully confident in the value of the study of secular literature, as his letter to Oxford University proves; by 1522 he had retreated to a more reactionary position:

> If there were anye questyon amonge menne, whyther the woordes of holy scripture, or the doctryne of anye secular authour, were of greater force and effecte to the weale and profyte of mannes soule, . . . yet this onely text written by the wise man in the seuenth chapiter of Ecclesiasticus[115] is suche, that it conteineth more fruitfull aduise and counsayle, to the formyng and framing of mannes maners in vertue, and auoyding of sinne, then many whole and great volumes of the best of old philosophers, or anye other than euer wrote in secular litterature.[116]

What was responsible for the change? Possibly the judicial murder of the third Duke of Buckingham in 1521[117] shocked More into recognizing that the history of King Richard III was beginning to be rewritten in his own time, and also forced him to confront the severe effects on his own moral being of having decided to enact Morus' advice in *Utopia*. The result was a retreat to the dualities and *contemptus mundi* of his earlier English poems.

The register of the change is the oppressive, unrelieved morbidity of *The Four Last Things*; it is choked with images of disease, pain and

---

[114] *EW* 1557, p. 84 B–C.

[115] 'In omnibus operibus tuis memorare novissima tua, / Et in aeternum non peccabis' (Ecclesiasticus 7:40).

[116] *EW* 1557, p. 72 B–C.

[117] Although the view that Buckingham's trial and execution amounted to judicial murder has been challenged (Barbara Harris, 'The Trial of the Third Duke of Buckingham: A Revisionist View', *American Journal of Legal History*, 20 (1976), pp. 15–26), most authorities agree that it was; see M. Levine, 'The Fall of Edward, Duke of Buckingham', in *Tudor Men and Institutions*, ed. A. J. Slavin (Baton Rouge, 1972), pp. 32–48, and G. R. Elton, *Reform and Reformation: England 1509–1558* (London, 1977), pp. 81–2.

execution, and there is no laughter to alleviate the perception of man's miserable condition, from which none can escape:

> as condemned folk and remediles, in this prison of the yerth we driue forth a while, some bounden to a poste, some wandring abrode, some in the dungeon, some in the vpper ward, some bylding them bowers and making palaces in the prison, some weping, some laughing, some laboring, some playing, some singing, some chidinge, some fighting, no man almoste remem-bringe in what case he standeth, till that sodeynlye nothyng lesse loking for, yong, old, pore and rych, mery and sad, prince, page, pope and pore soul priest, now one, now other, sometimes a gret rable at once, without order, without respect of age or of estate, all striped stark naked and shifted out in a shete, bee put to deth in diuers wise in some corner of the same prison, and euen ther throwen in an hole, and ether wormes eat him vnder ground or crowes aboue.[118]

This metaphorical depiction of the human situation, as conventional as it is, is little short of a cry of horror, as intense as anything in the *ars moriendi* tradition out of which it sprang.[119] Gone is the sense that there is anything that a man of good will, like Morton in the *History*, can do. All that is left to one is for each man

> by the labour of his minde and helpe of praier, [to] enforce himself in all tribulacion and afflicion labour paine and trauaile, without spot of pride or ascribing any praise to himself to conceiue a delite and pleasure in such spiritual exercise, and thereby to ryse in the loue of our lorde, with an hope of heauen, contempt of the world, and longing to be with God.[120]

More's hairshirt and self-inflicted scourging become immediately comprehensible.[121]

The cause of More's changed mood was probably the part he had

---

[118] *EW* 1557, p. 84 E–G.
[119] For an account of More's debt to medieval models, see H. W. Donner, 'St Thomas More's Treatise on the Four Last Things and the Gothicism of the Transalpine Renaissance', *Essential Articles*, pp. 343–55.
[120] *EW* 1557, p. 75 F.
[121] Roper, pp. 48–9.

had to play in Buckingham's execution. Shortly after the Duke's beheading, More had been sent to the Court of Aldermen to inform the Londoners that the king was displeased at their grumblings concerning it. Four days later he had been sent again to urge them to appease the king's wrath.[122] His complicity in these events must have reminded him, with a more than incidental force of irony, of the thoughts he had given the London citizens as they observe the sham reluctance of Richard in accepting the crown from the second Duke of Buckingham: 'there was no man so dul that heard them, but he perceiued wel inough, that all the matter was made betwene them. Howbeit somme excused that agayne, and sayde all must be done in good order though. *And menne must sommetime for the manner sake not bee a knowen what they knowe.*'[123] More, too, knew well enough, and his knowledge is expressed in *The Four Last Things* when he describes the example of a 'great Duke':

> if thou sholdest sodeinly be surely aduertised, that for secret treason lately detected to the king he shold vndoutedly be taken the morow his courte al broken vp, his goodes ceased, his wife put out, his children dysherited, himselfe caste in prison, broughte furth and arrayned, *the matter out of question*, and he should be condemned, his cote armour reuersed, his gilt spurres hewen of his heles, himself hanged drawen and quartered, how thinkeste thou by thy fayth amyd thyne enuy shouldeste thou not sodaynly chaunge into pity?[124]

Just as the Londoners had decided that 'thei that wise be, wil medle no farther' with the plays that kings stage, since they 'disorder the play and do themself no good',[125] so had More acted according to a belief that 'if thou can find no proper meane to break the tale, than excepte thy bare authoritie suffice to commaunde silence, it were paraduenture good, rather to keepe a good silence thy self, than blunt forth rudely, and yryte them to anger'.[126] Nevertheless, the effect on him had been severe, and one senses that *The Four Last Things* may

[122] Repertory of the Court of Aldermen, V, fol. 204, 204b, 5 July, 9 July, 1521; see Chambers, p. 192.
[123] *CW* 2, p. 80/23–7; my italics.
[124] *EW* 1557, p. 86 B–D; my italics. Rastell misprints 'enny' for 'enuy'.
[125] *CW* 2, p. 81/6–10.
[126] *EW* 1557, p. 76 C.

have been written out of remorse as a penitential exercise to concoct a 'tryacle' capable of restoring him in his own mind to spiritual health.

The close connections between *The Four Last Things* and the *History* suggest that More may have broken off the *History* once he realized that the third Duke of Buckingham was meeting the second Duke's fate, and that with respect to it he had had to assume Morton's political *modus operandi* to a degree that had compromised him morally, as Hythlodaeus had predicted it would. The validity of this speculation, however, depends upon whichever theory of the texts of the *History* one accepts; I shall therefore offer a textual hypothesis in support of the notion.

Both the extant Latin versions of the *Historia*, that of the Arundel MS and that in the 1565 Louvain *Opera omnia*, end with Richard's usurpation. As several scholars have suggested, the span of these texts may reflect More's original intention: to trace Richard's rise only as far as his coronation.[127] The English versions printed in Hardyng's *Chronicle* in 1543, Halle's *Union of the Two Noble Families* in 1548 and 1550, and Rastell's 1557 edition, however, continue the work to cover the murder of the princes and Morton's incitement of Buckingham to rebellion. In the version(s) upon which these texts were based, More clearly envisaged covering the full reign: 'King Richarde himselfe as ye shal herafter here, [died] slain in the fielde, hacked and hewed of his enemies handes, haryed on horsebacke dead, his here in despite torn and togged lyke a cur dogge.'[128] In addition, he promises a more detailed account of Perkin Warbeck, should he 'write the time of the late noble prince of famous memory king Henry the seuenth, or parcase that history of Perkin in any compendious processe by it selfe'.[129] The discrepancy between the English and Latin versions has led to the prevailing theory that the Latin texts reach only as far as the usurpation because, at the time when they were written, that is as far as More had taken the English text.[130] Nevertheless, another hypothesis seems equally possible. More could just as readily have written the English version to the point where we now have it in Rastell's 1557 version, having begun at some earlier stage, or written concurrently, a

---

[127] Sylvester, *CW* 2, p. li; Hanham, *Richard III and His Early Historians*, p. 201.

[128] *CW* 2, p. 87/4–6.

[129] ibid., p. 83/1–3. The Halle texts adjust the phrasing here to fit the disposition of Halle's continuation for the reign (adapted from Vergil).

[130] Hanham, *Richard III and His Early Historians*, p. 200.

Latin version which is now preserved in the text of the Arundel MS.[131] He could then have decided *subsequently* upon the limits of the final Latin revision, which formed the basis of the 1565 *Historia*. The Latin text upon which Louvain was based contains so much substantive material not found in the English *History* (witness the need Rastell felt to translate portions from it)[132] that it appears not to have been prior to the final English version; rather, it is more likely that More revised and augmented the Arundel text in such a way as allowed him to say as much as he wanted about Buckingham's motivation without showing anything of his treasonous plotting against the king. In fact, I would suggest that the section on Buckingham's ambition in the Louvain Latin appears where it does[133] because More had decided to cancel the more extended version of it he had composed in the later 'treasonous' context of the English version,[134] retaining for the Louvain Latin only as much of it as he could use with political discretion. This would explain why Rastell, anxious to preserve all parts of More's composition, achieved such a clumsy effect by including his translated portion at the place where it occurs in the Latin, which, as Sylvester says, gives 'a curiously conflated, almost *déjà vu*, version of the narrative'.[135]

This hypothesis is supported by evidence in Halle's English version. Just after the account of the death of the princes, Grafton adds a marginal gloss: 'From the beginnyng of Kynge Edward the fifte: hetherto, is of sir Thomas More's penning.'[136] Yet a few pages later the text includes the Morton/Buckingham episode as it appears in Rastell's 1557 version, with the addition of further feigned dialogue by Halle, but without acknowledging the Morean section as More's. If the Grafton/Halle texts are based on an edited version of the 1557 text as Alison Hanham suggests,[137] this would further support the idea that More himself cancelled the material relating to Buckingham's

[131] For a convincing case that the *History/Historia* was an exercise in dual composition, see Sylvester, *CW* 2, pp. liv–lviii.
[132] See Sylvester, *CW* 2, pp. xxxi–xxxii.
[133] *CW* 2, p. 42/23ff.
[134] ibid., p. 87/22ff.
[135] ibid., p. xxxi.
[136] *The Union of the Two Noble Families of Lancaster and York, 1550,* Scolar Press reprint (Menston, 1970), sig. AA5.
[137] Hanham, *Richard III and His Early Historians,* p. 205ff. One need not follow her conclusion that More was responsible for all the alterations in the G/H texts.

plot in the English version. Grafton printed it regardless, but this is not surprising if the edited manuscript came into either his or Halle's hands in a state comparable to that of the Valencia holograph of *De Tristitia Christi*, in which the cancelled passages are still eminently legible, as its modern editor has proved. Moreover, in the light of our certain knowledge that English versions of the *History* circulated in manuscript at least as early as 1538,[138] it would seem likely that Grafton should come upon the edited version rather than the copy from which Rastell printed, which may not have been circulated at all.

An illuminating analogy is provided by More's (and Rastell's) later treatment of the *Second Part of the Confutation of Tyndale's Answer*.[139] More originally intended to issue this work with a ninth book, and wrote a substantial part of it. Intervening political circumstances forced him to abandon it and direct his attention elsewhere. The printer received only Books 4 to 8 for publication; Rastell, however, printed the suppressed part in his own edition of the English works, presumably having found the fragmentary book 9 among More's papers. It is not hard to imagine that Rastell might have done much the same with the *History*, considering the draft in his possession to represent More's fullest intent, but ignorant in fact (as he was with the *Treatise upon the Passion*)[140] of More's final conception. It is also possible that More failed to complete the *History/Historia* across its projected span for the same reason he failed to complete book 9 of the *Confutation*: because a more urgent preoccupation intervened, in this case perhaps the need to answer Luther's *Contra Henricum regem Angliae* in 1522. But the nature of his transpositions and emendations in *Richard III* suggests that this was not the only cause, especially when More had ample time to continue with it during the hiatus in his polemical writing between the *Responsio ad Lutherum* of 1523 and the *Dialogue Concerning Heresies* of 1528–29. It is difficult to believe that More's personal and political response to Buckingham's trial and execution played no part, given the evidence in *The Four Last Things* that he had been extremely perturbed by it. Apart from the political indiscretion of putting forth a work depicting incitement to treason revolving around rival dynastic claims in the context of the 1520s,[141]

---

[138] Sylvester, *CW* 2, p. xxvii.
[139] See below, chap. 7.
[140] See below, chap. 9.
[141] See Pollard, *Essential Articles*, pp. 430–1.

More's equanimity must have been shaken by the way events in his own life were ratifying so shockingly his representation of those in time past. The force of the parallel had made More understand even more feelingly than when he wrote it the potency of the objections to the civil philosophy he had given Hythlodaeus in *Utopia*: by participating in political affairs, the philosopher merely becomes as tainted as the rest.

More's close encounter with the reality of politics had obviously taken its toll by 1522, and was tempting him to lose sight of the meaning of history and providence in the larger context. By *The Four Last Things* he had come close to repudiating the view he had attained in the writing of *Utopia* and *The History of King Richard III*, but the impulse to retreat into a withdrawn, interiorized spirituality was an overcompensation that More could not sustain. *The Four Last Things* remain unfinished,[142] and by the time the *Responsio ad Lutherum* had appeared in two versions by the end of 1523, he had not only reasserted his former view of the world, but had also been forced to contemplate implications in it of which, earlier, he had hardly dreamt.

---

[142] Had More persisted according to his original scheme, *De Quattuor Novissimis* would have been a massive treatise; as it is, he covered only the first of the four last things, and even then did not complete the digression on the seven deadly sins into which it led him, getting (ironically) no further than Sloth.

PART TWO

The Controversies

4

The Problem of the Controversies

By 1522 More had developed a personal view of the human situation together with a sense of the *modus vivendi* it required of a man of his talents and aspirations. *Utopia* and *The History of King Richard III* had represented his attempts to express this view in philosophical and historical terms, and his decision to enter the king's Council had been its practical outcome.

Up to this point the evolution of his intellectual career is coherent, if complex. One can observe a man of acute intelligence with an unusual capacity to combine all the diverse aspects of his being and experience into a unique, personal synthesis. From the time he entered into religious controversy until his imprisonment, however, the picture clouds. As one reads the polemical works the features and complexion of the man alter, the synthesis revealed in the earlier works becomes less and less apparent, and the coherence of the total man threatens to vanish from sight altogether.

The controversies, in fact, present the student of More with his greatest problem in understanding him. Paradoxically, they contain his most public and explicit utterances, yet at the same time they veil more completely than any of his other writings the inner experience of the private man. That experience was profound: it radically affected More's personality, it threatened to destroy his sense of providence, and it eventually brought him close to despair. Its existence is revealed not so much in More's intellectual argument, as in the external character of the controversies themselves. In them one can trace a pattern of progressive deterioration: dialogue gives way to debellation, self-control yields to loss of proportion and perspective, candour is replaced by dishonesty, and charity is displaced by violence. Until these changes can be explained, the real Thomas More must inevitably remain an enigma.

To gain a perspective on the problem, one needs to analyse the foundations of the two earliest assessments of More vis-à-vis the controversial works.

The view formulated by those impressed by his saintliness did not acknowledge any changes in him at all. William Roper, being concerned to show that his father-in-law was 'A Mirror of Virtue in Worldly Greatness', found all the evidence he needed in the outward character of More's life: in his meekness, wisdom, and love of learning,[1] his lack of ambition for worldly honour and rewards,[2] his spiritual exercises and devotions,[3] and in the heroic integrity of his death. Roper mentions that More wrote the controversies 'in defens of the true religion, against hereseies secreatly sowen abrode in the Realme',[4] but that is all; he does not assess them, or even describe them, and one senses that they held little interest for him. It seems altogether likely that More kept his family at a safe remove from his private feelings regarding his polemical task, just as he hid much of his devotional life. Only his daughter Margaret, for example, even knew that he wore a hairshirt until one of the other daughters saw it accidentally at supper, to More's consternation.[5] Likewise, 'He vsed also sometymes to pvnishe his body with whippes, the cordes knotted, which was knowen only to my [Roper's] wife . . . whom for secrecy aboue all other he specially trusted.'[6] A man inclined to conceal so much of his inner life was not likely to have directed Roper's attention to the area of activity where his passions were most deeply engaged, far less to have confessed any secret perturbation arising from his polemical war.

One particular anecdote well illustrates this point. Shortly before the king's divorce became a major issue, Roper tells us, he rejoiced to his father-in-law in the happy estate of the realm, 'that had so chatholike a prince that no heretike durst shewe his face, so vertuous and learned a clergy, so grave and sound a nobility, and so loving, obedient subiectes'. More at first commended all estates and degrees even more enthusiastically, but a heated disagreement developed when he continued:

[1] Roper, p. 21.
[2] ibid., p. 25.
[3] ibid., pp. 48–9.
[4] ibid., pp. 45–6.
[5] ibid., pp. 48–9.
[6] ibid., p. 49.

'And yeat, sonne Roper, I pray god' [said] he, 'that some of vs, as highe as we seeme to sitt vppon the mountaynes, treading heretikes vnder our feete like antes, live not the day that we gladly wold wishe to be at a league and composition with them, to let them haue their churches quietly to themselfes, so that they wold be contente to let vs have ours quietly to our selves.' After that I had told him many consideracions why he had no cause so to say: 'Well,' said he, 'I pray god, sonne Roper, some of vs live not till that day,' shewing me no reason why [he] should put any doubte therein. To whom I said: 'By my troth, sir it is very desperately spoken.' That vyle tearme, I cry god mercy, did I geeue him. Who, by thes wordes perceiuinge me in a fvme, said merily vnto me: 'Well, well, sonne Roper, It shall not be so, It shall not be so.'[7]

This exchange illuminates why Roper was so insensitive to any problematic aspect to the controversies. We can infer, although Roper did not mean us to, that More had been about to confide some perturbing foresight about the probability of an eventual Protestant victory. Possibly he already saw that the heretical cause would become allied with a deeper drive for political change, resulting in a radical transformation of the *status quo*. Roper's naïvely enthusiastic refusal to consider his insinuation had been enough to make him retreat into privacy, but without withdrawing the suggestion. In amazement, and quite unconsciously, Roper had accused him of despair, an act which retrospectively appalled him. This in turn had led More to humour him as someone whom it was unfair to draw into his own perturbed state of perception. The whole episode shows that there were areas of More's experience that he did not explain to his family because they were not prepared to acknowledge that they existed. It is little wonder, then, that the members of the More circle should have been blind to evidence in the controversies that More felt far more than his words ostensibly declared. Had Margaret written a

---

[7] ibid., pp. 35–6. For an argument that Roper deliberately created a naïve persona, see R. S. Sylvester, 'Roper's *Life of More*', *Essential Articles*, pp. 189–97: 'By dramatizing his own misunderstanding of More in the past, he provides us with a device through which we can come to comprehend something of the mysterious greatness embodied in a man who seldom failed to understand himself and his surroundings' (p. 190). While this is undoubtedly true in part, one does not always feel that Roper's misunderstanding was merely rhetorical.

life of More we might have learnt more about his real state of mind during this period, but that, lamentably, was not to be.

Once Roper's conception had been requisitioned for purposes of anti-Protestant polemic by the Marian hagiographers, the controversies were even less likely to be assessed critically or objectively. Harpsfield, for example, saw in them only 'the integritie, the sinceritie and vprightnes, the good and gratious nature and disposition, of the saide Sir Thomas More'[8] – precisely those qualities required by the function of his biography. The judgement is arrived at deductively, not inductively: More was an exemplary Catholic man, therefore it must follow that his writings manifest all the virtues attributed to him. Harpsfield does acknowledge the complaints of unfairness and partiality of More's opponents, but merely recites More's refutation of these charges from the *Apology* as if it is his own independent view of the matter.[9] As far as the substance of the controversies is concerned, his account is little more than a compendium of More's book and chapter headings, designed to illustrate More's doctrinal soundness as a champion of the Catholic position.[10]

What is true of the early hagiographies has also been true of all hagiographical accounts ever since. The controversies are either passed over briefly,[11] or else treated uncritically as a mine of evidence for More's Latin-church orthodoxy.[12] This is inevitable, because the polemical works do not easily accord with the inherited 'mythos' of More based upon the retrospective appearance of his life.

A second, very different view was created by the reformers themselves. Having a vested interest in scrutinizing the controversies critically, they found in them something far removed from Harpsfield's integrity, sincerity and good and gracious nature and disposition.

Tyndale saw evidence of inconsistency, appealing to *Utopia* and *The Praise of Folly* as proof that More had hypocritically repudiated the

---

[8] Nicholas Harpsfield, *The Life and Death of Sir Thomas More, Knight, Sometymes Lord High Chancellor of England*, ed. Elsie Vaughan Hitchcock with an Introduction by R. W. Chambers (London, 1932), p. 108.

[9] ibid., pp. 123–4.

[10] ibid., p. 114ff. Harpsfield describes at length only More's handling of Tyndale's mistranslations and his identification of the true church with the known Catholic church (pp. 116–17).

[11] As in Chambers, *Thomas More*.

[12] See, for example, Bridgett, *Life and Writings of Sir Thomas More*.

truth as he had earlier seen it, and for the basest of motives – a desire for promotion.[13] Although Tyndale's judgement was coloured by partisan bias, his charge has been repeated by many with a less subjective need to make it.[14]

To this charge Christopher St German added another: that of deliberate dishonesty. In *Salem and Bizance* he expressed bewilderment that More, against his own knowledge to the contrary, should have contrived to make it appear in his *Apology* that anticlericalism was not of long standing, had no justifiable basis, and was merely the product of heretical subversion; moreover, he took this as a sign that More was not as concerned to see the reform of abuses as he should have been:

> And surely considering not onely the wisedome and lerning that is in him, but also the great auctoritie and experience, that he hath had in this realme in tyme paste, whereby he myght right well haue perceyued, and as I thinke verily doth perceyue, that the gruges and murmures that hath ben and yet be betwixt the spiritualtie and the temporaltie in this realme, haue begunne by other thinges more than by heresies, so that although heresies were clerely extincted: yet al thinges were not quiet betwixt them: it is to me a right great merueille, that he hath done no more to acquiete those other thynges, then he hath done.[15]

St German's perplexity, one feels, was genuine rather than simply a polemical tactic.

Just as Tyndale and St German put More's integrity and sincerity in doubt, so John Foxe was soon to question his gracious nature and disposition. His most telling criticism comes in his discussion of the *Supplication of Souls*. Observing that More makes the dead men's souls speak out of purgatory 'by a rhetorical prosopopoeia', he impugns the manner in which they speak of Simon Fish, author of *A Supplication for the Beggars*: 'sometimes scolding and railing at him, calling him a fool, witless, frantic, an ass, a goose, a mad dog, a heretic, and all that

[13] *An Answer to Sir Thomas More's Dialogue*, ed. Henry Walter (Cambridge, 1850), p. 16; and *The Practice of Prelates*, in *The Works of the English Reformers: William Tyndale, Robert Barnes, and John Frith*, ed. Thomas Russell (London 1831), I. p. 448.
[14] See, for example, J. A. Froude, *History of England* (London, 1856–70), I, pp. 344–5; Seebohm, pp. 3545–8; and William W. MacDonald, 'Saint Thomas More and the Historians', *American Benedictine Review*, 21 (1970), pp. 428–9, 435–8.
[15] *Salem and Bizance* (London, 1533), sigs A6–A6ᵛ.

naught is. And no marvel, if these simple souls of purgatory seem so fumish and testy; for heat (ye know) is testy, and soon inflameth choler.'[16] In these few words, Foxe identifies one of the most disturbing aspects of the controversies: their immoderate tone and lack of charity. Roper claimed of More that 'in xvj yeares and more, being in house conuersant with him, I could neuer perceiue [him] as much as once in a fvme'.[17] Foxe shows that the souls, at least, succumb to choler of a most violent kind, and proceeds to suggest its culpability:

> But yet these purgatory souls must take good heed how they call a man a fool and a heretic so often; for if the sentence of the gospel doth pronounce them guilty of hell-fire, who say 'Fatue,' 'Fool,' it may be doubted, lest those poor, simple, melancholy souls of purgatory, calling this man fool so oft as they have done, do bring themselves thereby out of purgatory-fire to the fire of hell, by that just sentence of the gospel.[18]

More argued in the *Confutation* that the words and attitudes of his and Erasmus' dramatized personae could not be taken as representing his own,[19] but Foxe rightly observes that in the *Supplication* he did not keep '"decorum personae," as a perfect poet should have done', so that the souls speak with his own voice, and their fault becomes his.[20] He notes further that More's narrative quickly takes on the demonic character which he had imputed to Fish's book as a result of its having been inspired by Fish's evil angel, the devil, 'with hys enmyous and enuious laughter gnashing the teeth and grynning'.[21] This makes of the *Supplication*, says Foxe, 'all together . . . a very black "sanctus" in purgatory'.[22]

---

[16] *The Acts and Monuments of John Foxe*, ed. George Townsend (London, 1846), IV, pp. 664–5.

[17] Roper, p. 36.

[18] Foxe, IV, p. 665.

[19] *CW* 8, I, p. 178/3ff.

[20] Foxe, IV, p. 665.

[21] *EW* 1557, p. 289 H. Foxe was taking his cue from George Joye's observations at the end of *The Supper of the Lord* (ed. Henry Walter (Cambridge, 1850), p. 268).

[22] Foxe, IV, p. 666. C. S. Lewis reached the same conclusion: 'Instead of the psalms and litanies which resounded on the sunlit terraces of Dante's mountain from souls "contented in the flame", out of the black fire which More has imagined, mixed with the howls of unambiguous physical torture, come peals of harsh laughter. All is black, salt, macabre' (*Essential Articles*, p. 393).

In many ways, Foxe is the most percipient of More's early readers. Biased as he was, he was prepared to allow the devil his due, and was almost unique in attempting an explanation for the things he most detested in More:

> a man . . . of a pregnant wit, full of pleasant conceits . . . who, if he had kept himself in his own shop, and applied to the faculty, being a layman, whereunto he was called, and had not over-reached himself to prove masteries in such matters wherein he had little skill, less experience, and which pertained not to his profession, he had deserved not only much more commendation, but also longer life.[23]

Here is the picture of a man who, having taken on a task for which he was not naturally equipped, fell victim to his own hubris in attempting to achieve it.

How is one to weigh two such conflicting estimates? None would deny that More's natural virtues have been approved by the verdict of history, or that the controversies amply demonstrate them on occasions. The merry tales in the English works manifest the good humour and humane tolerance with which he could bring himself to look upon human folly at times, as when he describes 'a poore wyfe of the paryshe whyspering wyth her pewfellow' in church who, upbraided by the parson, 'waxed as angry agayne, and sodainly . . . start vp and cryed out vnto the frere agayne, that al the church rang theron: mari sir I beshrew his hart that bableth most of vs bothe. For I doe but whysper a woord wyth my neyghboure here, and thou hast babled there al thys houre'.[24] Equally, one is impressed by the depth of More's piety, his philosophical acumen, and the sheer diligence and courage required of him in taking on the polemical task almost single-handedly. Moreover, some modern scholars have argued that in certain respects the controversies are consistent with *Utopia*, claiming there is very little discrepancy, for example, between the Utopian attitude towards violent proselytization and the grounds More stated in *A Dialogue Concerning Heresies* for the forceful suppression of heretics.[25]

[23] Foxe, IV, p. 652.
[24] *The Debellation of Salem and Bizance, EW* 1557, p. 948 H.
[25] Chambers, pp. 264ff., 281–2. My own disagreement with this view will become plain.

Yet it would require self-imposed myopia to ignore the truth of many of the reformers' claims, and it is those that we must be concerned with here.

More's attitude towards reform did change. From being a cautious liberal prepared to speculate, like Morton in *Utopia*, on possible ways of improving the condition of the commonweal, More became the reactionary ultra-conservative who could declare in the *Apology* that he would sooner see no reform at all, even 'though the chaunge might be to the better', if it involved open public criticism of existing laws.[26] It is equally true that his defence of the clergy showed 'more legal acumen than philosophic candour'.[27] Although he disingenuously pretended to equate anticlericalism with heresy, the two were not identical, and he undoubtedly knew it. Charles V's ambassador wrote from London that 'nearly all the people here hate the priests',[28] and long before Tyndale fulminated against the English clergy, John Fisher, no less, had lamented their corrupt condition: 'But and we take hede and call to mynde how many vyces reygne now a dayes in crystes chyrche, as well in the clergy as in the comyn people. How many also be vnlyke in theyr lyuynge vnto suche as were in tymes past, perchaunce we shal thynke that almyghty god slombreth not onely, but also that he hath slepte soundly a grete season.'[29] When St German and Fish anatomized more precisely the grounds of complaint, More sought to defuse their charges through a strategy of evasion, cavillation and sophistry. A typical example occurs in *The Debellation of Salem and Bizance*. St German had charged that the clergy were still exacting tithes of wood and mortuaries, in spite of the statutes made against them,[30] by misleading their parishioners with false information.[31] More's rebuttal is a masterpiece of prevarication: in the first place, he says, he cannot remember one instance of such abuse, in the second, he will not believe there have been any until the 'Pacifier' (alias St German) can name those who have gained from it as well as those who have borne the loss; in any case, he cannot believe

---

[26] *Apology, CW* 9, pp. 96/27–97/13.

[27] G. G. Coulton, 'The Faith of St Thomas More', *Essential Articles*, p. 510.

[28] ibid., p. 511.

[29] *The English Works of John Fisher*, ed. J. Mayor (London, 1876), p. 170; cf. C. Cross, *Church and People, 1450–1660* (London, 1976), chaps. 1–2.

[30] The statute of *Silva cedua* (45 Edward III, chap. 3) and the statute of mortuaries (21 Henry VIII, chap. 6).

[31] *A Treatise Concerning the Division Between the Spirituality and Temporalty, CW* 9, Appendix A, pp. 193–6, 198.

that a parishioner would yield the exaction upon a parson's bare word that he should, and even if there were any that would, they were likely to be so few in number that it would be no cause for division anyway, especially if the tithe were yielded willingly; if it were exacted by compulsion, the whole parish would not suffer the parson to keep it, and even if it were taken indeed, the parishioner would recover 'a ryght large amendes' at the common law; and it would be highly unlikely that a parson would ever recover the tithe in the spiritual courts because of the danger of the suit in the face of the statute; therefore the Pacifier's charge is untrue.[32] More's specious argument makes one suspicious of its candour; it amounts to an assertion that because, hypothetically, such clerical abuse should not take place, ergo, it has not. Pages and pages of such reasoning in the controversies lend some substance to the reformers' complaint that all too often More was content 'to jest poor simple truth out of countenance' rather than be honest.[33]

As much as one would like to ignore it, one must also concede that More did display lack of charity and an almost demoniac emotional violence towards his opponents. In the *Apology* he claimed that, 'As touchynge heretykes, I hate that vyce of theyrs and not theyr persones',[34] but for all the prettiness of the distinction, More's conception of heresy was such that he was not likely to maintain it. Heresy, by definition, involved obstinate pride, malice and sedition, and More made quite clear what he thought should be done to the person of any infected with it:

who so be so depely grounded in malyce, to the harme of his owne soule and other mennes to, and so set vppon the sowynge of sediciouse heresyes, that no good meanes that men maye vse vnto hym, can pull that malycyouse foly oute of hys poysened proude obstynate harte: I wolde rather be content that he were gone in tyme, then ouer longe to tary to the destruccyon of other.[35]

---

[32] *EW* 1557, p. 1018 A–D.

[33] Foxe used this phrase to describe More's account of the Hunne case (IV, p. 198).

[34] *CW* 9, p. 167/19–20.

[35] ibid., pp. 167/36–168/4; cf. More's letter to Cochlaeus of 14 June 1533, in which he expresses satisfaction at the deaths of Zwingli and Œcolampadius; 'it is right for us to rejoice that such savage enemies of the Christian faith have been removed from our midst' (Rogers, *SL*, no. 45, p. 177).

Although he declared that he 'wolde not they were ouer hastely handeled / but lytell rygoure and moche mercy shewed where symplenes appered'.[36] More could not allow that any of his opponents (with the exception of St German) were motivated by anything but 'high heart' and malice. Consequently, he expressed his contempt for them with a vileness of sentiment that far outstrips the scurrility of, for example, Tyndale or Barnes.[37] Richard Bayfield, in fleeing back to the Continent before finally being caught and burnt, was 'lyke a dogge returnynge to his vomyte';[38] Thomas Hitton is 'the dyuyls stynkyng martyr' now that 'the spiryte of errour and lyenge, hath taken his wreched soule wyth hym strayte from the shorte fyre to the fyre euerlastyng';[39] William Roye has 'made a mete ende at laste', having been 'burned in Portyngale'.[40] The gloating satisfaction in these statements uncovers a vindictiveness that makes it impossible to believe that More could distinguish between the vice and the person. What disturbs one, as well as the intensity of his hatred of heresy, which seems unnatural even by the standards of the day, is his propensity for indulging a vice Foxe identified: 'in mordendo mortuos'.[41] More's polemical ferocity was not convention, even though some critics have claimed it was,[42] otherwise his opponents would not have complained of it so forcefully at the time,[43] nor would More have attempted to restrain it, as he appears to have done after those complaints were voiced. It does no service to More or More scholarship not to recognize that his experience of polemical warfare worked radical changes in him.

We are faced, then, with a paradox in More. The man of wit, wisdom and heroic personal integrity revealed traits in his controversial writings that seem to negate those very qualities. Unless the paradox

[36] *A Dialogue Concerning Heresies, CW* 6, p. 416/23–5.
[37] Cf., for example, the exordium of Barnes' 'Treatise on the Church' (*CW* 8, II, Appendix A, pp. 1039/1–1040/7) with More's reaction to it (*CW* 8, II, p. 833/9–18).
[38] *Confutation, CW* 8, I, p. 17/19.
[39] ibid., pp. 16/35–17/1.
[40] ibid., p. 8/23–4.
[41] Foxe, IV, p. 645.
[42] See, for example, Richard J. Schoeck, *The Achievement of Thomas More: Aspects of His Life and Works*, English Literary Studies, no. 7 (Victoria, BC, 1976), p. 57; also Louis A. Schuster, 'Thomas More's Polemical Career, 1523–1533', *CW* 8, III, p. 1265.
[43] More acknowledges this criticism in the *Apology* (*CW* 9, p. 43/18ff.) and the *Debellation* (*EW* 1557, p. 939 B–H).

can be explained, the whole man will never be grasped, and his intellectual career will remain incoherent to all but uncritical partisans or iconoclasts.

Critics from Tyndale onwards have posed the problem as a question of More's consistency, but to do so is a distraction. More may have changed, but he did not change his mind concerning his most essential beliefs. The idea that he was inconsistent depends upon an overly naïve interpretation of *Utopia* as an unambiguous blueprint for reform, and a false assumption that More's outlook between 1509 and 1517 was identical with that of Erasmus.

In the *Confutation* More himself easily exposed the lameness of the inconsistency charge. Even if *The Praise of Folly*, he says, contained heresies, which it does not, there would be no reason for any man to suppose that he was of the same mind, since it was written by another man. Besides, Erasmus narrated the book 'vnder the name and person of Moria, whyche worde in greke sygnyfyeth foly', so that her words need no more be assumed to represent his serious opinion than the Messenger's jesting represents More's own in *A Dialogue Concerning Heresies*. Men have become so prone to misconstrue anything they read 'to the colour and mayntenauns of theyr owne fonde fantasyes' that he would sooner burn some of his own earlier Latin works (presumably *Utopia*, the translations of Lucian, and certain of the epigrams) along with *The Praise of Folly*, rather than see them translated into English, 'all be yt there be none harme therin'.[44] Perhaps there is a hint of smoke-screening in More's rebuttal, but his main point stands: it is impossible to prove that he was formerly 'ferre otherwyse mynded' on the basis of simplified misreadings of his earlier works not recognizing their fictional, dramatized character.

Indeed, if one looks closely at *Utopia*, it is clear that More had alredy provided a philosophical justification for the manner in which he was to conduct his polemical defence of the church. The 'civil philosophy' described in book 1 assumes that, to make as little bad as possible that which cannot be made perfectly good, one may need to proceed indirectly, to act one's appropriate part according to the exigencies of the play at hand. In *Richard III* More had shown how Morton had been induced to play the part of a politically devious machiavel in the green world following the usurpation, his dubious means being justified by the end he sought. It is easy to see how More

[44] *CW* 8, I, pp. 178/3–179/17.

could have convinced himself that the situation in the early 1530s was so dangerous that he was morally obliged to act with a similar political pragmatism. If there were any danger of the heretics exploiting prevalent anticlericalism, he had to disguise the real extent of it; if justifiable legal and ecclesiastical reforms could in any way assist the heretics, he had to argue that they were not necessary; and if fairness to his opponents meant allowing them any degree of credibility in anything, he was justified in painting them as wholly black, whether he believed they were or not. One can put many labels on this strategy, but it was not inconsistent with the *modus operandi* Morus had urged in *Utopia*. To put it in positive terms, More was consistent in allowing himself freedom to be inconsistent.

Although the 'civil philosophy' helps explain some of More's tactics, it does not resolve the fundamental problem. The controversies reveal that something far more radical took place than a merely pragmatic adaptation of means to ends. To begin to see what it was one must contemplate its outward manifestations.

If viewed as a whole, not piecemeal, the polemics testify to a progressive loss of control, objectivity and any sense of proportion. More's failure to retain his self-possession is made all the more obvious by his attempts in the first three major polemics to safeguard it. The *Responsio ad Lutherum* (1523), *A Dialogue Concerning Heresies* (1529) and the *Supplication of Souls* (1529) are all cast in diverse fictional modes which allow for objective distance, a play of wit, and the interaction of comic and tragic perspectives.

In its first version, the *Responsio* is contrived to appear as if it is written by an impetuous young student, Baravellus, tricked into the task of refuting Luther by a friend's uncle who knows that Baravellus will answer Luther according to his own folly. This device allows More to compose the diatribe in the satiric spirit of the Brixius epigrams, without being himself identified with it, so that the book's effectiveness resides as much in its ridicule as its argument. However, More could not leave this conception alone to work by itself. In a revised version he substituted a new persona, Guilielmus Rosseus, from whose character the outrageous scurrility could never have issued, and inserted a long addition that shatters the prevailing satiric decorum and pulls the work on to a new level of seriousness.[45] More

---

[45] For an account of the revised *Responsio*, see J. H. Headley, *CW* 5, II, p. 760ff.

had become thoroughly involved with the issue in a way he had at first been concerned to avoid.[46]

More's descent into subjective involvement is equally apparent in *A Dialogue Concerning Heresies*. This work attempts a new kind of literary strategy by adopting the dialogue form of *Utopia*. By representing dramatically the interaction of two divergent personalities and viewpoints, More hoped to move his readers into agreement with the orthodox position through humane persuasion rather than dogmatic coercion. The dialogue itself was meant to create a living image of the process by which, in the course of history, the church had attained its understanding of the particular religious beliefs in question. The first three books work rather well, with More allowing his interlocutor, the young disgruntled Messenger, plenty of elbow room in which to express scepticism, anger and satiric outrage at ecclesiastical abuse. But by book 4 the dialogue collapses under the pressure of More's awareness of Luther. The Messenger grows unconvincingly pliant at the same time as More replaces debate with harangue, until by the final pages the work has turned into a monologue that brooks no contradiction.

In the *Supplication of Souls* it takes even less time for More to abandon his rhetorical conception. At the outset the souls in purgatory plead to the devout charity of all good Christian people 'for help, coumforte, and reliefe',[47] but within a few pages they start to sound like seasoned heresy hunters, far more concerned with political subversion in this world than with their pitiful plight in the next. After the *Supplication* More no longer even pretended to be able to objectify his feelings through the use of fictional frameworks.

Up to 1531 More had enjoyed a fair degree of latitude in which to manoeuvre as he sought to find an effectual way of writing against heresy. He could afford to cast his argument in fictive moulds because he had not yet been publicly attacked. All that changed with the appearance of Tyndale's *An Answere vnto Sir Thomas Mores Dialoge*. Once More was put on the defensive as well as the offensive the deterioration of his self-composure accelerated.

One sees the effects horrifyingly demonstrated in the massive *Confutation of Tyndale's Answer*, which appeared in two instalments in

---

[46] This issue is discussed at length in the next chapter.
[47] *EW* 1557, p. 288 D.

1532 and 1533 and yet still remained incomplete.[48] Opposition brought out the absolutist in More; he became, in C. S. Lewis' words, 'monotonously anxious to conquer and to conquer equally, at every moment: to show in every chapter that every heretical book is wrong about everything – wrong in history, in logic, in rhetoric, and in English grammar as well as in theology'.[49] No longer content merely to 'refute', he now sought to 'confute' Tyndale as he would soon seek to 'debellate', or vanquish completely by force of arms, his anonymous opponent, the 'Pacifier'. Whether he realized it or not, More was reliving the Utopians' response to warfare which he had depicted ironically 17 years earlier: 'They are not fierce in the first onslaught, but their strength increases by degrees through their slow and hard resistance. Their spirit is so stubborn that they would rather be cut to pieces than give way' ('nec tam primo ferociunt impetu quam mora sensim et duratione inualescunt, tam offirmatis animis ut interimi citius quam auerti queant').[50] He was probably insufficiently distanced from his writing to see that his determination to achieve absolute victory was putting him in danger of suffering the same fate: 'when it comes to hand-to-hand fighting, if the enemy stands his ground, the battle is long and anguished and ends with mutual extermination' ('si ad ipsorum manus uentum sit modo perstent hostes, longo et lugubri praelio ad internitionem usque decernatur').[51] The reformers, however, were quick to point out that the excessive length and tediousness of the *Confutation* indeed frustrated its very purpose.[52]

As well as destroying any vestige of form, this 'attempt to prove masteries' that Foxe had discerned gradually upset the finely balanced tragi-comic perspective More had tried to sustain. *A Dialogue Concerning Heresies* had been leavened with 'fansyes and sportes, and mery tales' brought in 'amonge the moste ernest maters'[53] so that human perversity could be viewed in its comic aspect as well as its tragic. Not only did these devices ease the burden of More's readers, but they also contributed to a truthful representation of the human

---

[48] More promised to answer Tyndale 'in euery chapyter that he hath impugned in the .iiii. bokes of my dyaloge' (*CW* 8, I, p. 36/1–3), and yet covered barely one quarter of Tyndale's *Answer*.

[49] *Essential Articles*, p. 394.

[50] *Utopia, CW* 4, pp. 210/12–14, 211/15–18.

[51] ibid., pp. 210/6–8, 211/8–10.

[52] *Apology, CW* 9, p. 5/7–9; for More's defence, see ibid., p. 8/27ff.

[53] ibid., p. 170/34–5.

situation; to paint everything black, as More had done in *The Four Last Things*, was to commit a libel on life,[54] and at his best he was able to restrain himself from doing so. After 1531, however, the merry tales begin to become infrequent islands in a sea of unsmiling argument and vituperation. The *Confutation* still contains some of the best merry tales More ever wrote, but relative to the bulk of the work they are few and far between, and their effect is therefore diminished. More's imagery grew progressively demonic, dominated by a sense of perversion, parody, disease and the unwholesome. Tyndale and his brethren are filled not with an 'apostolycall spyryt' but with an 'apostatycall spyryte'.[55] Master Masker, himself infected, like Chaucer's cook, with a diseased shin,[56] serves up an 'vnsauery supper' in two courses 'wythout ani corne of salte, and spiced al with poyson'.[57] The heretics' books, 'whych lyke the chyldren of vippara wold now gnaw out theyr mothers bely', beget a proliferating host of monstrous, unnatural progeny.[58] Everything to do with them consists of lies, deformity and darkness.

In the *Apology*, *The Debellation of Salem and Bizance*, and *An Answer to a Poisoned Book which a Nameless Heretic Hath Named the Supper of the Lord*, all written in 1533, the comic perspective practically vanishes altogether. He does attempt several merry tales in the *Debellation*,[59] but there are none at all in the *Answer to a Poisoned Book*. The snarling invective of the *Confutation* moderates in these works, but it is replaced by something even more deadly: diffuseness. More, one feels, scarcely knew any longer what he was doing.

He began to write the *Apology* as a personal defence against various charges that the reformers had levelled at him. One of their claims was that he could take a lesson in impartiality and good disposition from St German's *Treatise Concernynge the Diuision Betwene the Spirytualtie and Temporaltie*. After denying that it was well disposed and impartial, More adds: 'for as mych as the touchynge of the boke is here not my principal purpose / I wil therfore not peruse it ouer and touch euery point therof'.[60] Yet within the same paragraph he visibly succumbs to

---

[54] I have here purloined some phrases of C. S. Lewis (*Essential Articles*, p. 396).

[55] *CW* 8, I, p. 88/29–30.

[56] *Answer to a Poisoned Book*, *EW* 1557, p. 1088 E.

[57] ibid., p. 1038 C–D.

[58] *CW* 8, I, p. 6/31–5.

[59] For example, those of Grime the Mustard maker (*EW* 1557, p. 933 H), and of Henry Pattenson (p. 935 E–F).

[60] *CW* 9, p. 61/7–9.

the temptation of dealing with it in part, and thereafter its refutation does become his principal purpose against his own stated intention.

This waning ability to keep a grasp on the central issue is manifest again in the *Debellation*. In the *Apology* he had attacked a sermon reported to him in which the preacher had claimed that an imperfect translation of scripture were better than no translation at all. More claimed that this preacher had used the trope of poisoned bread being better than none.[61] In the Preface of the *Debellation* he declares that he has since heard of an answer asserting that the sermon referred only to 'moulden bread', and that he had 'misrehearsed' it. More's reaction shows how completely the impulse to attack indiscriminately had become a reflex, obscuring his ability to distinguish important matters from trivialities:

> come the booke abrode ones, I shal soone abate that corage. For first sith hee taketh recorde that he sayd but mouldy breade: if I bring witnesse also that he saied poisoned breade, than can his wytnesse stande him in none other stede, but for to proue for hym that hee sayed both.
>
> Secondly shall I proue that he sayd poisoned bread, by such meanes that men shall see by reason, that though the tother were possyble: yet was it farre vnlykely.
>
> Fynally shall I farther proue, that though the man had sayd not poysened breade but onely moulden breade: yet shall I proue I saye, that as the case stode, that same not poisoned bread but moulden breade, was yet for all that a very poisoned worde.[62]

Here we see the prevaricating play of a lawyer at a moot; More's problem was that he took it seriously. Not only is this passage a needless distraction and waste of space, energy and words, since the matter was inconsequential anyway, but it also exemplifies rationality run wild. Rather than concede even the slightest possibility that he had made a mistake, More was prepared to write yet another book to prove that his claim would have been true whatever the preacher had *actually* said. We are as far away from the reasonable world of *A Dialogue Concerning Heresies* as it is possible to be, and all for the sake of an issue that is completely peripheral to the concern of the book at

[61] *Apology, CW* 9, p. 12/4–6.
[62] *Debellation, EW* 1557, p. 930 D–E.

hand. It is not surprising that More found he had written a tome even larger than the *Apology,* instead of the 'three or foure leaues' he had originally contemplated.[63]

An Answer to a Poisoned Book marks the nadir. It is no longer even the diffuseness that strikes one, but the absence of all vigour and invention. More found it hard to rouse himself even into a posture of indignation against the anonymous 'Master Masker', and the book crawls tiredly towards its truncated close.

Significantly, when More picked up his pen again, he chose to write in a different mode. If he began *A Treatise upon the Passion* before entering the Tower, as the evidence suggests,[64] its tone and construction show that he had already begun to grapple with the destructive effects of his polemical career before imprisonment and leisure impelled him to.

Is the pattern of decline in the controversies ascribable solely to battle fatigue? I have already suggested that it sprang from something more: an inner experience which shook him to the core of his being. All the outward changes in his writings record the steps by which the desperation Roper fleetingly observed in him to his own incredulity before the polemical campaign began in earnest became a living, secret reality. In the course of his controversial career, More came close to losing faith in the understanding of the world he had framed for himself. What was at issue for him was not simply heresy alone, but the meaning of the whole historical situation that began to unfold before his eyes. To grasp this, one must retrace the process by which he was drawn into the struggle, examine the nature of his polemical argument, and identify his sense of the implications of contemporary historical circumstances.

---

[63] ibid., p. 931 A.

[64] See Garry E. Haupt, 'Introduction', *A Treatise upon the Passion, CW* 13, pp. xxxix–xli.

5

The Reluctant Champion: *Responsio ad Lutherum,*
Letter to Bugenhagen

External changes in the controversies chart More's progressively deepening personal involvement with the issues at hand, yet there is evidence that he had not wished to become involved at all. How and why he did, therefore, become questions of considerable importance.

Although More had taken sufficient interest in the spread of heresy to discuss it with his friends on the Continent as early as 1521,[1] whether or not that interest would have been strong enough by itself to make him pick up the polemical pen remains doubtful. We do not, for example, know how active he was in the composition of the king's *Assertio septem sacramentorum.* According to Roper, when More was accused of 'moste vnnaturallie procuring and provokinge' Henry to write the book, he claimed to have been 'only a sorter out and placer of the principall matters therein contayned' as distinct from 'the makers of the same'.[2] More himself declared in his letter to Cromwell of 5 March 1534 that 'at the fyrst reding' of the *Assertio* he had advised the king either to leave out the question of the pope's primacy, or else touch it more slenderly.[3] Clearly, he wished it to appear that his opinion had been sought after the event; given the political danger of his situation and Henry's temper in 1534, this would have been a foolish claim to make had it not been true. Similarly, we do not even know if he wrote the *Responsio ad Lutherum* of his own volition.[4] His position as royal councillor and confidant made him the obvious choice to answer Luther's derisive *Contra Henricum regem Angliae* in

---

[1] In a letter to Pace mentioning Luther's activities, Erasmus adds: 'Cetera cognosces e Mori litteris' (Allen, IV, p. 1218/404). The letter to which he refers is no longer extant.

[2] Roper, p. 67.

[3] Rogers, *Correspondence*, no. 197, p. 498/207–208.

[4] See Headley's discussion, *CW* 5, II, pp. 730–1.

kind, and presumably he was asked to; however, he never publicly acknowledged the *Responsio* as his own, and his desire to preserve his anonymity under pseudonyms in both versions may be a sign that he had undertaken the task reluctantly. Harpsfield thought the reason to have been that 'this kinde of wryting . . . seemed not very agreable and correspondent to his saide grauitie and dignitie'.[5] This may have been true to some extent initially, but More showed no such scruples later when he wrote the equally offensive *Confutation of Tyndale's Answer*, therefore another explanation seems just as likely.

The most explicit statement of More's own attitude occurs in the *Letter to Bugenhagen* of 1526. After describing how he had come to possess a copy of Bugenhagen's *Epistola ad Anglos*,[6] he expresses surprise that it should ever have been sent to him, who had never involved himself in the Lutheran business ('qui me Lutherano negotio nunquam immiscueram').[7] Furthermore, he declares, he was not the person to say anything on these matters, being neither a theologian, nor the person to whom the refutation of heresy pertained ('nec ego ea de re quicquam fere loquerer, quod neque Theologus eram, nec vllam personam gererem, ad quam eius vlceris cura pertineret').[8] Besides, he had absolutely determined to abstain from contagious contact with this kind of disease ('ego plane decreueram ab eiusmodi pestis attactu noxio semper abstinere').[9] Although disingenuous, these statements probably reflect the truth, with the difference that More was giving himself credit for the will rather than the deed. He would have preferred not to have become enmeshed in polemic, and possibly thought that his defence of the king's dignity and arguments against Luther's defamation did not amount to his having been. Even as he prepared to commit himself irrevocably, because publicly, he could still profess his wish for a detachment that had already been made impossible, but desirable nonetheless.

If one considers the personal understanding of things More had framed for himself by the early 1520s, his reasons for wishing to abstain from religious contention become clear.

[5] Harpsfield, p. 106.
[6] It had been left at his house by William Barlowe, later a zealous reformer; see E. F. Rogers, 'Sir Thomas More's Letter to Bugenhagen', *Essential Articles*, p. 449.
[7] Rogers, *Correspondence*, no. 143, p. 325/12–13.
[8] ibid., p. 325/17–19.
[9] ibid., p. 325/23–4.

He had come to accept that truth was as liable to be grasped through the experience of paradox and ambiguity as it was through absolute, rational definition. To this end he had evolved a mode of literary depiction capable of representing how contradictions may merge themselves in a higher truth that comprehends them. His own inclination towards poetry and history, rather than pure philosophy or theology, sprang from his belief that truth, especially religious truth, was neither self-evident nor complete in every respect, because its revelation was an historical process. Even when he had become immersed in dogmatic controversy, this conviction never left him:

> god doth reuele hys trouthes not alwayes in one manner / but sometyme he sheweth yt out at onys, as he wyll haue yt knowen and men bounden forthwyth to byleue yt. . . . Sometyme he sheweth yt leysourly, suffryng his flokke to comen and dyspute theruppon / and in theyr treatynge of the mater, suffreth them wyth good mynde and scrypture and naturall wisedome, with inuocacyon of his spirituall helpe, to serche and seke for the treuth, and to vary for the whyle in theyr opynyons, tyll that he rewarde theyr vertuouse dylygence wyth ledying them secretely in to the consent and concorde and bylyef of the trouth by his holy spirite.[10]

Only at the end of time would the full meaning of things be completely revealed; until then, men could only glimpse it in part, and it was more fruitful for a poet like More to depict the process by which men would eventually discover it than to dogmatize on what it might turn out to be.

More's view, in effect, precluded the very dogmatization that religious controversy required. We gain an insight into his own objections to it, I think, from *Utopia*. King Utopus, not venturing 'rashly to dogmatize' on matters of religion, prohibited religious coercion and polemic, believing this to be not only in the interests of peace, but also of religion itself:

> he foresaw that, provided the matter was handled reasonably and moderately, truth by its own natural force would finally emerge sooner or later and stand forth preeminent. But if the

---

[10] *Confutation*, *CW* 8, I, p. 248/11–22.

struggle were decided by arms and riots, since the worst men are always the most unyielding, the best and holiest religion would be overwhelmed by extremely empty superstitions, just as corn becomes overgrown by thorns and brambles.[11]

Far from clarifying religious truth, contentiousness obscured it and stifled its emergence. In the *Letter to Martin Dorp* written the same year, More defined his objections to controversy more precisely. If a heretic be unlearned, he says, he would not understand the subtleties of theological reasoning; if he be learned, there will never be any end to the debate: 'Those quibbles with which they are attacked furnish inexhaustible material to them for counterattacks, so that they are very much like two men fighting naked among piles of stones: each has plenty of weapons, neither has any defense.'[12] Although More was referring specifically to the ineffectuality of the scholastic *quaestio* method, his own experience later proved that his objection extended to all kinds of controversy. He tried at first to exploit fiction and rhetoric rather than dialectic once he had become irrevocably committed to polemic, but when Tyndale denounced this attempted virtue as a vice, he was reduced to the defence and use of the same scholastic subtleties he had earlier criticized, 'for the reprofe of those heretykes that wolde haue no dyuysyons nor dystynccyons, wherby the thynge sholde be made open and playne'.[13] He also discovered feelingly how right he had been to fear that there would never be any end to the debate: for him there was not.

There can be little doubt that in 1522 More would have liked to adopt the Utopian viewpoint and eschew polemic altogether. Previously he had not formulated his world view in dogmatic, doctrinal terms, and perhaps would have preferred it if circumstances had not required him to do so. History, however, was about to emphasize the difference between Utopia and Europe in ways More may not have anticipated in 1515.

---

[11] '. . . facile tamen praeuidit (modo cum ratione ac modeştia res agatur) futurum denique: ut ipsa per se ueri uis emergat aliquando atque emineat. Sin armis et tumultu certetur, ut sint pessimi quique maxime peruicaces, optimam ac sanctissimam religionem ob uanissimas inter se superstitiones, ut segetes inter spinas ac frutices obrutum iri' (*CW* 4, p. 220/15–20); my translation.

[12] Rogers, *SL*, no. 4, pp. 38–9; *Correspondence*, p. 53/894ff.

[13] *Confutation*, *CW* 8, I, p. 206/23ff.

The Utopians enjoy an unusual liberty to speculate becuse they are pagans. One advantage of their situation is that they are not forced to define dissent as heresy because they have very little established dogma by which to judge it. As More later said in *A Treatise upon the Passion*, 'vnto the Paynims and Gentils, to whom the law was not gyuen, nor neuer had heard of Christ, it was sufficient for their saluacion to belieue that two pointes onelye which saynt Paule . . . reherseth, that is to wit, that there is one God, and that he wyl reward them that seke him'.[14] These two points are very similar to the only dogmas that the Utopians are required to believe: that the soul is immortal, that the world is governed by divine providence, and that after this life vices are punished and virtues rewarded.[15] Only those who deny these tenets or contend too vehemently in expressing their religious views are punished by exclusion from the community.[16] In the halcyon days of the humanist revival, men like More and Erasmus seem almost to have been lulled into thinking that reform could arise from a Christianized extension of this liberal spirit.

Luther's attack on the institutionalized church shattered that illusion by forcing More to define his orthodoxy and so admit that what was possible for pagans was ultimately impossible for Christians. Christians, he concluded, 'be ratabli bounden to the beliefe of moe thinges' than pagans under a constraint of historical necessity.[17] Christ had promised that the church would be led unerringly into all truth by the Holy Spirit; accordingly, God positively required men to accept the beliefs and practices it had accumulated in its passage through time. From that it followed logically that much of what could be allowed in *Utopia* as creative speculation had to be condemned in Europe as heresy. In effect the church's official sense of itself precluded the degree of toleration allowed in Utopia, so that even if Luther had been less vehemently assertive, he would of necessity have needed to be condemned. Just as Christians were required to believe more than pagans, so were they obliged to suppress dissenters more rigorously and absolutely.

More, one feels, was reluctant to be forced by the Lutheran business to commit himself to such a rigid attitude, however much he may have fulfilled its requirements once he had done so. He would have

---

[14] *CW* 13, p. 43/8–13.
[15] *Utopia, CW* 4, p. 221/29–33.
[16] ibid., pp. 221/8–9, 221/34–223/14.
[17] *Treatise upon the Passion, CW* 13, p. 43/6–8.

preferred not to have been drawn back from the realms of gold, for it meant renouncing the degree of speculative freedom he had allowed himself.

Even though More was averse to assuming the dogmatist's role, he quickly found it irresistible after he had been forced into it. Part of the reason can be discerned in his treatment of his first polemic, the *Responsio ad Lutherum*.

A comparison of the two versions of the *Responsio* reveals that More, against his own expectation, became thoroughly captured by the fundamental issue in dispute. The first version, written under the pseudonym 'Baravellus', reinforces the impression that More undertook it simply as an official duty. The prefatory letter from Baravellus to Lucellus may, indeed, dramatize figuratively how this happened. Baravellus describes how he was tricked by his host into answering Luther's diatribe because of a rash pledge drawn out of him by an evil deception ('pactum . . . quod dolus malus elicuit').[18] Even after reading the *Contra Henricum*, he was reluctant to reply, because nothing of significance had been omitted by the king nor anything new added by Luther.[19] Nevertheless, he was not only held to his pledge, but also required to do violence to his nature by returning Luther's abuse in kind.[20] Between the lines one can read a hidden comment on the nature of More's commission and also his resentment at being unable to avoid it because of his position at Court.

The form and content of the first version suggest that initially he was working to rule and little else. He was content to let this argument be shaped by the matter of Henry's *Assertio* and conditioned by the tone of Luther's reply. As he was later to affirm in the second version, he had 'undertaken to refute nothyng but the trifling remarks with which the scoundrel stuffed the book in which he answers the prince' ('. . . non aliud, quam eas nugas eius desumpsi refellere quas in istum congessit librum: quo nebulo respondet principi').[21] Consequently, he confined his role to the defence and strengthening of Henry's main arguments: that the church had authority to decide the meaning of scripture, that tradition was valid against the self-sufficiency of scripture in the matter of the sacraments, and that the universal

[18] *CW* 5, I, p. 8/18–19.
[19] ibid., p. 10/11–12.
[20] ibid., p. 10/21ff.
[21] ibid., p. 138/14–16.

consensus was sovereign in founding laws and judging doctrine. All these notions were commonplace. Henry had been furnished with them by his team of advisors. All More had to do was restate the prefabricated argument in a manner befitting Luther's derisive assault on it.

To this end he created an appropriate rhetorical persona, one that would allow him, as Harpsfield observed, 'to represse and beate him [Luther] with his owne follye, according to Scripture, *Responde stulto secundum stultitiam eius*'.[22] In the figure of Baravellus we catch a glimpse of More the jester. Although the editor of the Yale *Responsio* rejects the suggestion, it is entirely possible that More chose the name 'Baravellus' with reference to Baraballo of Gaeta, the notorious poetaster and buffoon retained by Leo X.[23] Pastor records the antics of this fool when he had himself crowned as another Petrarch on the Capitol at Rome: 'Mounted on an elephant, the recent gift of the Portuguese king to Leo X, Baraballo in festal robes of ancient pattern had delivered some ridiculous lines outside the pope's window and then been led away to the sound of drums and trumpets, almost to be dumped on the bridge of St Angelo.'[24] This is precisely the kind of story that would have appealed to More, given his delight in fools, and he could easily have heard it by oral report, possibly through his Italian friend Bonvisi.[25] Since he was already renowned for playing the fool himself,[26] he may have seized upon the chance to requisition the robes of another fool whose folly, metaphorically speaking, held up a mirror to his own. The Baraballo association could also explain the Hispanic background of Baravellus.[27]

The advantages of the disguise were legion. More could be as scurrilous as he wished and yet still enjoy the same kind of immunity as Moria in Erasmus' *Praise of Folly*. If a fool attacks folly foolishly,

---

[22] Harpsfield, p. 106.

[23] The suggestion was first made by J. B. Trapp of the Warburg Institute, although he does not agree with the identification; see *CW* 5, II, p. 796.

[24] ibid.; Ludwig Pastor, *The History of the Popes from the Close of the Middle Ages*, 40 vols., ed. Frederick Ignatius Antrobus *et al.* (London, 1938–53), VIII, pp. 154–5. I use Headley's paraphrase.

[25] Bonvisi was Proctor-General in London to the Italian bishops of Worcester, and therefore a likely vehicle for the story; see Rogers, *Correspondence*, p. 87.

[26] A habit recorded by popular tradition in the Elizabethan play, *Sir Thomas More*, in which More dresses his fool as himself to see if Erasmus can tell the difference (Addition IV).

[27] *CW* 5, I, p. 4/15.

where is the blame? Above all else, the facetious persona was a device to keep himself distanced from the whole business, as he would have preferred to remain. It was also a self-reflective reminder to him of the absurdity of what he found himself doing.

The Baravellus version was printed and some copies bound up, but publication was withheld.[28] Its suppression shows how quickly More began to experience the self-generating power of controversy to draw participants to itself. Even though he had tried to remain detached, he discovered that one central issue did involve him deeply and personally: the nature and identity of the church.

In the Baravellus version, More had merely reasserted the king's argument: the church of Christ is identical with the papist church because of its universality and consensus. In the revised version, however, he inserted an enormous addition into the H gathering to expound his own definition: 'haec multitudo quae facit ecclesiam catholicam: istam dico, ex qua fides discitur, et scriptura discernitur, sit multitudo promiscua profitentium Christi nomen et fidem, etiam si professioni non respondeat uita';[29] or, as he was later to restate it in the *Confutation*: 'the comon knowen catholyke people, clergy, lay folke, and all / whych what so euer theyr lyuynge be . . . do stande to gether and agre in the confessyon of one trew catholyke fayth'.[30] By stressing that the church contained good and bad together, an issue that had not begun to worry Henry, More was setting up an idiosyncratic relocation of the whole argument according to his own personal insights. He was not primarily interested in the question of church government as Henry had been, and confesses that he would gladly have left the question of the pope out altogether, had not Luther entangled it inextricably into his discussion of the church.[31] In the *Confutation* he went even further to exclude explicitly the pope as a necessary part of the definition of the church.[32] The real focus of More's attention was Luther's claim that Christ's church was invisible, spiritual, sinless, and perceptible by faith alone.[33]

To appreciate the force of More's reaction against this idea, one must recall his earlier spiritual conflicts. In the early works he had

[28] Only one known copy now exists (*CW* 5, II, pp. 832–4).
[29] *CW* 5, I, p. 172/2–5.
[30] *CW* 8, I, pp. 480/36–481/1.
[31] *CW* 5, I, p. 139/1–16.
[32] *CW* 8, II, pp. 576/28–577/23.
[33] *CW* 5, I, p. 146/8ff.

betrayed perturbation at the world's mutability, tribulation, sinfulness and apparent futility. This had strengthened his impulse to withdraw into the cloister and an interiorized spiritual life; however, during his four years of self-trial in the Charterhouse, he had recognized that his sensuality was too powerful to permit this. He decided, therefore, to try and reconcile his piety and sensuality in marriage and a virtuous career in the world. Although the life of a layman did not require that complete chastity demanded of a priest, More nevertheless believed that Christ had still come 'to call and exorte the worlde frome all pleasure of the flesshe to the purytye and clennes of the body and soule / and frome the desyre of carnall generacyon to a gostly regeneracyon in grace'.[34] To live a married life in the world suppressing the pleasure of the flesh and in all respects bridling sensuality under the control of the will and reason was an arduous task, and More was more conscious than most of temptation and sinful motions, as his wearing of a hairshirt suggests. It was vital to his emotional security to believe that the church contained good and bad together, because the idea of a church 'militant' gave meaning to the experience of human frailty which he recognized in himself. Even good men, he declared, are constantly tainted by sin ('ecclesia Christi, dum uersatur in terris, non adeo adhuc depurata est: quin et peccata quaedam assidue maculent bonos').[35] Yet the experience of motions to commit sin or lapses into venial sins were no cause for despair because of Christ's promise to be perpetually present and assistant with his church; even the most sinful of men 'are somehow still alive and are nourished by a certain warmth of the divine Spirit who animates and preserves the church'.[36] While they remain in the church, no men are deprived of the chance of amendment, nor of the grace which enables them, as far as the limitation of their earthly condition allows, to achieve it.

Luther's assertion that the true church was sinless threatened More's entire understanding of the world and himself by denying any regenerative, instrumental purpose in human experience. If Luther was right, not only had More damned himself in making the choices he had, but the whole world was also as unredeemably satanic as he

---

[34] *Dialogue Concerning Heresies, CW* 6, p. 151/7–10.

[35] *CW* 5, I, p. 202/3–5.

[36] 'Nam adhuc, etiam si sani non sunt: tamen utcunque uiuunt, et aluntur calore quodam diuini spiritus: qui animat et conseruat ecclesiam, penetrans omnia fortiter, et disponens omnia suauiter' (*CW* 5, I, pp. 202/6–9, 203/8–10).

had once feared it might be. He therefore had an overpoweringly personal motive for seeking to confute Luther concerning the question of the church.

The expanded H gathering in the revised *Responsio* makes it a very different book from the one More first conceived, and the change in pose from satiric detachment to personal involvement is registered in a new persona. The new version purports to be written by Guilielmus Rosseus – William Ross, an Englishman living in Rome.[37] The use of a pseudonym at all suggests that More was still striving to remain detached through anonymity, but the shift from Spaniard to Englishman marks the first stage of the process by which he would eventually become at one with his polemical personae. In his next major controversy, *A Dialogue Concerning Heresies*, he projected himself into a character, 'Thomas More', who bears much the same relation to the real More as Morus does in *Utopia*. In spite of the narrowing gap between author and persona, his interlocutor, the Messenger, embodies almost as many aspects of More as the character 'More' does, and a degree of distance and imaginative play is thus maintained. From the *Supplication of Souls* onwards, however, More wrote unequivocally as himself, which reflects how completely he had come to view the dispute as his own.

Having acquitted himself of the *Responsio ad Lutherum,* More appears briefly to have been inclined to retreat from controversy once again. Neither circumstances nor his own perceptions were to let him.

The *Letter to Bugenhagen* shows him still at the point of irresolution. After professing uncertainty as to whether he should reply to Bugenhagen's *Epistola*, he plunges in to write a vituperative pamphlet of some 12,000 words, this time of his own free will. Then, having written it, he withheld it from the publication for which its form indicates it was intended.[38] Clearly, More was caught in a struggle between two contending impulses. His hesitancy about committing himself irrevocably to public contention one can understand, but the aggressive urge which overpowered it is more puzzling.

It is made all the more puzzling by More's efforts·to conceal its real causes. All the reasons he gives for going ahead with the reply to Bugenhagen are jejune: the thing was forced on him, he would not want to give any false hope to the heretics by remaining silent, and he

[37] On possible biographical identifications, see Headley, *CW* 5, II, pp. 798–801.
[38] Rogers, *Essential Articles*, pp. 443, 453; Jones, p. 89.

would sooner return a reply, however unskilled he might be in theology, than let it appear he was a Lutheran.[39] None of these ostensible reasons is convincing, especially in the light of More's own admission that the *Epistola* did not really need answering at all ('. . . nihil responsi tuae requirebant literae').[40]

The real stimulus for the *Letter* was More's desire to find a pretext for venting his indignation over several events that had taken place in 1525. This is revealed by the moments in which he loses his composure: when he rails at the Lutheran leaders as incestuous fornicators,[41] and when he expresses outrage at the slaughter of 70,000 rustics in Germany through what he believed was the malicious contrivance of the heretics.[42] The Peasants' Revolt and the marriages of Luther, Bugenhagen and Lambert in 1525 seem to have tipped the balance decisively. More's reaction to them combined with his existing nervousness at the idea of a sinless church to make an inflammable mixture which it would not need much to ignite.

More's horror of civil violence was as real as his belief in its connection with heresy was genuine. As early as 1523 he had discerned a potential threat to social and political order on the Continent, and prophesied direly in the *Responsio* that heretical subversion of the clergy would lead to anarchy: European princes would rejoice in a degenerating clergy and weakened church out of a greed for ecclesiastical possessions, the people would then look to shake off the yoke of the princes and, finally,

> drunk with the blood of princes and revelling in the gore of nobles, enduring not even common rule, with the laws trampled underfoot according to Luther's doctrine, rulerless and lawless, without restraint, wanton beyond reason, they will finally turn their hands against themselves and like those earthborn brethren, will mutually run each other through.[43]

In 1523 this prospect remained merely theoretical, but by 1525 More believed he had seen it happen in Germany just as he had predicted it would, confirming his worst fears:

[39] Rogers, *Correspondence,* no. 142, p. 325/24–8.
[40] ibid., p. 325/22–3.
[41] ibid., pp. 333/268ff., 353/1035ff.
[42] ibid., p. 364/1447ff.
[43] *Responsio, CW* 5, I, p. 691/26ff.

entendynge to bygyn at the feblest / there gathered theym together for the settyng forth of these vngracyouse heresyes / a boystyous company of that vnhappy sect / and first rebelled agaynst an abbot / and after agaynste a bysshop / wherewyth the temporall lordys had good game and sporte and dyssembled the matter / gapyng after the landys of the spyrytualtye . . .so was it shortly after that those vplandyshe Lutheranys toke so great boldnes and so bygan to grow strong / that thei set also vppon the temporall lordyes.

The tragic outcome was that the lords turned on the peasants, slaying more than 70,000 and reducing the rest 'to a right miserable seruitude'.[44]

More's dismay at this proof of the seditiousness of heresy was strong enough to provoke him into replying to Bugenhagen; once the danger approached closer to England his animosity towards the heretics and readiness to attack them increased. In 1526 England was still not immediately threatened. This was the year in which Roper could still enthuse happily that the realm was in such a good estate that no heretic dared show his face.[45] After 1526, however, events took a dramatic change for the worse. Tyndale's translation of the New Testament was printed by March 1526, and soon English bibles were being smuggled into England in large numbers, followed closely by other Lutheran books in the vernacular, such as Tyndale's *Compendious Introduccion . . . unto the Pistle off Paul to the Romayns*, Roye's *Brefe Dialoge* and Barlowe's *Beryeng of the Masse*.[46] Official repression could not quell the appetite for this literature, and the new doctrines rapidly gained adherents in the universities and the merchant fraternity of London.[47] Given More's conviction that heresy was inherently violent and seditious (at least Lutheran heresies), the spread of Lutheranism into England could only mean one thing: that England would slide relentlessly towards chaos unless heresy were exterminated. Indeed,

---

[44] *Dialogue Concerning Heresies, CW* 6, p. 369/15–29. The *Dialogue* repeats almost word for word More's assertion in the *Letter to Bugenhagen*, Rogers, *Correspondence*, p. 364/1407ff.

[45] Roper, p. 35.

[46] See Anthea Hume, 'English Protestant Books Printed Abroad, 1525–1535: An Annotated Bibliography', Appendix B, *CW* 8, II, pp. 1063–91.

[47] For a detailed account of this phase of the English Reformation, see A. G. Dickens, *The English Reformation* (London, 1964), pp. 68–82.

he came increasingly to believe in the existence of a Lutheran conspiracy devoted to that end.[48] All that the heretics looked for as the fruit of 'their sediciouse bookes and beggers bylles', he declared, was the destruction of Christ's faith so that they could advance 'al boldenes of sinne and wretchednes' and spur forth 'the deuilish vnbrideled appetite of lewde sediciouse and rebellion libertie, that slew in one somer . . . aboue .lx.M. of the poore vplandishe Lutheranis in Almaine'.[49] This would start in the same way with an attempt to destroy the power of the clergy, would be followed by the preaching of Luther's gospel and Tyndale's testament, and would eventually produce in the corrupted people 'obstinate rebellious mynde agaynst all lawes, rule, and gouernaunce, with arrogant presumpcion to medle with euery mannes substance'.[50] The result would be a fearsome bloodbath comparable to those More believed had already taken place in Germany, Switzerland and Italy:[51]

> For thei shall gather together at laste, and assemble themselfes in plumpes and in great rowtes, and from askyng fall to the taking of their almose themselfe, and vnder pretext of reformacion (bearing euery man that ought hath, in hand that he hath to much) shall assay to make newe diuision of euery mannes land and substance, neuer ceasyng yf ye suffer them, tyll thei make al beggers as they be themself, and at laste bryng all the realme to ruine, and this not without bocherye and foule bloudye handes.[52]

As a royal councillor concerned with the maintenance of law and order, More had a very practical reason for feeling that he could not remain aloof.

His sense of the social, political and ecclesiological implications of Lutheranism would probably have been enough by itself to bring him

---

[48] See Steven W. Haas, 'Simon Fish, William Tyndale, and Sir Thomas More's "Lutheran Conspiracy"', *Journal of Ecclesiastical History*, 23 (1972), pp. 125–36.

[49] *Supplication, EW* 1557, p. 312 F.

[50] ibid., pp. 312 H–313 B.

[51] More was appalled by the sack of Rome by imperial troops in 1527, an event that he erroneously ascribed to Luther's supporters, describing it graphically in *A Dialogue Concerning Heresies* (*CW* 6, p. 370/28ff). See also Richard C. Marius, 'The Sack of Rome', *CW* 6, II, Appendix C, pp. 773–7.

[52] *Supplication, EW* 1557, p. 313 B–C.

eventually into the conflict, but one precise event seems positively to have inflamed him: Luther's marriage.

Several of the other reformers had married earlier – Bugenhagen and Karlstadt in 1522, Lambert in 1524. While More knew of these marriages, they did not arouse undue indignation in him; in the *Responsio* he mentioned the breach of clerical vows only in passing as a further sign of shameless impiety.[53] It was only Luther's marriage to Katherine von Bora in 1525 that really upset his equilibrium. That he should have become incensed out of all proportion at this particular marriage is perplexing until one recognizes the different status Luther had in More's imagination.

Luther appears to have become a personal demon for More because in many respects he was very like him. They both shared an Augustinian revulsion against sensuality on one hand, and a propensity to indulge it on the other. Luther's plea for an invisible, sinless church was also related to the same manichean sense of the world More had expressed in his early poems. After rigorous trial, More had decided to be a chaste husband rather than an unchaste priest, as Erasmus tells us in the *Letter to von Hutten* ('Maluit . . . maritus esse castus quam sacerdos impurus');[54] when Luther married, More must have felt particularly outraged that his counterpart was daring to gratify both flesh and spirit in a way he could not allow for himself, even though his contemplation of a married order of priests in *Utopia* suggests that in the sphere of fantasy he may have wished to. Even worse, Luther was reviving old heresies which allowed him to participate in the world's corruption at the same time as he condemned it and declared himself free from it. To More this was the most monstrous manifestation of spiritual hypocrisy conceivable.

One can detect the influence of Luther's marriage in the perceptible change in More's attitude to him after 1525. In the *Responsio* he had portrayed Luther as a 'Luder', a laughable, rather simple-minded buffoon for whom a fitting epitaph could already be written:

> men will recall and say that once long ago there was in a former age a certain rascal by the name of Luther who, when he had got the better of cacodaemons in impiety, in order to adorn his sect

---

[53] *CW* 5, I, pp. 686/33–688/4.
[54] Allen, IV, no. 999, 18/167.

with fitting emblems, surpassed magpies in chatter, pimps in wickedness, prostitutes in obscenity, all buffoons in buffoonery.[55]

In *Dialogue Concerning Heresies* he is presented as something much more sinister: 'an apostate . . . an open incestuouse lechour / a playne lymme of the deuyll / and a manyfest messenger of hell'.[56] And instead of being a mere farrago of buffoonish words ('mera farrago uerborum scurrilium'),[57] his books provoke men 'to wronge opynyons of god and boldnesse in synne and wretchednes'.[58] Luther's doctrines had not changed so drastically between 1522 and 1528 as to justify More's shifting of the note from comic to tragic, but his lifestyle had, and one can gauge the effect on More from the incessant references to Luther's 'shamefull inceste and abominable bycherye' that infest the earlier English polemics.[59] These references are not merely the result of polemical convention as some critics have claimed; as far as I know nobody has yet found anything analogous in any other controversialist of the time (or since, for that matter). Nor do the reiterated taunts amount merely to 'comic abuse'.[60] The language More uses is often so violently disgusted and disgusting as to suggest an obsessive pre-occupation that is far from being objectively rhetorical. Katherine von Bora is 'Cate calate', a nun 'runne out of relygyon' to do 'foule stynkyng sacrifyce to that fylthy idole of Priapus, that frere Luther bereth about to gather in his offerynge wyth';[61] Luther is a 'luske' who 'hath often tymes played out his luste' with his 'lewde lemman', for whom burning 'fyrste here in fyre of foule fylthy luste' is merely a foretaste of the 'euerlastynge fyre of hell';[62] and because Luther and his fellows preach that lechery is no sin, 'of all shamefull shamelesse sectys that the deuyll can dyuyse, these be the botome of the draffe

---

[55] '. . . recordentur et loquantur homines, fuisse olim aliquando apud seculum prius nebulonem, quendam, cui nomen Luthero fuerit: qui quum cacodaemones impietate uicisset, ut dignis emblemmatis ornaret suam sectam, picas garrulitate, lenones improbitate, prostibula obscoenitate, scurras omnes scurrilitate superarit' (*CW* 5, pp. 684/22–7, 685/25–30).

[56] *CW* 6, p. 346/13–14.

[57] *CW* 5, I, p. 692/5.

[58] *CW* 6, p. 347/13–14.

[59] See, for example, *CW* 8, I, pp. 41–2, 49, 181, 191, 204, 207, 209, 228, 262, 306, 443, and so on.

[60] Schuster, *CW* 8, III, p. 1265. For another rejection of this idea, see G. R Elton's review of the Yale *Confutation*, *English Historical Review*, 89 (1974), pp. 382–7.

[61] *CW* 8, I, pp. 181/3, 207/19–21.

[62] ibid., pp. 496/6, 262/23–4.

tubbe and the moste poysoned dregges'.[63] In all the instances where he raises the matter, More's rhetoric becomes so aurally heightened and emotionally overcharged as to imply lack of objective control.

It is possible that More's whole attitude towards heresy after 1525 may have been conditioned by an interior psychological conflict arising from a continuing preoccupation with problems of sexuality.[64] Certainly, he often describes heresy as if it were a sexual sin. This is most apparent in his habit of associating the fire of hell with the fire of lust, and both with the image of a flaming firebrand; for example, the 'lyghtesome lanterne' by which the world may see Luther and his nun 'luskynge togyther in lechery' is described as a 'fowle fyrebronde' of 'helly lyght';[65] similarly, Tyndale is warned that if he does not amend in time, when he comes to hell he is likely to find 'an hote fyrebronde burnynge at hys bakke, that all the water in the worlde wyll neuer be able to quenche'.[66] The collocation is significant, for as well as being an emblem of damnation,[67] a firebrand was a traditional phallic emblem associated with Venus. In Chaucer's *Merchant's Tale,* for instance, Venus 'with hir fyrbrond in hir hand aboute / Daunceth biforn the bryde and al the route' at the wedding of January, the lecherous *senex amans*.[68] The squire Damian, too, is 'ny wood' with desire, 'So sore hath Venus hurt him with hir brond, / As that she bar it daunsinge in hir hond.'[69] Through a curious process of conflation, More on one hand uses the symbol to express the damnable character of lust, and on the other to liken Tyndale's eternal punishment to the unquenchable experience of it. He may have had in the back of his mind Chaucer's description of Venus' Temple in *The Parliament of Foules* (a work which he echoes on another occasion in the *Confutation*):[70]

> Within the temple, of syghes hote as fyr
> I herde a swogh that gan aboute renne;

[63] *CW* 8, II, pp. 766/32–767/10.

[64] A suggestion made forcefully by G. R. Elton in 'Thomas More, Councillor', in *Studies in Tudor and Stuart Politics and Government* (Cambridge, 1974), I, pp. 149–50; and 'The Real Thomas More?', in *Reformation Principle and Practice*, pp. 29–30.

[65] *Confutation, CW* 8, I, p. 181/1–8.

[66] ibid., p. 22/36–7.

[67] See, for example, the *Responsio, CW* 5, I, p. 686/3.

[68] *Complete Works*, E 1727–8.

[69] ibid., E 1775–8.

[70] When he adapts the idea of a parliament of birds to describe the heretics (*CW* 8, II, p. 723/9ff.).

Which syghes were engendred with desyr,
That maden every auter for to brenne
Of newe flaume.[71]

It seems that More thought the worst conceivable punishment for
heresy would be to be deprived of the sexual gratification Luther had
procured for himself.

More's peculiar identification of heresy with violence and sexual
misconduct had been apparent as early as 1526 in the *Letter to
Bugenhagen,* and even though he drew back from the irrevocable step of
publishing it, his complex set of reactions to Luther and Lutheranism
was bound to draw him into controversy sooner or later. He was
primed and ready. The spark that ignited him was struck from the
commission to launch a polemical campaign in the vernacular from
Cuthbert Tunstal on 7 March 1528:

> Because you, dearest brother, can excell Demosthenes himself
> in our vernacular as well as in Latin, and are accustomed to
> being a most keen defender of the Catholic truth on all occasions
> of conflict, you could not spend your leisure hours more profit-
> ably, if you can snatch any away from your official duties, than
> by publishing something in our language that may expose to
> simple and unlearned men the cunning malice of heretics, and so
> make them better prepared against these impious subverters of
> the church.[72]

This time More showed no hesitancy or reluctance, but fulfilled his
commission with a vengeance. *A Dialogue Concerning Heresies* and the
Supplication of Souls were the first fruits, being published in 1529; while
he was Lord Chancellor he published *The Confutation of Tyndale's
Answer,* books 1–3, in 1532; then after his resignation he published in

[71] *Complete Works,* p. 104/246–50.
[72] 'Et quia tu, frater charissime, in lingua nostra vernacula, sicut etiam in Latina,
Demosthenem quendam praestare potes, et Catholice veritatis assertor acerrimus in
omni congressu esse soles, melius subsiciuas horas, si quas tuis occupationibus
suffurari potes, collocare nunquam poteris, quam in nostrate lingua aliqua edas, que
simplicibus et ideotis hominibus subdolam hereticorum malignitatem aperiant, ac
contra tam impios Ecclesie supplantatores reddant eos instructiores' (Rogers,
Correspondence, no. 160, p. 387/19–26).

quick succession *A Letter Impugning the Erronious Writings of John Frith* (1533), books 4–8 of the *Confutation* (1533), *The Apology of Sir Thomas More, Knight* (1533), *The Debellation of Salem and Bizance* (1533), the *Answer to a Poisoned Book Which a Nameless Heretic Hath Called the Supper of the Lord* (1533), and wrote at least part of *A Treatise upon the Passion of Christ* before his imprisonment in April 1534.[73] This output amounted to approximately one million words of exhaustive and exhausting argument in the space of four years – a staggering achievement, particularly given that much of it was composed outside the hours of More's official duties.

Why did More throw himself into the task with such alacrity and overkill? As always, the reasons he himself gave were convenient rather than fully candid. Even though there were others equally qualified to write against the heretics, he claimed, the role particularly appertained to him by virtue of his office and oath; the king had admonished all the justices of the peace in every quarter of his realm to warn every one of his subjects of the grievous punishment to be incurred by importing, reading, or possessing heretical books, therefore he was bound to do the same, 'wyth openynge . . . the malyce and poyson of those pernycyous bokes . . . that hys people . . . maye be farre from infeccyon / and therby from al suche punyshement as . . . [follows] theruppon'; moreover, the king had set a notable example to imitate by writing the *Assertio septem sacramentorum*.[74] These reasons, however valid in themselves, do not account either for the bulk or the scope of the English controversies, and when More declares that 'the cause is of my wrytynge, not so mych to debate and dyspute these thynges [religious matters] wyth them . . . as to gyue men warnynge what myschyefe is in theyr bookes', one simply does not believe that he is stating the whole truth.[75]

More did indeed debate with the heretics, because he had acquired a considerable self-interest in the issues. Had he been seeking merely to warn men of the mischief in their books, he need have written no more than *A Dialogue Concerning Heresies* and the *Supplication of Souls*, which together charge the heretics with all the malicious intentions he was ever able to think of. By continuing to write one book after another, he was seeking to prove a central, private conviction: that human imperfection was no cause for despair or desperately radical

---

[73] See Haupt, *CW* 13, p. xxxix.
[74] *Confutation*, *CW* 8, I, pp. 27/26–28/34.
[75] ibid., p. 27/15–19.

action, however exaggeratedly it manifested itself in contemporary society, because God had created the postlapsarian world to be instrumental in its imperfection rather than perfectible. This idea underlines every stance More ever assumed, no matter what the precise issue. It explains in particular his fixation with proving that the church is a mixed body containing good and bad together, both in the temporality and spirituality. On that belief depended his whole understanding of human history, for the experience of the church provided a paradigm, illuminated by the Holy Spirit, of the meaning of life itself.

To prove his point, More invested his whole polemical argument with the personal convictions he had achieved in his humanist years. The controversies thus conceal a private attempt at self-justification within More's public execution of his official duty. It was probably inevitable that More would commit himself body and soul to a bellicose activity he found intrinsically abhorrent, but tragic that he did so; for having linked his own fortunes with the polemical cause, More had no option but to win, whatever the cost.

The cost was enormous, for More was soon so deeply involved that he turned the war into a personal crusade. He admits as much at the opening of *The Debellation of Salem and Bizance*; after boasting that he has changed Salem and Bizance from Englishmen back into towns and chased them back to Syria and Greece where they belong, he adds: 'And if the Pacifier conueie them hyther againe, and tenne suche other townes with them, embatailed in such dialogues: Sir Thomas More hath vndertaken, to put himselfe in thaduenture alone against them all.'[76] This boast would have been funny coming from the usual kind of *miles gloriosus,* but Sir Thomas meant it seriously, and wrote accordingly. The effort to achieve total victory brought out the worst in him, just as it had in his Utopians, as he was forced to become more and more ruthless, obstinate, and unreasonable, and suppressed the most attractive aspects of his nature.

The deterioration in More accelerated as it grew obvious to him that he was going to lose: that history was taking a new turn which led to nowhere but the Apocalypse, and that nothing anyone could do was going to alter its course. His fear of this prospect brought him close to despair; to understand why, one must appreciate the stakes he had invested in his controversial cause.

[76] *EW* 1557, p. 929 F–G.

6

More's Doctrinal Argument: *A Dialogue Concerning Heresies, The Confutation of Tyndale's Answer*

Once he had accepted Tunstal's commission, More's task was clear: to expose the error of heresy to ordinary Englishmen. The positions he was to defend were doctrinally predetermined, and it was part of the argument that they inevitably should be, but how he conducted his defence was another matter. The strategy More chose was deeply personal. Underlying his treatment of every topic were two concerns: to show that the Lutherans misunderstood the nature of the human situation and God's ways, and to prove that orthodox beliefs and practices embodied a right perception of them.

At the heart of More's thought was his sense of the Fall and man's postlapsarian condition; from that all other things followed.

Men had been placed originally in an earthy paradise in which they should have endured for a time 'without age, werines, or payn, without spot or wem or any decay of nature, preserued continually by the holesome frutes and helpe of Gods hand', until they 'shulde haue had theyr bodyes chaunged sodenly into a glorious form, and without death depart out of the earth, caryed vp wyth the soule into the blysse of heauen'.[1] To safeguard them against pride, God had given them precepts and commandments whereby they should have been reminded of their dependence on him,[2] and also set them to work in the Garden of Eden.[3] Adam and Eve, however, had failed in their spiritual duty. According to divine justice, their disobedience should have been punished by 'an ineuitable necessity of dyeng'[4] – not only temporal death, but the death of 'the whole entire man', body and

---

[1] *A Treatise upon the Passion* (hereafter cited as *Passion*), *CW* 13, p. 13/24–31.

[2] *A Dialogue Concerning Heresies* (hereafter cited as *Dialogue*), *CW* 6, pp. 138/35–139/21.

[3] *Passion*, *CW* 13, p. 12/26–30; cf. *Answer to a Poisoned Book*, *EW* 1557, p. 1047 H.

[4] *Passion*, *CW* 13, p. 13/7.

soul, with the irreparable loss of heaven.[5] Nevertheless, God took pity
upon man and determined upon a means of restoring him that would
satisfy both justice and mercy: 'that by the cruel painefull death of
that innocent person, that should be both god and man, the
recompence should be made vnto God for man. For that person both
being God, shuld be of that nature that was able to do it, and beinge
man, should be of that nature that was bounden to do it.'[6] Christ was
the person, and all those professing his faith are redeemed by the
merits of his passion and made 'enheritable' again'.[7] This includes all
pagans who, even if they do not know that Christ is the means, believe
that a means exists for man's reward and salvation.[8]

God, More believed, could have restored men straight-away to the
liberty of their former state, living in paradise, but 'hys high wisdome
well wist it was for oure selfe not best':

> For as the scripture saith: *Homo cum in honore esset, non intellexit.*
> When man was in honour, hys vnderstanding fayled him, he
> coulde not knowe hymselfe. And therefore to the keeping of hym
> from synne, and specially fro pryde the roote of al synne, a more
> base estate was better. And better was it also for hym to haue
> two enemies, that is to wyt the dyuel and hys owne sensuality
> both, than for to lacke the tone. For the hauinge of both, is a
> cause of double fear, and therfore of double diligence, to set his
> reason to kepe sure watche to resist theym, and for double helpe
> to cal double so much vpon almighty God for grace. And then
> wyth hys so doing, he is more able and more sure nowe to subdue
> them both, than with lesse looking for Gods helpe, he was before
> the tone: and hath yet also thereby for his double victory against
> his double enemies, thoccasyon of double rewarde.[9]

Although the state of innocence was the best that men could have
enjoyed, its very felicity allowed for men's negligence. Having given
them the chance to have possessed it – 'Sufficient to have stood,
though free to fall', as Milton later said[10] – God placed them in a

---

[5] ibid., p. 39/16–22.
[6] ibid., p. 27/5–9.
[7] ibid., p. 44/8–9.
[8] ibid., p. 43/20–8.
[9] ibid., pp. 46/25–47/17.
[10] *Paradise Lost,* III, 99; cf. *Passion, CW* 13, p. 13/7–13.

postlapsarian situation providentially tempered to give additional safeguards against human weakness. Sensuality, the most immediate consequence of the Fall, became instrumental to this end:

> sensualyty laboured soo busyly to cause man to set by delyte aboue good and conuenyente / that for the resystence thereof / it then bycame to be the spyrytuall busynesse and occupacyon of man / so to preserue and brynge vp the body / that it were not suffered to mayster the soule / and so to rule and brydyll sensualyte / that it were subiecte and obedyent vnto reason.[11]

In this perpetual warfare between body and soul, sensuality, assisted by the devil, was to send in ceaseless occasions for the deadly sins 'by all the dores and wyndowes of the body by felyng / tastynge / smellyng / sight and herynge', which reason, working with grace, would need to resist.[12] The effects were to be painful, for God's justice required that man should be 'somewhat punished' for his original transgression;[13] yet however harsh any man's tribulation may seem to be,

> all thys dothe god for the beste, vsynge our euyll to goodnes as we vse his goodnes to euyll. For whan a wanton chylde feleth ones a fall, and hathe all to rayed his gaye cote and broken bothe hys shynnes / than wyll he fynde hys owne faute and loke better to hys fete, and holde faster after on the mannes hande that ledde hym.[14]

Out of this sense of the providentiality of the fallen human situation grew More's whole view of the order God had used in governing men from the beginning.

Because God had determined to bring men to salvation not inevitably, but conditionally upon their repentance, contrition, and willing conversion towards him,[15] it followed that human will must be free, not servile. Even though it was true that men could do nothing

---

[11] *Dialogue, CW* 6, p. 139/27–33.
[12] ibid., p. 140/19–22; cf. *Confutation, CW* 8, II, p. 744/6–16.
[13] *Passion, CW* 13, p. 25/31.
[14] *Confutation, CW* 8, I, p. 527/21–6.
[15] ibid., pp. 510/37–511/1; cf. *Passion, CW* 13, pp. 53/30–54/3.

without the assistance of God's grace, 'the staf without help wherof no man is able to ryse out of syn',[16] it was equally true that God would never withhold from any man the prevenient grace that enables their free will to operate: 'though man can not turne vnto hym without preuencyon and concurraunt helpe of goddes especyall grace . . . the goodnesse of god prouydeth that his grace is euer redy to hym that wyll vse it'.[17] Ordinarily, God calls upon men of all sorts, using outward means and instruments, to turn to him as long as they live in the world;[18] however, even though God calls men perpetually to be saved, his calling is no constraint of necessity, for 'it is not the custome of God by force to make menne good whether thei wyll or no, nor in his eleccion hee chooseth not folkes by violence, but by good aduyce and mocion'.[19] Salvation depends entirely on men's obedience to God's commandments 'bothe in the bylyefe and the worke'.[20] They are fully capable of choosing to be good because God never tempts any man more than he can withstand,[21] nor leaves him 'withoute so moche helpe of his grace, as were sufficient for hym bothe to stande and walke with if hym selfe wolde'.[22] No man who purposes to remain good, therefore, can be carried one hair's breadth towards sinful deeds against his will.[23]

The frailty of human nature is such, however, that men's endeavour 'seldome constantely standeth eny whyle to gether in good workys / but that the perseueraunce is interrupted / often spotted / and bysprent with synne'.[24] This means that a man's life will be in a constant state of flux, 'now vp now downe, now fallynge by synne and now rysynge agayne by grace'.[25] Even the righteous man is liable to fall seven times a day and rise again: 'Septies in die cadit iustus / et resurgit.'[26] As a result, men are kept in a perpetual condition of responsiveness, forced by their weakness to acknowledge their dependence on God at the same time as they are obliged to overcome their

---

[16] *Supplication, EW* 1557, p. 323 C.
[17] *Confutation, CW* 8, I, p. 511/1–5; cf. *Dialogue, CW* 6, p. 404/13–16.
[18] *Confutation, CW* 8, I, pp. 520/38–521/7.
[19] *Answer to a Poisoned Book, EW* 1557, p. 1075 H.
[20] *Confutation, CW* 8, I, p. 464/3–17.
[21] ibid., pp. 453/34–454/1, 532/33–6.
[22] ibid., pp. 527/36–528/2.
[23] ibid., p. 454/10ff.
[24] *Dialogue, CW* 6, p. 395/21–3.
[25] *Apology, CW* 9, p. 108/24–5.
[26] *Dialogue, CW* 6, p. 395/24.

sinfulness. Although they can never completely succeed in this life, they are bound to sustain their effort to do so, and thus perhaps shorten their time in the cleansing fires of purgatory in the next.[27]

More translated all of these theological conclusions into a comprehensive view of history which profoundly influenced his ecclesiology and political thought. The rudiments of this view had already been expressed in *Utopia* and *The History of King Richard III*, but in the controversies More refined his sense of the full extent of its ramifications.

History had revealed that the world was in no way perfectible because of the continuous struggle in human nature between good and evil. Man was caught in the middle ground between two rival contenders: the devil seeking to pervert him through sensuality to sin and damnation, and God seeking to draw him back into obedience and salvation through reason and faith. Just as fast as God cleansed good corn from the cockle, so did the devil turn the corn back into cockle, and vice versa, and 'thys meruailouse straunge turning, neuer ceaseth nor neuer shall whyle thys world endureth'.[28] Hence men could never look to create heaven on earth.

Indeed, history showed that the natural tendency of human nature was towards degeneration, but throughout history God had provided special assistance to arrest this drift. The effect was to impose on history a rhythmic pattern of decline followed by providentially assisted renewal.

This pattern could be seen in the history of the church itself, which More considered in its largest sense as having been begun in paradise before being subsumed within Christ's new church.[29] After the Fall, men received assistance from their own natural reason, aided by 'good spyrytes appoynted by god', and divine grace.[30] God gave them further knowledge of anything necesary to be known that reason and nature could not plainly discern 'by specyall message' through patriarchs such as Noah, Lot and Abraham.[31] Even so, after a time the Hebrews began to drift into sin:

> the worlde waxynge worse, ryght good and vertuous lygnages declyned and decayed . . . and . . . fell by dysorder in suche a

[27] *Supplication, EW* 1557, p. 316 A–D.
[28] *Confutation, CW* 8, II, p. 1020/28ff; cf. *Letter to a Monk* (Rogers, *SL*, p. 129).
[29] ibid., II, p. 1007/33ff.
[30] *Dialogue, CW* 6, p. 140/24–6.
[31] ibid., p. 140/32–4.

blyndnes / that all be it some were there alwaye that perceyued
well theyr dutye / yet were the commen people of the chyldren
of Israell by custome of synne soo darked in theyr naturall
knowledge / that they lacked in many thynges the ryght
perceyuynge.[32]

God, however, did not turn his back on them as they deserved, but
sought of his endless mercy to revive their responsiveness. His first act
was to remind them again by the ten commandments of certain
conclusions of the law of nature, 'whiche theyr reason (ouerwhelmed
wyth sensualyte) hadde than forgotten'.[33] Having restored the precepts by which they should live, God gave them in addition 'a great
hepe' of laws and ceremonies 'to kepe them in straytely for [from?]
strayenge abrode in ryot', wrought miracles to arouse their awe and
devotion, and gave a warning of Christ to come.[34] Thereafter the Jews
never lacked knowledge of Christ's life, death and resurrection, for
God did not cease to foreshow the future 'by Patriarkes and
prophetes / by fygures and prophesyes'.[35] As well, he continued to
send good men from time to time whose words, living and miracles
ensured that the Jews were never destitute of sufficient understanding
of the written law to enable them to fulfil and keep it as far as human
frailty could allow.[36] They were thus left better fortified to remain
faithful than they had been before their degeneration.

In spite of all this, the same pattern of decline began to repeat itself:
'Very trouth it is, that lytle and lytle the same knowen churche
decaied, and waxed weake in faith . . . and the weede beganne to ouer
grow the corne.'[37] In the synagogue, which was then the church, evil
members began to sow new doctrines against Christ's coming until a
great confusion had arisen. Nevertheless, God, 'of his goodnes not
wylling to suffer the people to fall in perplexitye, but that they should
easely and readelye bee sure of the true doctrine', once again specially
intervened, this time in his own incarnate person, coming down to
begin his own new church,[38] leave a new covenant, and write a new
law more effectually in men's hearts.[39]

[32] ibid., p. 141/9–15.
[33] ibid., p. 141/21–2.
[34] ibid., p. 141/25–6.
[35] ibid., p. 141/31–2.
[36] ibid., p. 142/5–10.
[37] *Confutation*, *CW* 8, II, p. 1008/25–8.
[38] ibid., II, p. 1009/5–22.
[39] *Dialogue*, *CW* 6, p. 142/12–23.

With the incarnation of Christ and the founding of his church, men were to receive even more assistance than they had enjoyed previously. Christ's words were to be proved by his wonderful works, and his doctrines were to be confirmed by the miracles of his apostles and of saints ever after.[40] Furthermore, he left his church with a promise,

> one of the grettest, most solempne, most assuredly made, and therto most frutefull and most necessary that euer he made / that is to wyt that he wold be wyth hys chyrch of crysten people all dayes vnto the ende of the worlde, and that he wolde sende also the holy ghoost vnto them that sholde teche them all thynge and lede them in to euery treuth.[41]

In addition, he promised that the faith professed by Peter would never fail, and that the gates of hell should not prevail against it.[42] From those promises it followed that the church could never err 'in the ryght fayth necessary to be byleued',[43] nor be led to make a law 'dampnably displesaunte' to God.[44] Men, therefore, should never lack certain knowledge of God's behests thereafter.

Moreover, since Christ had come and damned sin in the flesh by the passion of his flesh, men 'may yf they wyll farre more easyly folowe the spyryte and resyste the flesshely mocyons' than men under the old law.[45] The instruments for this were the sacraments, which God had instituted 'as meanys by whiche we come to clensyng of the soule and to saluacyon'.[46] Far from being mere bare tokens (as the Lutherans claimed), the sacraments provided 'a quycke lyuely workynge medycyne, meane, and instrument'.[47] Any man who receives them reverently and with good will also receives grace and assistance from God through the merits of Christ's passion,[48] so that the outward sensible signs of all the sacraments 'do sygnyfe and that ryght effectually, an inwarde secrete gyfte and inspiracion of grace effused in

---

[40] *Confutation*, *CW* 8, I, pp. 244/30ff, 276/17–18.

[41] ibid., I, pp. 107/31–108/1.

[42] *Dialogue*, *CW* 6, p. 108/2–25.

[43] ibid., p. 112/9–10; cf. p. 178/11ff.

[44] ibid., p. 147/6.

[45] *Confutation*, *CW* 8, II, p. 755/21–34.

[46] ibid., I, p. 105/6–7.

[47] ibid., pp. 101/26–8, 102/3–6.

[48] More later expounded at length what he thought this involved in *A Treatise to Receive the Blessed Body of Our Lord* (*CW* 13, pp. 191–204).

to the soule . . . by the holy spirite of god'.[49] With all this additional
help, men had even less excuse than before for failing in their spiritual
duty.

Nevertheless, the old pattern had reasserted itself in Christian
history as much as in Old Testament history, proving that the greater
the good use of anything, the more it is susceptible to abuse. Human
perversity was manifest almost immediately in outbreaks of heresy:

> forth with vpon the deth of Cryste in the begynnynge of the
> chyrch / many sectys and heresyes began (as well appereth by
> the apocalyps of saynt Iohn the euangelist / and the epystles of
> the apostle Poule) and after almost contynually dyuers heresyes
> sprange in dyuers places (as we playnly se by the story
> of the chyrche by the bokys of saynt Hyerome / saynt
> Augustyne / saynt Eusebye / saynt Basyle / saynt Ambrose /
> saynt Gregory Nazianzenus / saint Chrysostome / and many
> other doctours of the chyrche.[50]

Even scripture itself was perverted when Wyclif, 'the great arch-
heretyke', purposely corrupted it in his English translation.[51] And just
as Wyclif had revived the old heresies of those ancient heretics, so was
Luther reviving his.[52] This recurrence of heresy had led frequently to
violence and destruction, as with the Donatists in North Africa,[53] and
even to 'the vtter subuersyon of that hole realme both in fayth and
good lyuyng / with the losse also of many a thousand lyues' in
Bohemia during the time of John Huss.[54]

It was thus clear to More from biblical history that although
particular circumstances may change in the course of time, the
prevalent condition of men remains the same. However active God
may be in assisting men, his providential intention was that all men
should always experience the same degree of trial and effort in

---

[49] *Confutation, CW* 8, I, pp. 77/35–78/10.

[50] *Dialogue, CW* 6, pp. 406/27–407/2. The extent of More's patristic scholarship and
knowledge of actual church history is questioned by S. L. Greenslade, 'The Morean
Renaissance', *Journal of Ecclesiastical History*, 24 (1973), pp. 395–403.

[51] *Dialogue, CW* 6, pp. 314/23–315/4.

[52] ibid., p. 315/8–13.

[53] ibid., p. 409/4–8.

[54] ibid., p. 315/6–8.

choosing to be obedient or disobedient. For this reason he had in the first place created the world not perfectly but willingly, 'not to the vttermost of his power, but with suche degrees of goodnes as his hye plesure lyked to lymyt'.[55] Even after he had intervened to arrest the degeneration of the Jews with the ten commandments, he had imposed upon them the obligation of observing the ceremonial laws of the Old Testament, thus requiring them to exercise greater responsibility in return for their greater help. When the old law was abrogated by Christ, that responsibility had increased even further in ratio to the greater assistance offered by the new law, as More declared in *A Dialogue Concerning Heresies*:

> It is I trow more harde not to swere at all / than not to forswere / to forbere eche angry worde than not to kyll / contynuall watche and prayer then a few dayes appoyntyd. . . . What say ye than by deuorsys restrayned / and lybertye of dyuerse wyuys withdrawen. . . . What ease also call you this / that we be bounden to abyde all sorow and shamefull dethe and all martyrdome vpon payne of perpetuall damnacyon for the professyon of our fayth. . . . Called he not them [the apostles] to watchynge / fastyng / prayeng / prechyng / walkyng / hunger / thurst / colde / and hete / betyng / scourgyng / prysonement / paynfull and shamefull deth?[56]

As well as suffering more tribulation in the course of trying to achieve a more holy life, Christians were also required to believe more things than had been the Jews.[57] Furthermore, God had contrived many of these things to be harder to believe than before:

> lyke as our nature fyrst fell by pryde to the dysobedyence of god with inordynate desyre of knowledge lyke vnto god / so hath god euer kepte man in humylyte / straynynge hym with the knowledge and confessyon of his ygnoraunce / and byndynge hym to the obedyence of byleue of certayne thinges / whereof his owne wyt wolde verely wene the contrary. And therfore are we bounden not onely to byleue agaynste oure owne reason /

[55] ibid., pp. 74/34–75/2.
[56] ibid., pp. 105/29–106/17.
[57] *Passion*, *CW* 13, p. 43/7–8.

the poyntes that god sheweth vs in scrypture / but also that god
techeth his chyrche without scrypture and agaynste our owne
mynde also.[58]

Scripture, in fact, had been 'so deuysed and endyted by the hyghe
wysedome of god / that it far excedeth in many placys the capacyte
and perceyuyng of man'.[59] It had been deliberately tempered by God
so as 'to quykken and exercyse . . . some mennys myndes in the studye
and deuysynge theruppon / whyche yf all were open and playne,
wolde waxe neglygent and dull'.[60] To remain obedient, Christians
were required, paradoxically, both to apply reason diligently in
discovering the grounds of their faith,[61] and then – which was more
difficult – to subdue it into subservience to suprarational belief, for, as
More said in his letter against Frith,

> alasse for the dere mercy of god, yf we shoulde leaue the letter
> and seke an allegory . . . in euerye place where we finde a thing
> that reason cannot reach vnto . . . faine would I wit what one
> article of all our fayth thys yonge man coulde assigne me spoken
> of in the scripture, from which his reason shal not driue away the
> strength of his proofe.[62]

The additional burdens of Christian responsibility meant that men's
spiritual business was proportionately just as testing and effortful as it
had always been since the Fall; More did not believe that there was
any escape from the perpetual trial, both punishingly and redemp-
tively purifying, that divine wisdom had disposed as the lot of fallen
man.

More's sense of postlapsarian history and the realities of the fallen
human condition influenced his stand on all the particular issues in
dispute with the reformers.

Chief among them was the question of the church. The inevitable
frailty of human nature meant that Luther's assumption of a sinless,
invisible church was, for More, an absurdity. While men are on earth,

[58] *Dialogue, CW* 6, p. 166/9–18.
[59] ibid., p. 335/5–7.
[60] *Confutation, CW* 8, I, p. 331/7–10.
[61] *Dialogue, CW* 6, pp. 131/18–132/16.
[62] *EW* 1557, p. 837 F–G.

they are bound to lapse many times, some eventually to fall into sin and wretchedness and so cast themselves away, and some to 'tourne agayne wyllyngly by grace vnto grace / and so passe at the laste thorowe grace into glory'.[63] Consequently, the church must inevitably be in a continuously militant, dynamic state while it is here on earth, comprising both good and bad together. Inevitably, therefore, the church is 'in thys worlde very sikely, and hath many sore membres / as hath somtyme the naturall body of a man, and some sore astonyed, and for a time colde and dede / whyche yet catcheth hete and lyfe agayne, yf it be not precyded and cut of from the body'.[64] Far from being without spot or wrinkle as Barnes, for example, claimed, the church on earth was suffering the process by which God was washing out her spots and stretching out her wrinkles in preparation for her entry into 'the pleasaunt weddyng chambre to the bed of eternall rest' after the last judgement;[65] but in the meantime, 'as faste as her husbande wassheth she spotteth, and as faste as he streccheth she wryncleth'.[66] By refusing to accept that the church would inevitably be 'as scabed as euer was Iob' as long as it is here, the heretics, More believed, were seeking to 'bylde vp in the ayre a chyrche all so spyrytuall / that they leue therin at length neyther god nor good man'.[67]

More's sense of the militancy of the church reinforced his objections to the doctrine of predestination. Luther and his followers, he believed, had overlooked a crucial distinction in asserting their predestinate, sinless church: 'yf the questyon were of the chyrche tryumphaunt in heuyn / than sayd they well. But we speke of the chyrch of Chryst mylytaunt here in erthe'.[68] He saw their error as arising first from Luther's belief that even with the help of God's grace, no man is able to observe the commandments of God,[69] and, second, from the Lutherans' refusal to admit that God's prescience could accord with human free will.[70] This had led Luther to the conclusion that 'all thyng hangeth onely vpon desteny', which More

[63] *Dialogue, CW* 6, p. 197/26–9, *Confutation, CW* 8, II, p. 957/22–3.
[64] *Confutation, CW* 8, I, p. 398/31–5.
[65] *Dialogue, CW* 6, p. 206/1–3.
[66] *Confutation, CW* 8, II, p. 865/28–32.
[67] *Dialogue, CW* 6, pp. 206/7, 196/25–7.
[68] ibid., p. 196/28–30.
[69] ibid., pp. 395/33–396/17.
[70] *Letter Impugning Frith, EW* 1557, p. 839 H.

thought 'the very worste and most mischieuous heresy that euer was thought vpon' because it assumed that God was indifferent to men's deeds, whether good or bad; his predestinate elect could do nothing displeasing to him, however wicked, while those not chosen could do nothing pleasing, 'be it neuer so good'.[71] More also detected an even more sinister implication in this heretical determinism. If men could not choose of their own free will to do good, then they could not be held responsible for doing bad. Luther's doctrine of the servile will thus implicitly laid 'to the charge and blame of god / all the malyce and myschyefe frome the fyrste fawt to the laste / that euer was wrought or thought by man woman or deuyll'.[72] This made God 'the cause of all euyll / and [of] suche cruell appetyte as neuer tyraunt and tourmentoure had'.[73] To More, God was indeed active in his creation, but rather than causing human evil, he worked continuously to bring goodness out of it, by assisting men to find occasions of amendment therein.

It was precisely because he believed that God was creatively present and active in human affairs that More rejected the doctrine that all things necessary to be believed were left by the apostles written in scripture.

Scripture was not the full extent of God's revelation, because 'his testament is not the wrytyng onelye, but *al the whole thing* reueled by God vnto hys church'.[74] Since history was the medium of this total revelation, it would not be complete until the end of time. Until then, God knows many things that men do not: 'he can yf yt please hym reuele and shew vs any of those, and commaunde vs to byleue them when so euer he lyste. . . . And he maye when yt please hym commaunde vs to do some other thynges that he hath not commaunded yet. . . . And he maye commaunde to leue vndone some thynges that he hath byfore commaunded to be done.'[75] In fact, it had been God's perpetual order from the beginning to require from men unconditional obedience. For this reason he reveals the truth by degrees, disclosing more and more things 'as it shall lyke his hygh goodnes and wysdome

---

[71] *Dialogue, CW* 6, p. 400/1–9. For More's most detailed rebuttal of this notion, see *Confutation, CW* 8, I, pp. 445–61.
[72] *Dialogue, CW* 6, p. 377/12–14.
[73] ibid., pp. 402/32–403/2.
[74] *Answer to a Poisoned Book, EW* 1557, p. 1083 H.
[75] *Confutation, CW* 8, I, p. 284/14–23.

to dyspence and dyspose'.[76] Whereas in matters to be believed
nothing that is revealed subsequently in history can ever be contrary
to what was revealed before, the possibility for change in things to be
done is endless: 'For in dyuerse tymes, dyuerse thynges may be
conuenyent / and dyuerse maners of doynge.'[77] Men are bound to
perform these things just as surely as they are bound to believe the
articles of faith, because all measures deriving from the church's
deliberations have the authority of an inspired consensus:

> in a counsayle of crysten men the spyryt of god inclyneth euery
> good man to declare hys mynde, and inclyneth the congregacion
> to consente and agree vppon that that shall be the beste, eyther
> precysely the beste, or the beste at the leste wyse for the season:
> whyche when so euer yt shall be better at any other tyme to
> chaunge, the same spyryte of god inclyneth his chyrche eyther at
> a new counsayle, or by as full and whole consent as any
> counsayle can haue, to abrogate the fyrste and turne yt into the
> better.[78]

Upon this secret leading into a sanctified, unerring consensus, the
whole authority of the earthly church, for More, depended.[79] It was
the basis of his insistence that men were bound to observe unwritten
traditions that had been evolved after the time of the apostles, such as
the Lenten fast, the changing of Saturday into Sunday, the hallowing
of chalices, vestments, holy water, and other things, the reverence
owed to images, and certain practices concerning the sacraments.[80]
These traditions and practices formed the unwritten continuation of
scripture, which, metaphorically speaking, was still in the process of
being written. More likened the unwritten scripture to the laws of
England, many of which resided only in custom, precedent and usage,
but which were effectual and binding nonetheless.[81]

Just as God had not enshrined all his revelation in writing, so, More
believed, had he deliberately tempered even the written scripture to

---

[76] *Dialogue, CW* 6, p. 146/33–4; *Confutation, CW* 8, I, pp. 248–9.
[77] *Confutation, CW* 8, II, p. 923/13–14.
[78] ibid., pp. 922/33–923/5.
[79] For the current dispute over this point, see the authorities listed above,
Introduction, note 7.
[80] *Confutation, CW* 8, I, p. 366/34ff.
[81] ibid., p. 291/16–24.

be dark and mysterious in many places. Such things as the coming of Antichrist and the day, manner and fashion of the small judgement, for example, 'shall neuer be fully dysclosyd / tyll the tymys appoyntyd by goddys hye prouydence mete and conuenyent for them'.[82] When the time is ripe for men to understand such things, God 'dothe insumate and inspyre them into the brestys of his crysten people / that by the secrete instyncte of the holy gost they consent and agre togyther in one' as to the meaning.[83] In this respect there was an analogy between the nature of scripture and the nature of historical experience at large; the one illuminated the other, but neither would be fully understood until God's purpose had worked itself out in time. In the meantime, men were dependent on the understanding into which Christ had promised the church would be led, and the church's understanding was that scripture alone did not suffice. Besides, only the church's consensus could decide what was true scripture and what was not,[84] and only the church could be certain that it had grasped whatever degree of right understanding of it that God had vouchsafed.[85]

More's belief in free will and his sense of men's appointed responsibility both in belief and action made him equally hostile towards the idea of evangelical liberty.

He recognized that the Lutherans' view that the elect were justified by faith arbitrarily and deterministically disposed logically implied an irrelevancy of all temporal laws:

> all lawes they sette at nought. And they holde that no man is bounden to obaye any / but wolde be at lybertye to byleue what they lyste / and doo what they lyste / as they saye that god dothe wish vs not what we deserue / but what hymselfe lyste . . . and thus the bestys be not ashamyd to say . . . that whan they wyll do a thynge they do it. And whan they lyst they leue it.[86]

---

[82] *Dialogue, CW* 6, p. 146/17–19.

[83] ibid., p. 146/22–4. The Yale edition emends the 'insumate' of the 1529, 1531 and 1557 editions to 'insinuate' (see *CW* 6, p. 647, note to p. 146/22), but 'insumate', from Latin *insumere* ('to take in', 'absorb'), used transitively, seems to me to render far more precisely More's sense of the consensual process involved.

[84] ibid., p. 181/1ff.

[85] ibid., pp. 183/22–184/27.

[86] ibid., pp. 403/32–404/11; cf. *Responsio, CW* 5, I, p. 269/30ff.

As well as asserting that the elect act deterministically, Luther had also argued that human laws could be replaced by the law of the gospel alone, if the faith were truly preached and magistrates good.[87] Against this, More claimed not only that human laws were necessary, but also that men were positively bound to develop them.

He vehemently rejected the plea for evangelical liberty on the grounds that inherent human sinfulness would inevitably frustrate any attempt to achieve it: 'As if even the best magistrates could manage either that the whole Christian people would want to live in common or that the wicked would not want to steal or that the preaching of the faith could procure that no one anywhere would be wicked.'[88] Positive laws were necessary to restrain crime through providing a deterrent in accordance with natural law; for example, 'If the law of the gospel does not permit stealing, surely the human law which punishes stealing is not useless' ('Si lex euangelica furtum non permittit: certe nec inutilis est lex humana: quae furtum punit').[89] As well as administering retributive justice, positive law had a prescriptive function. Even in a society where all men lived in common ownership, More argued, the obligation to work, for example, would still need to be prescribed for certain classes ('certis ordinibus').[90] In a society organized around property, the prescriptive function is even more necessary. In both its retributive and prescriptive aspects, positive law served the same purpose as the 'great heap' of laws given to the Jews in the Mosaic code – to constrain men more forcefully to the observance of God's commandments. Law, More realized, could exploit fear to be the ally of conscience.

Human laws, moreover, were necessary for the administration of distributive justice, as More had declared in the *Responsio ad Lutherum*:

> hardly any judgment is rendered justly which is not rendered according to some established law. For the law of the gospel does not apportion possessions, nor does reason alone prescribe the forms of determining property, unless reason is attended by an

---

[87] *Responsio, CW* 5, I, p. 275/29–31.

[88] 'Quasi uel optimi magistratus possent efficere: ut aut totus populus christianus uiuere uellet in communi: aut mali nolint furari: aut ulla fidei praedicatione posset impetrari: ut nulli usquam sint improbi' (ibid., pp. 274/26–9, 275/31–5).

[89] ibid., pp. 274/29–30, 275/35–7.

[90] ibid., p. 276/5–6.

agreement, and this a public agreement in the common form of mutual commerce, which agreement, either taking root in usage or expressed in writing, is public law.[91]

Men were bound to obey secular laws propounded in such a way for much the same reason they were bound to obey the laws of the church: because of the consensus and customary usage that had ratified them. In fact, there was an implicit analogy in More's thinking between the law and the church: both were institutional instruments through which the virtues of divine and natural law could be developed in history;[92] both required men to exercise their free will and reason before these virtues could be brought into being; and both bound men authoritatively to the observance of the measures they propounded. Any society where the law failed became vulnerable to two of the worst manifestations of human sinfulness: the anarchy of thieves and murderers on one hand, or else despotic princes ruling lawlessly according to their whim on the other.[93]

More's conviction that men were responsible for maintaining their own temporal order influenced his view of kingship. He could accept neither what he took to be Luther's view, that people need not obey kings at all, nor Tyndale's view that kings must be obeyed unconditionally in all things good or bad.[94] He considered both doctrines to be opposite forms of the same vice: a wish to evade the daily burden of political responsibility – evangelical liberty by denying the need for the elect to conform their actions to the law, and Tyndale's doctrine of obedience by replacing consensus with regal voluntarism.

More's own view was less absolute and extreme than either. Men, he argued, were indeed bound to obey and revere kings for several

---

[91] '. . . uix ullum iuste redditur iudicium: quod non ex aliqua lege lata redditur. Nam neque lex euangelica diuidit possessiones: neque sola ratio praescribit formas discriminandi proprij: nisi rationi consensus accedat, atque is in communi forma commercij mutui publicus: qui consensus aut coalescens usu, aut expressus litteris, publica lex est' (ibid., pp. 276/20–5, 277/24–30).

[92] More's view of positive law is very close to that of Fortescue; see *De natura legis naturae*, in *The Works of Sir John Fortescue*, ed. Thomas (Fortescue), Lord Clermont (London, 1869), pt. 1, chap. 43: '. . . jam liquet omnes leges humanas quasi instrumenta esse quibus lex Divina in humanis actibus explicat virtutes suas' (p. 109).

[93] *Responsio, CW* 5, I, p. 276/25ff.

[94] See *The Obedience of a Christian Man*, in *Works of the English Reformers*, ed. Russell, I, pp. 213, 228.

good reasons. First, order depended on it, since 'there is nothynge earthlye, that so muche kepeth themselfe in quyete, reste, and suretie, as dooeth the due obedyence of the people to the vertuous mynde of the prynce'.[95] Justice and order would fail in any realm where there was no ruler to see them kept, and even if the rulers were bad, 'yet wolde the people be myche worse yf they were all wythout'.[96] Second, every Christian man or woman was duty bound to give honour and reverence to princes because of the sacred nature of their persons and office. Together with priests, kings formed one of the two most eminent orders 'of speciall consecrate personys' that God had ordained on earth.[97] To emphasize their sacredness, More alleged the example of David, who

> dyd so moche esteme the holy oyntemente with whiche kynge Saule was consecrated, that all be it he was reiected agayne of god, and hym selfe receyued and anoynted kynge in his place, and was also persecuted by hym / he nat onely put the man to dethe that sayd he hadde slayne hym for touchinge of goddes anoynted / but also for all that he spared hym and sauyd his lyfe, and beynge his dedely enemye, dyd hym yet no bodely harme. He repented and forthought that he hadde so moche done to hym, as secretely to cutte his garment.[98]

This sacerdotal character of the king meant that his subjects were not free to obey or disobey him as they pleased.

In return for the obedience of their subjects, kings were bound by their oath and office to fulfil certain responsibilities. They might not, More declared, 'vpon the parell of theyr soules wyttyngly suffer amonge the people whome they haue in gouernaunce any one to take away anothers horse'.[99] They were thus responsible for the maintenance of justice down to the most humble cases. Equally, 'bothe nature / reason / and goddys byheste byndeth . . . the prynce to the sauegarde of hys peple with the parell of hym selfe / as he taught Moyses to know hym selfe bounden to kyll the Egypcyans in the defence of Hebrewe'.[100] This comprised the defence of the realm

[95] *Supplication, EW* 1557, p. 295 H.
[96] *Confutation, CW* 8, II, p. 911/7–14.
[97] *Apology, CW* 9, p. 50/31.
[98] *Confutation, CW* 8, II, p. 595/10–20.
[99] *Dialogue, CW* 6, p. 415/22–4.
[100] ibid., p. 414/36–415/4.

against invaders, particularly infidels, and the protection of men's souls against corruption by heretics.[101] (On these grounds More rejected pacifism and approved the use of bodily violence against heretics.)[102] The relation between rulers and those ruled was of the nature of a sacramental contract in which subjects were to return reverence and obedience for the benefits that princes had been ordained to provide for them.[103]

Although dutiful obedience was a religious obligation, men were nevertheless also required to ensure that the prince rules virtuously, and not according to the leadings of his own nature. In this respect More diverged from Tyndale's belief in the need for servile obedience as much as he had from Luther's notion of liberty. Subjects must obey, but what they needed to obey lay partly in their own hands. Magistrates must not be allowed to prosecute imperiously anything they pleased, More declared, because the people would then be reduced into a condition of servitude ('seruitutis conditione') and justice would be likely to fail.[104] However, the restraint and correction of princes was a problematical affair. Public defamation or criticism of princes was forbidden not only by the dignity of their office, but also by the common laws of England and plain statute;[105] nevertheless, there were indirect ways of influencing them for the better:

> if priuate affection towarde theyr owne fantasies, happened in any thynge so far to myslede theyr iudgement / for helpe of suche happes serue their confessours and counsaylours / and euery man that of good mynde wolde in good maner declare his owne good aduyce towarde his prynce and his countrey, eyther to his owne person or suche other of his counsayle, as by them it may be brought vnto him.[106]

Individual and collective counsel could go some way towards restraining the whims of the prince, and once persuasion had led to a

---

[101] ibid., p. 415/11–26.

[102] ibid., pp. 406/4–416/8.

[103] More's view of the sacramental relation between king and subjects meant that he did not consider the king's authority to be derived 'immediately from the people through their representatives in Parliament' (asserted by Brian Byron, *Loyalty in the Spirituality of St Thomas More* (Nieuwkoop, 1972), p. 35), or absolute by inherited right.

[104] *Responsio, CW* 5, I, p. 276/29.

[105] *Confutation, CW* 8, II, p. 592/21–6. More was referring to the statute *De scandalis magnatum* (3 Edward I, chap. 34; 2 Richard II stat. 1, chap. 5).

[106] *CW* 8, II, p. 591/12–18.

consensus which had taken root in usage or had been expressed in writing ('consensus aut coalescens usu, aut expressus litteris'),[107] the resulting law acquired a force of binding a king (mediately, if not immediately), even though his regal discretionary power could override it.[108] Customary privileges and procedures evolved in the various orders could also be invoked as a means of restraining the prince's wilfulness. More suggested, for example, that King John's despotic designs had been frustrated by the assertion of the convent of monks at Canterbury of their right to elect their own archbishop, 'to whom as the king well knew and denied it not, the eleccion of the archebishop at that time belonged'.[109]

Thus in spite of his apparent authoritarianism, More did not ultimately equate obedience with servility, and so found himself caught awkwardly between the extreme positions of Luther and Tyndale. A particular problem arose from his belief that when Christ had ordered the Jews to obey the commandments of their governors, he had not meant by that generality that 'they sholde obaye any commaundement that by god were forbeden, nor to set goddes law asyde for mennys tradycyons', but that they were forbidden 'to refuse to fulfyll the commaundement of theyr rulers, wherof there were no mencyon made in scrypture, where the commaundement tended to vertue, good maners, or goddes honour'.[110] The theoretical dilemma posed by this distinction between legitimate commands to be obeyed and sinful ones that must not be obeyed, but also not resisted, was acute. Where, and how, was one to draw the line? Even allowing that the church's unerring consensus could decide what was legitimate or illegitimate, which was questionable (especially once More had admitted that a provincial council of the church could err),[111] a man was still left with the problem of how to reconcile his conscience and conduct. Because subjects were forbidden to defame a prince publicly or rebel against

[107] *Responsio*, *CW* 5, I, p. 276/24–5. Although More was speaking specifically of property, the idea stands as a generality.

[108] This is implicit in the totality of More's works, and coincides with the view described by G. R. Elton, *The Tudor Constitution: Documents and Commentary* (Cambridge, 1960), p. 13: 'Tudor kingship inherited not only potential absolutism (always implied in medieval kingship) but also certain limitations. To be obeyed – in theory – a king needed only to be king; in practice it was tacitly assumed that he should be a just king.'

[109] *Supplication*, *EW* 1557, p. 296 E.

[110] *Confutation*, *CW* 8, I, p. 353/6–15.

[111] *Apology*, *CW* 9, p. 100/8–10.

him, anyone who found himself unable to fulfil a command because it seemed to be forbidden by divine law had ultimately no redress – as More would later discover at the cost of his life. Any human society, therefore, was at the mercy of its prince. It could not do without him, for the alternative was chaos, but equally it could not suffer him to gallop unbridled; men were bound to obey him, but forbidden to accept the sinful despotism unquestioning obedience could promote. That left them faced continuously with a need to find some way of steering the ship of state between Scylla and Charybdis without the helm being fully in their control. Here, then, was yet another circumstance to abase men's pride.

All of More's arguments eventually returned to their point of origin: his assumption that the postlapsarian world is so ordered as to keep men in a perpetual struggle to attain a victory that their condition will never allow them definitively or securely to win. His concern to prove that this was so, and providentially so, underpinned his defence of every orthodox dogma in dispute with the heretics.

With the advantage of hindsight, one can see that More, whether he knew it or not, was attributing to the world, and the church in particular, characteristics deriving from his own sense of himself: both were in a state of militant, unresolvable warfare, both were subject to an order of experience that was baffling in its paradoxicality, and both were governed by the unsearchable dispose of God's providence. Furthermore, he had decided to conduct his polemical campaign as if the dogmatic formulations, beliefs and practices of the Roman church adequately and accurately expressed the understanding of the world he had developed for himself years earlier in *Utopia*. Having hitched his own intellectual wagon to the orthodox train, he had ventured everything on its successful passage. It was absolutely imperative that history prove him right with the success of his cause; when events began to suggest that this might not happen, the effects on him were catastrophic indeed.

7

Political Commitments and Encounters: *Supplication of Souls, Apology, Debellation of Salem and Bizance*

The ultimate purpose of More's doctrinal argument was to assert the imperfectible condition of the world. Lutheranism, by suggesting that men were not bound inevitably by it, provided an unimaginable affront to his understanding of things, so that by the 1530s his opposition had become total, subsuming private inclination within public duty, and fuelled by personal psychological reactions as well as intellectual disagreement.

Even the extreme degree of More's hatred of heresy, however, cannot fully explain the scope or intensity of the controversies. From almost the very beginning More stepped beyond the strict terms of his brief. He had been licensed to read and refute heretical books, yet almost half his polemical output does not really concern heresy at all. Simon Fish's *Supplication for the Beggars*, which elicited More's *Supplication of Souls*, was not overtly heretical apart from a few qualified objections to the doctrine of purgatory, and those objections were not the main target of More's attack on it. Likewise, there is not a trace of heresy in either Christopher St German's *Treatise Concernynge the Division between the Spirituality and Temporality*, or his *Salem and Bizance*, yet they provoked More into writing two books and more pages than his entire *Dialogue Concerning Heresies* in reply. More himself indirectly admitted the truth when he referred to the 'Pacifier' St German as a man 'whom I for hys playne confession of the true fayth, tooke and take yet for a man good and catholyke'.[1] Whatever the views St German was to express later in the *Power of the Clergy* and the *Answer to a Letter*,[2] in late 1532 and early 1533 he was no more a heretic than Henry VIII − or for that matter, most of his Parliament.

All this leads one to suspect that More was dealing with much more

---

[1] *Debellation, EW* 1557, p. 932 D.
[2] See *CW* 9, p. lii.

than heresy alone. Indeed, the evidence suggests that the *Supplication of Souls*, the *Apology* and the *Debellation* were written both as a response to political events, and also as a covert attempt to influence their outcome. The campaign against heresy had become practically identical in More's mind with a desire to frustrate a momentous political revolution he saw in train within the commonwealth.

More knew, and had long known, that at the heart of the contemporary European and English crises was a failure to achieve reform, especially within the church. His close association with Erasmus' *Moriae encomium*, his own satiric epigrams and his *Letter to a Monk* testify to his awareness that much was rotten in the late-medieval condition of religion, learning and the body politic. *Utopia* itself analysed some of the problems: the rapacity of the nobility in England, the imperial ambitions of European princes, the destructiveness of recurrent wars, and the irresponsibility of popes in failing to rebuke rulers for breaking faith. It also contemplated the extent to which any redress was possible. More concluded that, although the world was not perfectible because of the sinfulness of human nature, much could be done, and that it was a perpetual necessity for men to keep on trying to do it, however doomed their best efforts might be to frustration. Even as late as 1529 the urgent need for reform was very much on More's mind. In the speech with which he opened the Reformation Parliament on 3 November, he declared that many of the existing laws had become outmoded through time and social change, that reform was necessary in both church and state, not least because of Wolsey's negligence, and that having been summoned to reform the realm, Parliament would be asked to enact appropriate legislation.[3]

More knew that the church in particular was in desperate need of reform, 'for vndoutly yf the clergye be nought we [the laity] must nedes be worse'.[4] Since 1515, with the cases of Richard Hunne and Friar Standish,[5] popular discontent had shown that many Englishmen did think that their clergy were wicked. The very lengths to which More went to disprove allegations arising from Hunne's death 15 years later reflect his awareness of the force of this anticlericalism.[6]

---

[3] I follow the reconstruction of More's speech, based on a conflation of reports by Halle and Chapuys, given by Guy, pp. 113–14.

[4] *Dialogue, CW* 6, pp. 297/36–298/2.

[5] For an account, see Elton, *Reform and Reformation*, pp. 51–7.

[6] *Dialogue, CW* 6, pp. 317–30; *Supplication, EW* 1557, pp. 297–9.

The church should have been able to reform itself from within, but More knew that this had not happened, and while he was sufficiently discreet not to rebuke the church universal for failing to remedy abuse,[7] he was not so reticent in condemning the slackness of the provincial English clergy:

> as for my dayes as farre as I haue herd, nor as I suppose a good parte of my fathers neyther / they came neuer to gether to conuocacyon, but at the request of the king / and at theyr suche assembles concernynge spyrytuall thynges haue very lytle done.
>
> Wherfore that they haue ben in that great necessary poynt of theyr dewty so neglygent, whyther god suffer to growe to a secret vnperceyued cause of dyuysyon and grudge agaynste theym, god whome theyr suche neglygence hath I fere me sore offended, knoweth.[8]

At the time when his polemical campaign commenced, More seems to have been ready and willing to participate in a drive to achieve ecclesiastical reform. In *A Dialogue Concerning Heresies* he went so far as to suggest his own remedies for certain defects. First, he proposed far stricter standards of selection for the priesthood as a first step towards dispelling the truth of the proverb that 'yf a preste be good than he is olde'.[9] Second, he emphatically disassociated himself from those members of the clergy who refused to countenance a vernacular translation of scripture in case seditious people should do more harm with it than honest men would benefit: 'whiche fere I promyse you nothynge fereth me. . . . For els yf the abuse of a good thynge sholde cause the takyinge awaye thereof frome other that wolde vse it well / Cryst sholde hym selfe neuer haue bene borne / nor brought hys fayth into the worlde / nor god sholde neuer haue made it neyther.'[10]

---

[7] John Fisher was not so discreet when he charged the Fifth Lateran Council with not having been gathered in proper meekness and charity (*English Works of John Fisher, Bishop of Rochester*, p. 338; see also Headley, *CW* 5, II, pp. 770–1). When St German rehearsed the account in the *Declaratio defectuum virorum ecclesiasticorum* (*CW* 9, pp. 182–3) of clerical abuses that the earlier councils had been meant to reform, More simply ignored it in his *Apology* on the lame excuse that Gerson had written in Latin (*CW* 9, p. 60/15–20). The *Declaratio*, although attributed to Gerson in More's time, was in fact, written by Heinrich von Langenstein (see *CW* 9, pp. xlvi, lvi, 339).

[8] *Apology*, *CW* 9, pp. 144/33–145/4.

[9] *CW* 6, p. 301/14–15.

[10] ibid., p. 332/9–17.

He expressed amazement, in fact, that God had not provided a satisfactory English bible already.[11] To allow for the good use of an approved English bible should it eventuate, More proposed a system of supervised reading overseen by the ordinaries.[12]

Those liberal sentiments were penned probably in the latter half of 1528. Within two years his attitude towards reform had altered radically. The change is first registered in the proclamation against heretical books of 22 June 1530, promulgated on the advice of More and Fisher.[13] Not only did this proclamation proscribe heretical books and forbid the importation of all English books printed abroad, but it also declared that the bible in English was 'not necessary'.[14] Since the proclamation had More's full support, he presumably approved this reactionary step, which was a far cry from his opinion in the *Dialogue* that the 'lewdnes and foly' of those who misuse an English bible 'were not in my mynde a suffycyent cause to exclude the translacyon'.[15] By the time he wrote the *Apology* in early 1533 he had succumbed to the very fear which, in the *Dialogue,* he had condemned as pusillanimity, being now prepared to countenance a translation only 'yf the men were amended and the tyme mete therfore'.[16]

More's changed attitude towards an English bible in 1533 was merely symptomatic of a more pervasive change. It appears also in his opposition to St German's proposals for equitable legal reform. Whereas in his speech to the 1529 Parliament he had urged the need for reform of the law, in 1533 he had become determined to preserve the *status quo* at all costs:

> surely yf the lawes maye be kepte and obserued without perel of soule though the chaunge might be to the better: yet out of tyme and place conuenient to put the defawtes of the lawes abrode among the people in wrytynge, and wythoute any surety of the chaunge geue the people occasyon to haue the lawes in derysyon . . . that way wyll I not as thus aduysed neyther vse my selfe nor aduyse no frende of myne to do.[17]

[11] ibid., p. 331/27–31.
[12] ibid., p. 341/6–27.
[13] Guy, p. 171.
[14] ibid., p. 172.
[15] *CW* 6, p. 338/3–4.
[16] *CW* 9, p. 13/33–4.
[17] *Apology, CW* 9, p. 97/3–11.

More's appeal to a 'time and place convenient' is a cavillation that does not successfully conceal the real drift of his statement: better no reform at all than that which is in danger of being enacted.

What had happened to transform More's attitude so completely? Clearly it did not concern any deterioration in the effort to contain heresy. More's campaign of detection and extermination had been remarkably effective: six notable offenders had been brought to the stake, and a rigorous system of press censorship had been imposed.[18] More had even devised a way of bypassing the bishops for the sake of efficiency, by having suspected heretics tried and sentenced in Star Chamber for breaches of the two proclamations he had helped contrive.[19] Furthermore, his campaign had had the full backing of Henry VIII, as More himself implied in a letter to Erasmus of June 1533: 'the King appears to be more antagonistic toward heretics than even the bishops are'.[20] More changed his mind not primarily because of an escalation of heresy, but because of his sudden realization of political dangers arising from Henry's desire for a divorce.

To appreciate this, one must recall certain events of 1529. By the summer of that year it was obvious that Wolsey's efforts to procure a divorce had failed; worse still, they had resulted in the humiliation of Henry's having been cited to Rome.[21] There had long been an aristocratic faction at Court, led by the Dukes of Suffolk and Norfolk, who were eager to bring Wolsey down for having aspired too high. In June and July they saw their chance. At the instigation of Suffolk and Norfolk, Thomas Lord Darcy prepared a memorandum of matters to be raised at the next session of Parliament in response to Wolsey's misrule. At the same time Suffolk circulated literature at Court inviting the king to strip the clergy of their temporal possessions.[22] Both tactics amounted to a single aim: to diminish the power of the clergy by enlarging the king's regal sovereignty. One item of the Darcy memorandum, for example, explicitly proposed that Henry oversee reformation himself: 'Item better and much more merit, honour and virtue is it for the king's grace to proceed and determine

---

[18] See Guy, p. 164ff.
[19] ibid., p. 173.
[20] Rogers, *SL*, no. 46, p. 179.
[21] See J. J. Scarisbrick, *Henry VIII* (London, 1968), p. 227ff.
[22] Guy, pp. 106–7; Scarisbrick, ibid., p. 247.

all reformations of spiritual and temporal [matters] within this realm. . . .'[23] Fate had thus converged three separate interests into a single, mutually convenient focus: the anticlericalism of the laity, Henry's indignation and impatience over the delay of his divorce, and the heretics' attempt to throw off the repressive authority of the church.

More must have been horrified to see this informal alliance materializing. He had already seen Tyndale cast the lure of an unconditional regal absolutism to Henry VIII in *The Obedience of a Christian Man and How Christian Rulers Ought to Govern* of October 1528. In that book Tyndale had conceded to the king a divinely sanctioned, arbitrary power upon which neither pope nor clergy could encroach: 'the king is in this world without law, and may at his lust do right or wrong, and shall give accounts but to God only': moreover, 'heads and governors are ordained by God, and are even the gift of God, whether they be good or bad. And whatsoever is done to us by them, that doth God, be it good or bad.'[24] Simon Fish had quickly followed up these propositions with some specific proposals in his *Supplication for the Beggars* of early 1529: because the clergy had usurped so much wealth and rule in England that the king was powerless in his own country, he declared, Henry should reassert his regal rights, dispossess the clergy, and reclaim his temporal jurisdiction. Anne Boleyn had ensured that the king had read both the *Obedience* and Fish's *Supplication* in mid-1529, and given More's close attendance on Henry at this time, he can hardly have failed to notice how receptive Henry was to the suggestions in them. When Henry had finished Tyndale's work, he is reported to have said: 'this is a book for me and for all kings to read',[25] and according to Foxe he kept Fish's pamphlet 'in his bosom three or four days' and accorded Fish his personal protection.[26] Yet even though Henry let it appear briefly that he was flirting with heresy, More had no reason to doubt his orthodoxy, and there is no evidence that he ever did. What he did have to fear, however, was Henry's decision in autumn 1529 to accept the invitations being offered him of allying himself with anticlericalism.[27]

---

[23] The whole memorandum is printed in Guy, Appendix 2, pp. 206–7.

[24] *The Works of the English Reformers*, I, pp. 213, 228.

[25] John Strype, *Ecclesiastical Memorials; Relating Chiefly to Religion . . .* (Oxford, 1822), I, pp. i, 172.

[26] *CW* 8, III, p. 1187; Guy, pp. 108–9.

[27] See Scarisbrick, *Henry VIII*, p. 245.

More's opposition to this alliance was as absolute as his opposition to heresy, and in fact the two seem to have merged together in his mind.

In the first place, he rejected completely the validity of the proposed divorce *per se*. When Henry had opened his 'great matter' to him at Hampton Court in late September 1527, he had declared his unfavourable opinion as he did on several later occasions; however, he had declined to meddle in the subsequent legatine commission on the grounds of incompetency, and had allowed Henry to gain the impression that he would withdraw from considering the matter further.[28] Years later, in his letter to Cromwell of 5 March 1534, More declared: 'after this did I never nothing more therein, nor never any word wrote I therein to the impairing of his Grace's part neither before nor after, nor any man else by my procurement, but settling my mind in quiet to serve his Grace in other things, I would not so much as look nor wittingly let lie by me any book of the other part [i.e. the queen's]'.[29] Although More was telling the literal truth – that he had not *written* anything against the divorce or incited others to do so – he was taking refuge in an equivocation, as he often did. It is now known conclusively that he was part of an organized opposition to the divorce.[30] He did not need to write against it because Fisher, Tunstal, Nicholas West and others were busy on that behalf.[31] More's task was different: to remain as a mole in the Council and leak news of impending government moves so that they could then be countered in advance by public sermons and propagandist treatises.[32] Chapuys, Charles V's ambassador, who was co-ordinating the opposition, records the care with which More tried to remain outwardly uncompromised so that he could retain his freedom in the Council.[33] Even so, he came close to dismissal in 1530 when Henry, furious at finding that Council matters were being leaked to the queen's faction, directed his displeasure against More.[34]

[28] Rogers, *SL,* no. 53, pp. 207–8.

[29] ibid., p. 210.

[30] See Elton, 'Sir Thomas More and the Opposition to Henry VIII', in *Essential Articles,* pp. 79–91.

[31] For a discussion of Fisher's theological work on the divorce, see Scarisbrick, *Henry VIII,* pp. 166–80; for a list of the works by West, Tunstal and Fisher composed *ex parte Regine,* see *Letters and Papers, Foreign and Domestic, of the Reign of Henry VIII,* ed. J. S. Brewer *et al.,* 21 vols. (London, 1862–1932), IV, 5768(1).

[32] Guy, pp. 138–41.

[33] Elton, 'Opposition', pp. 86, 88–9.

[34] Guy, pp. 139–40.

It is also known that on at least one occasion, More actively encouraged resistance in Parliament. Sir George Throckmorton in his confession to the king in 1537 described how More had sent for him to go and speak with him 'in a little chamber within the Parliament chamber'. At this meeting More had praised him as a good Catholic man, and promised that he should deserve to be rewarded if he continued 'in the same way that . . . [he] began'.[35] Typically, More's words were calculated to be so discreet that they could not be used against him, but considering that Throckmorton spoke not only against the divorce in Parliament, but also against the bill of appeals, the drift of More's meaning is clear.[36]

More thus had no reason to write against the divorce, being so actively engaged in the campaign to frustrate it in other ways. Nevertheless, at one point in the *Dialogue Concerning Heresies* he could not prevent his true feelings from showing through. One of the added tribulations of Christ's new law, he declared, was its restraint of divorces and withdrawal of the right to marry diverse wives, whereas before men had 'had lyberte to wed for theyr plesure'.[37] This may have been an unconscious expression of More's sense of Henry's true motives. If so, it placed Henry about equal with Luther in More's estimation as a lecher engaged in the pursuit of 'abominable bychery' – although in the king's case, More dared not say so. At the deepest level, the same psychological motives probably fuelled More's opposition to Henry as operated in his attack on Luther: a loathing of their efforts to justify indulging an unlawful concupiscence he had denied himself.[38]

Apart from considering the divorce unjustifiable, More was appalled at the shift of sovereignty that was being proposed to bring it about. From his earliest maturity, he had loathed tyranny, yet he knew that, even according to the view of kingship he himself accepted, there was ultimately nothing to restrain a king from absolutism, should he incline towards it, except the force of custom.[39] To his

[35] The text of Throckmorton's confession is printed in Guy, Appendix 2, pp. 207–12.
[36] ibid., pp. 210–11; see also Stanford E. Lehmberg, *The Reformation Parliament, 1529–1536* (Cambridge, 1970), p. 180.
[37] *Dialogue, CW* 6, p. 106/1–4.
[38] See above, pp. 141–4. The fable of the lion, ass and wolf at confession in Margaret Roper's letter to Alice Alington seems to reflect More's revulsion at Henry's lust disguised under a scruple of conscience (Rogers, *Correspondence*, no. 206, p. 513).
[39] See above, p. 165.

dismay, More saw Henry's advisors systematically expound a new theory of royal supremacy and empire.

Recent research has shown that Henry derived much of his caesaropapism from a manuscript called *Collectanea satis copiosa*, compiled by Edward Foxe, Nicholas de Burgo and John Stokesley.[40] This work drew upon scriptural, patristic, canonical and historical sources to argue that Henry possessed by right 'what amounted to a Byzantine sovereignty, part of which had been "lent" to the priesthood by previous English monarchs'.[41] When Henry was shown the *Collectanea* in September 1530 he was deeply impressed, as his annotations show, and it further confirmed his opinion that his cause was justified.

It is probable that More saw this very manuscript, for in his letter to Cromwell of March 1534 he recalled that before the legatine suit began, the king had commanded him 'to commune further with Master Fox . . . and to read a book with him that was then in making'.[42] Again in late 1529 or early 1530, when More desired 'to have some conference in the matter with some such of his Grace's learned Council as most for his part had labored and most have found in the matter', Henry had assigned him to Edward Foxe and Nicholas de Burgo, along with Cranmer and Lee, with whom he had 'diligent conference', as well as reading everything he could find that had been written on the divorce.[43]

There can be no doubt that More knew what was shaping up, or that he realized that Thomas Cromwell's promotion in late 1530 was designed to effectuate it.[44] More's advice to Cromwell as recorded by Roper is not so much an utterance of gnomic wisdom as a cynically cryptic remark aimed at conveying to Cromwell that More knew what was afoot:

'Master Cromewell,' quoth he, 'you are nowe entered into the service of a most noble, wise and liberall prince. If you will followe my poore advise, you shall, in your councell gevinge vnto

[40] See Guy, pp. 131–3, who draws upon the unpublished thesis of G. D. Nicholson, 'The Nature and Function of Historical Argument in the Henrician Reformation' (Ph.D., University of Cambridge, 1977).

[41] Guy, p. 132.

[42] Rogers, *SL*, no. 53, p. 208.

[43] ibid., pp. 209–10.

[44] On Cromwell's rise, see Guy, pp. 133–4.

his grace, ever tell him what he owght to doe, but never what he is able to doe. So shall you shewe yourself a true faithfull servant and a right worthy Councelour. For if [a] Lion knewe his owne strength, harde were it for any man to rule him.'[45]

The comment makes a lot of sense if More had read the *Collectanea* and knew that its aim was precisely to tell the king what he could do, rather than what he should do.

The implications of the divorce stretched even further, as far as More was concerned. In September 1529 Chapuys sent a detailed analysis of the situation in England to Charles V. Many people, he wrote, were liable to support a call from Suffolk for a breach with Rome. The strategy would be threefold: to secure the trial of Henry's divorce in England, to satisfy the laity's grudge against the clergy, and to confiscate church property. As a result, the door would be open for Lutheranism to creep into England.[46] This analysis bears the hall-mark of someone with detailed inside information, and since Chapuys had only arrived in England in late August 1529, being presented to Henry on 14 September,[47] it is unlikely that he could have attained such an acute insight in so short a time unless it had been supplied to him. The association between an attack on ecclesiastical possessions and the incursion of heresy suggests that More may have been Chapuys' informant, especially since he had just argued precisely the same connection in his *Supplication of Souls*, published in the same month. Even if More had not supplied Chapuys with his information, the fact that Chapuys possessed it means that More could just as easily have foreseen the breach with Rome in late 1529.

He was violently opposed to it, not primarily because of any deep commitment to the papal primacy, but because he believed that a breach would cut England off from the evolution of God's purpose in history and rupture the unity of Christendom.

As far as the pope's primacy was concerned, More allowed an area of legitimate speculation:

For I wyste very well that the chyrche beynge proued thys comon knowen catholyke congregacyon of all chrysten nacyons, abydyng to gyther in one fayth, neyther fallen of nor cut of: there

[45] Roper, pp. 56–7.
[46] Guy, pp. 109–10.
[47] Lehmberg, p. 4n.

myghte be peraduenture made a secunde questyon after that whyther ouer all that catholyke chyrche the pope must nedes be hed and chyefe gouernour or chyefe spyrytuall shepherde / or ellys that the vnyon of fayth standyng among them all, euery prouynce myghte haue theyr owne chyefe spyrytuall gouernour ouer it selfe, wythout any recourse vnto the pope, or any superyoryte recognysed to any other outwarde person.

And then yf the pope were or no pope / but as I say prouyncyall patryarces, archbysshoppes, or metropolytanes, or by what name so euer the thynge were called: what authoryte and what power eyther he or they sholde haue among the people, these thynges well I wyste wolde rayse among many men many mo questyons then one.[48]

As he asserted in his letter to Cromwell of 5 March 1534, his own personal opinion – that no member of Christendom could lawfully depart from its common head – was irrelevant to his argument. He had, he continues, gathered together material pertaining to the issue which he had intended to include in his *Confutation,* but when he saw the breach between Henry and the pope develop, he had 'suppressed it utterly'.[49] More's concern that the king should not, 'either by laws making or books putting forth, seem to derogate and deny not only the primacy of the see apostolic, but also the authority of the general councils too', sprang from his perception of 'a great urgent cause in avoiding of schisms'[50] rather than a conviction that the papacy was an essential part of the definition of the church.[51] Although this argument was ultimately specious, More meant what he said at the time.

At the provincial level, he feared that a breach with Rome, combined with an enlargement of regal dominion, would exclude the English church from an active role in the body politic. Apart from their spiritual authority deriving directly from God, such as that of administering the sacraments, the clergy, More argued, had gained authority to do 'dyuerse thynges by the graunte of kynges and prynces'.[52] These comprised the right to formulate canons in their

---

[48] *Confutation, CW* 8, II, p. 577/3–17.
[49] Rogers, *SL,* no. 53, p. 214.
[50] ibid., pp. 212–13.
[51] See *CW* 8, II, p. 576/23–37.
[52] *Apology, CW* 9, p. 99/9–12, 21–6.

provincial convocations, their representation in Parliament, and the ecclesiastical legal jurisdiction, governing such matters as marriage, wills and the trial of heretics. In More's view there were two advantages in the clergy's participation in government. First, it brought to bear on English polity the influence of laws and viewpoints which had been 'thorow the whole corps of chrystendome bothe temporalty and spyrytualty, by longe vsage and custome ratyfyed agreed and confyrmed'.[53] Second, conclusions deriving from the clergy's consensus could only be to the good, since 'in that congregacion to goddys honour gracyously gathered together, the good assystence of the spyryte of god is accordynge to Crystes promyse as veryly present and assystente as it was with his blessed apostles'.[54] More feared that if Henry and his party got their way and stripped the clergy of their power, not only would English polity be deprived of the sustaining influence of the Holy Spirit, but the king would also be more liable to rule despotically according to the leadings of his own nature, reducing his subjects to a condition of servitude. More was not to know, of course, that Cromwell would aim to create a sovereignty residing in Parliament and statute rather than mere monarchic despotism,[55] but had he so known, he would have mistrusted it equally. Unlike an ecclesiastical consensus, a secular consensus had no assurance of the Holy Spirit's inspiration; indeed, 'myche people maye sometyme byleue some one mannys lye',[56] and agreement can just as easily be inspired by 'the spyryte of errour and lyenge, of dyscorde and of dyuysyon, [and of] the dampned deuyll of hell'.[57]

The very worst aspect of the imminent political revolution for More was that it paved the way for a mode of reform which he believed to be as futile in its expectations as it was misguided in its methods. To this extent Henrician political radicalism was as bad as Lutheran doctrinal radicalism. Both assumed that the existing state of things could be substantively altered. Lutheranism aimed at freeing the elect from the corruption of the institutionalized church and providing transcendental escape from the frailty of human nature; the political reformers aimed at a secularized equivalent: 'order, improvement, the active

[53] ibid., pp. 99/35–100/1.
[54] ibid., p. 100/3–6.
[55] G. R. Elton, 'Thomas Cromwell Redivivus', *Archiv für Reformationsgeschichte*, 68 (1977), pp. 198–203.
[56] *Apology*, CW 9, p. 112/12–13.
[57] ibid., p. 41/24–5.

removal of all that was bad, corrupt or merely inefficient, and the creation of a better life here and now in preparation for the life to come'.[58] If the Lutherans believed heaven could be reached through the absolutism of the divine will, the political reformers believed that the earthly utopia could be largely attained through the absolutism of the state expressed in rational positive law.[59] More, on the other hand, had persuaded himself philosophically and doctrinally that the world was irremediably imperfect according to God's deliberate design. Reform for him meant renewal, not reformation. Any hopes either of avoiding the realities of the human condition, or of radically transforming them were therefore not only stupid, but also faithless.

More had thus every motive for opposing the political revolution as totally as he opposed heresy – mind, body and soul. It is not surprising to find him doing exactly that, as much through his·polemical books as through his political contacts. I would go further to suggest that the *Supplication of Souls*, the *Apology* and *The Debellation of Salem and Bizance* were an integral part of the covert campaign to oppose Henry VIII and his administration.

Both the *Supplication* and the *Apology*, in particular, were written as political propaganda thinly disguised as anti-heretical polemic in the first case, and as apologetic in the second. As might be expected, their political role was oblique. After his promotion to Lord Chancellor in October 1529 More could not speak openly against the divorce and its corollaries by virtue of his office – not if he wished to retain it, as he appears to have done. In any case, the author who had urged political machiavellianism in *Utopia* and had exemplified it in his mentor and model, Cardinal Morton, in *Richard III*, would have chosen an oblique method by instinct. Nevertheless, the political intention behind the *Supplication* and *Apology* emerges if their content is correlated with their contexts.

Both were occasional works, although the occasions must be inferred.

[58] Elton, 'Thomas Cromwell Redivivus', p. 197.

[59] Thomas Starkey, for instance, was soon to propose a programme of laws that he believed could ensure that men were good. Englishmen could be safeguarded against vice, for example, by prohibiting the importation of any foreign goods capable of luring them to vain pleasure. To make these laws effective, Starkey hypothesized a state in which administration is regulated to such a large degree that sinful administrative acts would be impossible (*A Dialogue between Reginald Pole and Thomas Lupset*, ed. K. M. Burton (London, 1948), pp. 144, 155–6).

In the case of the *Supplication of Souls* the matter is particularly complex. Fish's anticlerical pamphlet, the *Supplication for the Beggars,* was available to More at least as early as 2 February 1529 when, according to Foxe, it was 'thrown and scattered at the Procession in Westminster, on Candlemas Day before king Henry the Eighth, for him to read and peruse'.[60] More had finished his *Dialogue Concerning Heresies* by this time,[61] but did not publish his own reply to Fish until seven months later in September.[62] The time lag is suggestive. If More was seriously worried by Fish's strictures on purgatory (which eventually received only secondary attention), or even by his proposals to strip the clergy of their temporal possessions, why did he not write a refutation straightaway? He can hardly have been over-burdened with work, not yet being Chancellor, and having no other book in progress; besides, pressure of work did not stop him in the years ahead. The answer is that he probably hoped the commotion aroused by the *Supplication for the Beggars* would die a natural death, as it probably would have, had not events at Court altered radically with the fall of Wolsey. It was only when More saw Suffolk and Norfolk in June–July focus the anti-Wolsey backlash into the specific Parliamentary proposals of the Darcy memorandum,[63] and when he realized that Henry was inclined to listen to them because of fury at the adjournment of the legatine court in July,[64] that he seized his pen to write a reply, probably with the express purpose of influencing opinion against the measures to be raised in the pending session of Parliament. As I have already suggested, Chapuys' letter of late September may have reflected More's sense of the dangers and what his own *Supplication* was calculated to resist.[65]

If More were to defuse the plot, he had to persuade his readers of the falsity of two main notions: that England's chronic miseries were due to the greed and rapaciousness of a corrupt clergy, and that the king was powerless in his own kingdom because of the strength of the clergy in Parliament and the extent of their jurisdiction. To achieve this end, he adopted a threefold strategy: to argue that the situation in

[60] Quoted by Schuster, *CW* 8, III, p. 1187.
[61] The statement of the title page, 'Made in the yere of oure Lord, M.D.xxviii', established March 1529 as the latest possible *terminus ad quem*.
[62] Schuster, *CW* 8, III, p. 1190.
[63] Printed in Guy, Appendix 2, pp. 206–7.
[64] Scarisbrick, *Henry VIII*, p. 227.
[65] See above, p. 176.

England was much the same as it had always been, to try and equate anticlericalism with heresy, and to play on the psychology of Henry VIII himself.

In the first place, More argued, it was wrong to suppose that poverty and beggary were recent products of ecclesiastical oppression,[66] as he has the souls in purgatory declare:

> If we shoulde tell you what number ther was of poore sick folke in dayes passed long before your time: ye wer at libertie not to beleue vs . . . wherefore we must . . . be fain to remit you to your own time. . . . And so dooyng we suppose if the sorye syghtes that menne haue seene, had left as great impression styll remaynynge in theyr heartes, as the sight maketh of the present sorowe that they see, menne should thinke and say that they haue in dayes passed seen as many sicke beggars as they see now. For as for other sicknes, thei rain not God be thanked, but after such rate as they haue done in times passed.[67]

The existence of sickness, pain and deprivation is a historical reality of the human situation itself: 'for of trouth there were pore people and beggars, ydle people, and theeues too, good plentye bothe then [in the time of the apostles] and alwaye before, sence almost as longe as Noyes floude and yet peraduenture seuen yere afore that to'.[68] Fish was therefore as misguided as he was malicious in claiming that the clergy are the sole cause, 'as though the clergye by theyr substaunce made men blinde and lame'.[69] Indeed, if the church had not been engaged in a persistent effort to alleviate poverty, its effects would have been far worse, especially 'in the last two deare yeres' when the poor would have 'dyed vp of likelihod almost euerichone' had it not been for the alms of the clergy and other charitable men.[70] Furthermore, it is only the clergy who provide hospitals for the sick, and by dispossessing them of their wealth, Fish would destroy this remedy without providing for another.[71] On top of everything else, Fish's

---

[66] For Fish's charges, see *A Supplicacyon for the Beggers*, (Antwerp, 1528), p. [5]; More rehearses some of them in the *Supplication of Souls* (*EW* 1557, pp. 290–1).

[67] *EW* 1557, p. 292 F–H.

[68] ibid., p. 311 H.

[69] ibid., p. 300 B.

[70] ibid., p. 293 C–D.

[71] ibid., p. 300 H.

arithmetic was wildly inaccurate, More claimed, particularly in his calculation of the church's revenues, of which he reckoned £43,333 6s 8d (very little short of half the crown's ordinary income before the dissolution) to be derived from the alms of begging friars alone![72]

Having diluted the potency of Fish's case against the church's wealth through reason and ridicule, More switched his attack to their supposed overmighty power and disloyalty. Fish had claimed that the English clergy persistently laboured to make the king's subjects fall into disobedience and rebellion. As proof he cited the reign of King John when the treason of the clergy had allowed the pope to render the king servile, had made England a tributary of the see of Rome, had enforced the payment of Peter's pence, and had forced John to accept the election of an archbishop he did not want.[73] He claimed further that the clergy had usurped a legal jurisdiction which they boasted was 'a kingdome' superior to the king's own, and which effectively destroyed the temporal jurisdiction.[74] Even worse, they were so powerful in Parliament that the king was powerless to legislate against these iniquities, especially since they outnumbered the temporal lords in the Upper House.[75]

More at once denounced these charges as an attempt 'to enflame the kynges hyghnesse against the church'[76] – an all too accurate assessment informed by his own inside knowledge of Suffolk's campaign to do the same. The need to rebutt these claims forced More into an awkward corner, for some of them were hard to deny. Some of his arguments were equivocating, if not downright specious. He countered that no king of England could ever make the realm a tributary of Rome even if he so wished, and that even if Rome could show any proof of such a grant – which it could not, because none existed – 'it were right nought worth'; furthermore, 'no such moneye is there payde, nor neuer was'. As far as the Peter's pence were concerned, 'they wer payde before the conquest to the apostolike sea towarde the mayntenance therof, but only by way of gratitude and almes'.[77] The election of Stephen Langton was an even more delicate

---

[72] ibid., pp. 293 G–294 H.
[73] See *EW* 1557, p. 295 Hff.
[74] ibid., p. 296 G.
[75] ibid., pp. 300 H–301 A.
[76] ibid., p. 295 H.
[77] ibid., p. 296 C–D.

issue. More had to prove that although the election was in defiance of the king, it nonetheless did not amount to disobedience. He was driven to the dubious expedient of claiming that John in some vague way should have been bound by the custom the Canterbury monks had acquired of electing their own archbishop, although More knew full well that there was nothing to bind the king to observe it, except the very canon law that Fish was citing as evidence of disloyalty. He then, by a fantastic sleight of hand, insisted that John had not resisted the election because of any treason laid against Langton, but because he was discontented at his candidature – a desperate measure indeed.[78] Still content to press his luck, More proceeded to justify the spiritual jurisdiction on grounds that 'the good princes passed haue graunted, and the nobles in their tymes, and the people too, haue by plain parliamentes confirmed them'.[79] This was a bold line to take, considering More's acute awareness that any consensus that may have ratified the ecclesiastical jurisdiction in the past no longer existed, however much he might wish that it still did. On the question of the clergy's power in Parliament he was on firmer ground, and quickly ridiculed Fish's claims as springing from pretension and ignorance: 'it well appereth of hys wyse wordes [that] he neyther canneth anye skill therof, nor neuer came in the house'.[80] The clergy could never be more powerful than the laity in the House of Lords because the presence of the king's own royal person more than outweighs all the other lords, spiritual and temporal combined, and the king in any case could call by writ as many more temporal lords to attend as he pleased.[81] Moreover, it is often the temporal lords who prove themselves the stronger, sometimes out of sheer perversity:

> it hathe bene seene that the thing which the spiritual lordes haue moued and thought resonable the temporal lordes haue denied and refused: as appereth vpon the mocion made for legitimacion of the children borne before the mariage of their parentes. Wherin albeit that the reformacion which the lordes spirituall moued, was a thing that nothing partayned to their owne commoditie, and albeit that thei layed also for theyr parte the constitucion and ordynaunce of the church and the lawes of

---

[78] ibid., p. 296 E.
[79] ibid., p. 296 G.
[80] ibid., p. 301 B.
[81] ibid., p. 301 B–C.

other christen countries: yet coulde thei not obtaine againste the lordes temporal that nothing alleged to the contrari but their own willes.[82]

As far as the House of Commons was concerned, More dismissed Fish's charge that all the learned men of the realm are bribed to speak for the clergy as absurd, for, he adds sardonically, 'if he had bene in the comen house as some of vs haue ben: he should haue sene the spiritualtie not gladly spoken for'.[83]

Up to this point one senses that More knew his case was weak; nevertheless, he had at least to mount a show of demolishing Fish's specific charges, and he gathered all his legalistic acumen to do it. His main ammunition, however, was of a far more deadly order.

His first telling coup is an attempt to expose Fish's proposals (and hence by implication those of Suffolk's Court faction) as covert heresy. This was a daring diversionary tactic, but one which More, knowing the king's pride in his orthodoxy and Defender's title, hoped would transmute Henry's tacit support into suspicion, then anger, and finally indignation. After a flourish mocking Fish's aureate rhetoric, More suddenly switches tack with the effect of a thunderbolt:

But it is ethe to see, wherof springeth al his displesure. He is angry and freteth at the spirituall iurisdiccion for the punishe-ment of heretiques and burning of theire erroniouse bookes: for euer vpon that stringe he harpeth: very angry with the burning of Tyndals testament. . . . And for the rancour conceiued vpon this displesure, cometh vp all hys complaint of the possessions of the clergye.[84]

Having thus sown the seeds of a dilemma for Henry – whether to persist in the anticlerical plan at the risk of being duped by heretics, or reject it to satisfy his opinion of himself – More goes on to fire a salvo at the nobles. It takes the form of an attempt to switch the accusation of treason and disloyalty away from the clergy towards any of the laity who support the plan to dispossess them. More draws upon English history for evidence that attacks on church land have always been

[82] ibid., p. 301 C–D; More is prevaricating here, for the event was not a Parlia-mentary occasion (see F. Pollock and F. W. Maitland, *The History of English Law*, 2nd edn (Cambridge, 1968), I, p. 127, and II, p. 397).

[83] *EW* 1557, p. 301 F.

[84] ibid., p. 302 B–D.

equatable with heresy, and that this has always led to rebellion against the king, especially on the part of over-ambitious nobles. In the reign of Henry IV, he says, after one John Badby was burned for heresy, a bill was presented at the next session of the Commons declaring how much land was held by the spirituality and proposing that it be repossessed, but good men soon perceived that the maker of the bill had no real knowledge of the extent of church lands, and that it had been devised out of rancour by some who had favoured Badby and wanted to see his heresies go forward.[85] If More did know of the Darcy memorandum, as he must have, the intended political allegory is chilling in its clarity: Fish is merely the simple-witted tool of those who, like the heretics in Henry IV's reign, were conspiring to aid the spread of heresy. The warning to Suffolk and Norfolk is clear: if they were to proceed with a similar bill in the forthcoming session of Parliament, they would do so at their own peril, since he, More, was thus informing Henry of their intent. Resuming the historical narrative, More makes the analogy even more menacing in its implications:

> So happed it then sone after that in the first yere of the kinges moste noble progenitour king Henry the fift those heresyes secretelye creping on still amonge the people: a great number of theim had fyrst couertly conspired and after openly gathered and assembled theim selfe, purposing by open warre and battaile to distroy the king and his nobles and subuert the realme. Whose traitorouse malice that good catholike king preuented, withstode, ouerthrew and punished.[86]

This passage conflates two simultaneous invitations; the first invites the dukes to desist from conspiracy in case they find themselves cast in the role of Lord Cobham, the second invites Henry to imitate his noble Catholic forebear by recognizing the danger to himself, disassociating himself from the plan, and punishing those who are seeking to perpetrate it. In case anyone had missed the parallel, More reinforces it with several other instances from the earlier reigns illustrating the same archetypal situation.[87]

More, one feels, believed he knew his man. As if to nurture in Henry the seedling of piety that he hoped he had planted in his mind, More

[85] ibid., p. 302 D–E.
[86] ibid., p. 302 F.
[87] ibid., p. 302 G–H.

reminds him that he had written the *Assertio septem sacramentorum,* referring to it as 'his graces most famouse and most graciouse boke, that his highnes as a prince of excellent erudition, vertue, and deuocion toward the catholike faythe of christ, made . . . against the furiouse boke of Martin Luther . . . with thacceptacion of hys godly well deserued title of defensoure of the faith giuen hys grace by the see apostolique'.[88] Having launched an appeal to Henry's vainglory with this fulsome flattery, More had the effrontery within half a page to denounce Fish's attempted flattery as insulting irreverence, 'open playn dispite and contumely'.[89]

Here then is evidence of a political endeavour in More so subtle and devious as to set not only Machiavelli, but also Richard III and Iago to school. One should not be surprised to find him acting in such a way, for as he had expounded in *Utopia,* he considered it the Christian duty of a councillor to act indirectly to influence things for the better, not least the mind of the prince.[90] Whether or not the *Supplication of Souls* influenced opinion to any great extent is impossible to determine. Henry did reassure Campeggio soon after its publication that he would crush Lutheranism and defend for ever the liberty of the English church, but he implied quite the opposite to Chapuys about the same time.[91] The force of popular anticlericalism probably meant that the battle was already lost, for when Parliament assembled on 3 November 1529 there was almost immediately a tremendous airing of grievances against the clergy, even though the actual statutes framed in the first session were relatively innocuous, dealing only with probates, mortuaries and non-residence.[92]

After this first literary excursion into politics, More retreated into other covert forms of opposition, devoting his writing energies to the confuting of Tyndale's *Answer* to his *Dialogue.* However, within four years he was drawn back into political propaganda; the *Apology* and *The Debellation of Salem and Bizance* mark his last desperate bids to impede the administration's reform policy.

As with the *Supplication of Souls,* the *raison d'être* of these two works only becomes fully apparent when they are placed in their immediate contexts.

[88] ibid., pp. 310 H–311 A.
[89] ibid., p. 311 E–F.
[90] *CW* 4, pp. 97–101.
[91] *LP,* IV, p. 5995; cited by Guy, pp. 110–11.
[92] Lehmberg, p. 81.

In the first session of the Reformation Parliament (3 November–17 December 1529), the most radical anticlerical legislation in the minds of the dukes, if not of Henry himself, had been forestalled. But before the second session opened on 16 January 1531, Henry had acquired a new minister with considerably more acumen and steel – Thomas Cromwell. Among Cromwell's papers a document survives from the session of 1531 which proves that he was orchestrating, or at least preparing, a new concerted attack on the church; whether this was on his own initiative, the king's or someone else's is impossible to tell.[93] Half the document is concerned with the reform of the clergy. It proposed a standing council to investigate the ecclesiastical jurisdiction, consider the possibility of a vernacular bible, and enquire into the spread of heresy, taking over the initial investigations and reserving only the most serious of cases for the ordinaries. Certain abuses were to be abolished, such as the exaction of fees for obits and trentals, and a more strict observance of ecclesiastical laws for the good order of spiritual men was to be enforced to assuage the division that had sprung up between the laity and the clergy. The other half of the draft proposes a barrage of remedies for poverty and unemployment.[94]

Despite its superficial appearance of moderation and reasonableness, this document really only picks up where Fish and the dukes had left off in 1529; its proposals amount to a sugar-coated version of the same thing, so tempered as to be rendered more palatable to the Commons. Most importantly, it is written partially in the hand of Christopher St German, More's future antagonist, with corrections, afterthoughts and revisions wholly by St German.[95] Here is clear evidence that Cromwell was in collusion with this respected lawyer from the first few months of his entry into the Council.

The implications are tremendous as far as More's later ferocious attacks on St German are concerned. There is no evidence that the reform document from the 1531 session was ever discussed formally in Parliament; even in their watered-down form, Cromwell probably

---

[93] For diverse opinions on the authorship and import of this document (*LP*, V, p. 50), see G. R. Elton, *Reform and Renewal: Thomas Cromwell and the Common Weal* (Cambridge, 1973), pp. 71–7; J. J. Scarisbrick, 'Thomas More: the King's Good Servant', *Thought: Fordham University Quarterly*, 52 (1977), pp. 259–65; and Guy, pp. 151–6, whose summary and conclusions I largely follow.

[94] Guy, pp. 152–3.

[95] ibid., p. 151.

judged the disguised proposals for encroaching upon the liberty of the *ecclesia Anglicana* to be politically premature. But many of its provisions were to find their way into another draft bill of 1533,[96] upon which both St German's *Treatise Concerning the Division between the Spirituality and Temporality* and More's *Apology* bore closely. Altogether, the cumulative evidence suggests that from late 1530 onwards Cromwell and St German were working in collusion to further Cromwell's reform strategy, and that More knew it.

Having had to lower his sights in 1531, Cromwell took the next step during the third session of the Reformation Parliament (January–May 1532), by engineering a new hearing of the anticlerical grievances of 1529.[97] In particular, he had worked up the anticlerical petition of 1529 against ecclesiastical legislation and jurisdiction into a new draft: the so-called 'Supplication of the Commons against the Ordinaries', delivered to the king on 18 March 1532,[98] in which the Commons declared, among other things, 'howe the temporal men of [the] realme were sore agrevèd with the cruel demeanoure of the prelates and ordinaryes, which touched bothe their bodyes and goodes', and begged the king to take appropriate action.[99] Eventually Henry was persuaded to demand from Convocation that the clergy surrender their legislative power and submit all existing canons to the scrutiny of a committee appointed by the king, which they did in their Submission of 16 May.

Although More could not appear openly to be aligned against the administration during the third session, especially since he was still Lord Chancellor, Fisher and other clerics performed this role with such hastily whipped-up treatises as *Clerici sunt exempti de jurisdictione laicorum, etiam de jure divino* and Fisher's *That the Bishops Have Immediate Authority to Make Such Laws as They Shall Think Expedient for the Weal of Men's Souls*[100] (which later caused More acute embarrassment when St German cited it as evidence of the clergy's contumacy).[101] More himself was bound to maintain his cover as an essential part of the opposition strategy, so that until a book came forward which he could

---

[96] *LP,* VI, p. 120(2).
[97] Elton, *Reform and Reformation,* pp. 151–6, Guy, p. 164.
[98] Elton, ibid., pp. 151–2.
[99] Cited in Lehmberg, p. 140.
[100] Lehmberg, pp. 149–50.
[101] *CW* 9, Appendix A, p. 180. For More's reply, see ibid., p. 97/28ff.

answer under the pretext of exposing heretical malice, he had to remain publicly silent. Nevertheless, it was during these early months of 1532 that he was most active in furthering the opposition of the Aragonese party in Parliament, with some degree of success, apparently, for Cromwell's extant bill for a Parliamentary submission of the clergy was not passed during the third session, either because it was never actually introduced, or because it encountered unexpectedly strong resistance.[102] As it turned out, a submission enforced by statute was replaced by a surrender to the person of the king.[103] Even though this was probably less than Cromwell hoped for and More feared, it was still sufficiently decisive to provoke More into resigning as an act of defiance.[104]

Some historians have thought that More withdrew totally from politics after his resignation, having decided to tend to religious matters and his conscience. This was precisely the illusion that More tried to foster.[105] He may have intended that initially, being genuinely concerned with his health, and may even for a short time have done so, but the matter of the clergy's Submission was no more concluded in his mind than it was in Cromwell's. The Submission had not been ratified by statute, and both Cromwell and More knew that until it was, the political revolution was neither secure nor fulfilled. When More was informed of a new initiative to secure this ratification, he could not prevent himself from galloping to intercept it.

Cromwell's further move came with the drafting of two complementary Acts for the fourth session. The first, a bill in restraint of appeals, has been much discussed.[106] The earliest of the eight surviving drafts of this statute can be dated to September 1532.[107] Its preamble states, explicitly and unambiguously, claims adumbrating all the most radical suggestions of the *Collectanea satis copiosa* and the St German document of 1531: England is an empire and therefore totally independent under one supreme head governing both temporality and spirituality; all jurisdiction within the realm depends from the king

[102] Lehmberg, pp. 153–4.
[103] Elton, *Reform and Reformation*, pp. 152–5.
[104] Guy, p. 201.
[105] As, for example, in his letters to Erasmus of 14 June 1532 and June 1533 (Rogers, *SL*, nos. 44, 46), and in his epitaph (Rogers, *SL*, p. 182).
[106] G. R. Elton, 'The Evolution of a Reformation Statute', *English Historical Review*, 64 (1949), pp. 174–97.
[107] Lehmberg, p. 164.

with no possibility of appeal to any external authority; unlawful usurpation of power and possessions by the see of Rome must be reclaimed according to the measures proposed.[108] After having undergone several stages of revision and the king's scrutiny, the bill reached a form in which it was ready to be introduced into Parliament in January 1533. Cromwell, however, appears to have been extremely cautious. Not only was the opening of Parliament delayed from November 1532 until February 1533 to allow the bill to be perfected, but the final draft was also offered to a team of divines for examination.[109]

The second bill has been largely overlooked. In the words of the Calendar's summary, it was a

> draft Act of Parliament to restrain bishops from citing or arresting any of the King's subjects to appear before them in cases of heresy, unless the bishop or his commissary be free from any private grudge against the accused, and there be three or at least two credible and indifferent witnesses; a copy of the libel to be in all cases delivered to the accused with the names of his accusers.[110]

This bill sought to achieve what the administration had dared not put to Parliament during the first three sessions, and Cromwell must have considered it a vital corollary to clinch the Act in Restraint of Appeals. Furthermore, St German, whose participation the contents of the second bill unmistakably betray, was given the task of preparing the climate of opinion for the introduction of both bills in advance of the forthcoming session. His *Division between the Spirituality and Temporality* was set up in the last two months of 1532, and was published either at the end of 1532 or very early in 1533.[111] This chronology suggests that the *Division* was written specifically as a propaganda tool to smooth the way for the passage of the two bills.

Whether or not More knew of St German's earlier 1531 document cannot be determined,[112] although one suspects that if there had been

---

[108] ibid., pp. 164–6.
[109] ibid., pp. 166–8.
[110] *LP,* VI, p. 120(2).
[111] J. B. Trapp, *CW* 9, pp. xcii–xciii.
[112] Guy suggests that their antagonism arose when St German devised his draft of 1530/31 (p. 155).

any way for him to detect it, he would have made it his business to do so. He almost certainly, however, knew what was afoot between late November 1532 and the opening of the fourth session in February 1533. Late in February, Chapuys reported that Gardiner and Lee had refused to consent to 'a "strange" bill' drawn up according to the king's wishes.[113] This bill was most likely a late draft of the bill of appeals; More could, therefore, have been alerted to the strategy of the administration either directly by Gardiner, who had been his ally in 1532,[114] or through Chapuys, his former contact, who had known (probably from More) as early as May 1532 that 'the King . . . wishes bishops not to have the power to lay hands on persons accused of heresy'.[115] That being so, More would have recognized at once the covert purpose of St German's *Division* from its contents alone, if he did not already know through his intelligence network; therefore it is understandable that he launched into a furious effort to discredit it.

Several other pieces of external evidence support this hypothesis. After his resignation, More had been engaged in writing books 4–8 of his *Confutation of Tyndale's Answer* (books 1–3 having been published separately in the spring of 1532). The *Second Part*, published in the early months of 1533, shows signs of having been very hastily dropped. In contrast with More's usual practice, it contains no list of errata – this appeared only at the end of the *Apology*. In addition, there are signs that a further book was envisaged at the time of printing, since the 1533 text contains no 'Finis', date of printing, or colophon.[116] The unfinished ninth book exists, of course; it was printed by William Rastell in the 1557 edition. More's decision to leave it out completely, substantial though it already was, testifies to the extreme urgency with which he turned to grapple with St German's *Division*.

More must have felt he had a fair chance of influencing opinion against both bills. The bill of appeals was held off for six weeks until 14 March, which implies much caution on the administration's part and, possibly, judicious lobbying.[117] Perhaps the second bill was delayed along with it. This delay was a godsend to More because it gave him time to race his counterpropaganda into print.

One can trace the pace at which he wrote the *Apology*, because it

[113] Lehmberg, p. 169.
[114] Guy, p. 194.
[115] *LP*, V, p. 1013 (Chapuys to Charles V).
[116] James P. Lusardi, *CW* 8, III, pp. 1421, 1424.
[117] Lehmberg, p. 172.

reflects his awareness of the intervening matters being discussed in Parliament; namely the debate on the statute of apparel, which may have triggered More's comments on 'the proud and pompose appareyll that many prestes in yeres not long paste, were by the pryde and ouersyght of some few, forced in a maner against theyr own wyllys to weare'.[118] Seeing as the apparel bill was before Parliament in early March, it is probable that More had finished the *Apology* by mid-March when the appeals bill was introduced. Ironically, the publication of the *Apology* a little before Easter[119] coincided almost exactly with the passage of the Act in Restraint of Appeals by Palm Sunday on 6 April. It is difficult at this distance to tell whether this amounted to defeat for More, or not. The second bill against the heresy laws was not passed; perhaps it never reached Parliament in the fourth session – in which case the *Apology* may have been a futile exercise.

More's tactics in the *Apology* were almost identical to those he had used in the *Supplication of Souls*: an attempt to paint the anonymous author of the *Division* as merely the tool of a secret, more sinister organization of heretics, a defence of the *status quo* as answering to the realities of the human condition, and a fugue upon the civil horrors arising from failure to contain heresy.

There can be little doubt that More knew who the 'Pacifier' really was. John Rastell, More's brother-in-law, had been a close associate of St German at the Middle Temple, as well as the printer of his *Dialogus de fundamentis legum Anglie et de conscientia* [*Doctor and Student*] in 1528. Given that More had become involved by implication in the dispute arising from *Doctor and Student* and the *Replication* it provoked over the Chancellor's equitable jurisdiction,[120] it is unlikely that he would not have been aware of St German and his theories when he so easily could have been. More was also in the habit of pretending not to know anonymous authors when it suited him. For instance, in his *Letter to a Monk* of 1519–20 he flatly denied knowing that Erasmus was the author of the notorious *Julius exclusus e coelis*,[121] whereas only three years earlier he had discussed with Erasmus a manuscript of the dialogue written in Erasmus' own hand, and had acknowledged it to

[118] *CW* 9, p. 98/13–17.
[119] The date can be inferred from More's comments in the *Debellation*, *EW* 1557, p. 930 F–G; cf. Trapp, *CW* 9, p. xviii.
[120] See Guy, pp. 42–8.
[121] Rogers, *SL*, no. 26, p. 121.

be the latter's own work.[122] The simple truth is that St German's decision to issue the *Division* anonymously was a godsend to More, for given St German's intimate collusion with the administration, he could hardly have dared answer it had he not been able to pretend that he did not know either its real purpose or the identity of its author. As it was, More was able to exploit mock-ingenuity for the sake of deflation, by affecting to deduce variously that either the Pacifier had been 'of symplycyte by some sotle shrewe deceyued',[123] or that he had been motivated by wily malice under a guise of charitable indifference,[124] or that he was a priest (!) who was grossly exaggerating the vices of the clergy 'leste he sholde seme parcyall to hys own parte'.[125]

More takes some time in the *Apology* getting to the issues with which he is really concerned. The pretext is disposed of quickly and summarily; namely, the reformers' charges that his books are too long and tedious and have been confuted in sundry sermons, that he lacks charity and impartiality, and that he had treated Tyndale's works dishonestly.[126] Then at the eighth chapter he turns to face St German through a sleight of hand allowing him to pretend that he had not meant to. His sequence of declarations shows the oblique Morean approach at its most transparently subtle:

(i)   for as mych as the touchynge of the boke is here not my principal purpose / I wil therfore not peruse it ouer and touch euery point therof. . . .

(ii)   And yet bycause the bretherns boste hath made it an incydent vnto my mater . . . and *leste a better opynyon of the boke then the mater may bere (yf yt be pondered ryght) may be occasyon to moue men in some great thynges to do no lytle wronge* . . . I shall for a sample of handlynge, touch by the waye one or two places of hys.

(iii) And leste folke sholde thynke that I pyke oute here and there two or thre lynes of the wurst: I wyll take his fyrst chapiter whole.[127]

---

[122] ibid., no. 12, pp. 86–7.
[123] *Apology, CW* 9, p. 103/3–4.
[124] ibid., pp. 56–7.
[125] ibid., p. 103/22.
[126] ibid., p. 5/7ff.
[127] ibid., p. 61/7–30; my italics.

In this passage More effectually gives himself a *carte blanche* to treat the *Division* as extensively as he wishes – since its first chapter contains the essence of all the rest – while safeguarding himself against any possible charge of political malice aforethought. His real intent is nevertheless insinuated in the clauses I have italicized, and the attention of the judicious is drawn towards them by the antithesis and litotes they contain. No wonder More was able (with more than a hint of irony) to boast to Erasmus in a letter of June 1533 that 'so far, no one has advanced a complaint against my integrity. Either my life has been so spotless or, at any rate, I have been so circumspect that, if my rivals oppose my boasting of the one, they are forced to let me boast of the other.'[128]

Even once More launches into his refutation, he is careful to approach the central issue obliquely, moving by degrees from the general to the particular.

His first step is to give a general defence of the clergy in the manner of his other works. The Pacifier, he says, is trying to make mountains out of molehills by asserting that many priests and religious do not keep the perfection of their order, and that there are worse men in the spirituality than in the temporality: 'For whan was it otherwyse? not euyn in Crystes owne dayes. For Iudas that was one of hys owne apostles, was not onely wurse then the comon sorte of all those that loued theyr belyes and theyr ease amonge Crystes dyscyples were they men or women / but wurse also than the very wurste in all the world bysyde.'[129] Both the clergy and temporality contain wicked members, but the faults of individuals are not to be imputed to the whole body.[130] Besides, even the best men have faults: 'who so prye vpon euery mannys dede so narowly, as to spy that faute and fall at variaunce of greate zele with euery man that doth not to the very poynt and perfeccyon, euyn all that he shold do / shall waxe within a whyle at varyaunce wyth euery man and euery man wyth hym'.[131] There is thus no more cause for anticlerical grievance than had always existed. The contemporary grudge, apart from being far smaller than the Pacifier pretends, was merely the artificial contrivance of the

---

[128] Rogers, *SL*, no. 46, p. 180.
[129] *CW* 9, p. 68/27–31.
[130] ibid., p. 53/13–16.
[131] ibid., pp. 67/32–68/3.

heretics, and had arisen 'euyn of late synne Tindals bokes and Frythes and frere Barons beganne to go abrode'.[132]

Having dismissed contemporary anticlericalism as a mere storm in a teacup, having extolled the benefits flowing from the clergy to temporal men,[133] and having justified the harsh treatment recently meted out to suspected heretics by the ordinaries,[134] More launches into his prime objective: a defence of the ecclesiastical jurisdiction in general, and of the heresy laws in particular.

Significantly, More argues as if the Supplication against the Ordinaries and the Submission of the Clergy had never even taken place. He knew that while the clergy's surrender of its jurisdictional independence remained unenacted by statute, there was a faint hope that the situation could be retrieved. St German apparently knew it too, for he cites as one of the chief causes of division the summoning of heresy suspects before ordinaries *ex officio*; that is, on the initiative of an ecclesiastical judge without the intervention of a private party and without the indictment process customary in the common law.[135] This procedure, St German argued, violated the fundamental laws of the realm. He singled out as particularly unjust the provision in the *Extravagantes* entitled *Ad abolendam*, by which a man, unconvicted of heresy, could be put to his purgation and then punished by excommunication if he refused to abjure. Equally pernicious were provisions allowing perjured witnesses to give evidence, and bishops to withhold the names of accusers.[136] Apart from the intrinsic corruption of these laws, St German objected to the presumption in the clergy they reflected: 'for as moche as it shulde seme, that spyrytuall men somwhat pretende to punysshe heresyes only of theyr owne power, without calling for any assistance of the temporal power / therfore they make suche lawes / as may helpe forthe theyr purpose, as they thynke'.[137] As a remedy he proposed that 'the kynges grace and his parliamente' should intervene to find a way of settling this grievance.[138]

[132] ibid., p. 64/26–8.

[133] ibid., chaps. 28–34.

[134] ibid., chaps. 35–8.

[135] The provisions are set forth in *Decretales Gregorii IX*, lib. V, tit. VII, *De hereticis*, in *Corpus iuris canonici*, ed. E. A. Friedberg (Leipzig, 1879–81), II, pp. 780–2; see also Trapp, *CW* 9, pp. 376–7.

[136] *Division, CW* 9, Appendix A, p. 188.

[137] ibid., p. 190.

[138] ibid., pp. 190, 193.

More sought by all means possible to discredit these allegations. His first move was to try scare tactics; if the summoning of heretics *ex officio* were to be abolished, 'the stretys were lykely to swarme full of heretykes before that ryght fewe were accused, or peraduenture any one eyther'.[139] He then developed a series of analogies between the heresy canons and the common law to prove that they were not inconsistent, and that to do away with one would imply the need to abolish the other. For example, just as an ordinary can detain a man *ex officio* and put him to abjuration, so

> by the comen lawe of this realme, many tymes vppon suspycyon the iudges awarde a wrytte to enquyre of what fame and behauour the man is in hys countrey / and hym selfe lyeth somtyme styll in pryson tyll the retourne / and yf he be retourned good, that is to wyt yf he be in a maner purged, then is he delyuered, and yet he payeth his fees ere he go. And yf he be retourned nought / then vse the iudges to bynde hym for his good aberynge, and somtyme suertyes wyth hym to, suche as theyre dyscrecyon wyll allowe.[140]

In both the canon and common law, he argued, the plain realities of experience required exceptions to be made to the general rules according to 'the necessyte whych the nature of the mater wurketh in the profe'.[141] St German's proposal that the king and his Council could ensure that neither the innocent should be punished nor the guilty go without correction rested upon two impossible conditions:

> The tone is, yf they prouyde that neyther men that be proude nor couetouse, nor haue any loue to the worlde, be suffered to be iudges in any cause of heresy.
>
> The tother is, that the bysshoppes shall arrest no man for heresy, tyll the desyre that spyrytuall men haue to cause men to abiure heresyes and to punyshe them for heresyes, be ceased and gone.[142]

---

[139] *CW* 9, p. 130/29–31.

[140] ibid., p. 132/6–14.

[141] ibid., p. 136/18–19. This is an idea that More developed further in *The Debellation of Salem and Bizance* (*EW* 1557, pp. 990 B–C, 997 E.

[142] *CW* 9, p. 152/1–6.

Thus, just as St German's attack on the clergy and the heresy laws was misjudged, so were his remedies futile. In fact, More concluded, great harm would come of his 'mytygacyons'.[143]

As in the *Supplication of Souls*, More's final coup was an appeal to English history as proof that heretics lurk behind all attacks on the clergy, and that Henry's most noble regal forebears had found it necessary to ratify and reinforce the clergy with even harsher temporal statutes.[144] He concludes that he would have to see it before he would believe that the Pacifier could ever induce '*thys prudent parlyament*' to tamper with this legislation; rather, he hopes that it will 'lette those lawes stande and make mo such to them besyde'.[145]

More's *Apology* appears to have had no influence on the passage of the Act in Restraint of Appeals, but it may have been instrumental in delaying the passage of the second, complementary Act to which More's words quoted above refer. The full intent of the Supplication against the Ordinaries was not embodied in statute until the fifth session of Parliament, when in March 1534 the two Houses finally established the long-mooted open trials for heresy (although they retained punishment for relapsed heretics by burning according to the writ *De hæretico comburendo*).[146] By then More was on the verge of imprisonment, so that his influence counted almost for nothing. The *Apology*, however, was sufficiently damaging to provoke St German into a defence of his assertions in *Salem and Bizance*, and More himself gloated that 'As soone as mine apologie was ones come out abrode, anone herde I worde that some were very wrothe therwith . . . very wroth wer they with me.'[147] With affected innocence, he added that he could not at all understand why, 'for I had but spoken for my selfe, and for good folke, and for the catholike faith'.[148]

Although *The Debellation of Salem and Bizance*, which More wrote in late 1533 to demolish St German's arguments once and for all, adds nothing of substance to the *Apology*, More must have felt that sufficient hope remained of impeding any further reformist legislation to justify writing it. Either that, or else he had so completely lost his sense of

---

[143] ibid., pp. 163/27–166/20.
[144] ibid., pp. 161/12–162/26.
[145] ibid., p. 162/27–36; my italics.
[146] Lehmberg, pp. 186–7.
[147] *Debellation, EW* 1557, p. 929 H.
[148] ibid.

realism and self-control that he could not recognize when the battle was irreversibly lost.

One fascinating little passage suggests that by late 1533 he may have been on the verge of perceiving that the policy espoused by Cromwell and openly urged by St German aimed ultimately at a parliamentary, not a regal, sovereignty,[149] for he tried to flaunt it as a device to arouse Henry's suspicions. In a fashion worthy of Iago, he insinuates a suggestion that the Pacifier's proposals to regulate mortmain more precisely by statute may be covertly designed to trim the royal prerogative:

> As for his acte of parliament that he speaketh of . . . such actes are there alreadye made mo then one, good and sufficient, *but if he meane to set an addicion therto, that the kings grace should expresselye be bounden by the act,* that if he gaue any licence of mortifying into the church, it should be voyde, except such cases as thys good man lyst to lymyt and gyue him leaue.[150]

Cynically, More's next statement veils a hint that, if the king has already been in connivance with the political reformers, he is unwittingly being gulled: 'Syth hys highnes is now moued by thys good man here thereto: hys grace maye agree to it when it pleaseth him.'[151] Did More still hope that Henry could be detached from his partisans?

The *Debellation* ends with More's ritual plea for unity and adherence to the harmonious consensus of the realm, general councils, and the whole of Christendom. When More laid down his pen he had finished with political controversy this time, even if his political opposition had by no means ended.

---

[149] Franklin Le Van Baumer, 'Christopher St German: The Political Philosophy of a Tudor Lawyer', *American Historical Review*, 42 (1937), pp. 631–51; Guy, p. 154.
[150] *EW* 1557, p. 942 G; my italics.
[151] ibid.

8

The Dark Night of the Soul

I suggested at the beginning of this consideration that More under-
went a perturbed inner experience in the course of writing the
controversies. It should now be apparent that he had good reasons for
the loss of proportion, charity and candour that reflected it.

More had become trapped by circumstances into committing himself to a viewpoint that required of him nothing short of complete
success in his endeavours. According to his deepest convictions,
neither radical doctrinal nor radical political reformation could
succeed, and therefore might not be allowed to proceed. God's
purpose was realizing itself in history through his chosen instrument,
the known church; all that was necessary to be believed was gradually
being revealed to the church through its inspired consensus, and the
church was also being instructed on things necessary to be done.
Although More tried to avoid being trapped into the logical inference
that the church was infallible by asserting a distinction between things
which men were bound to do and believe and things which were
merely convenient for the occasion,[1] in practice his view implied that
all the church's beliefs and practices must necessarily be observed.
Hence, no divergence could be tolerated. Not only did God require
men to suppress dissent, but he would also never allow it to prosper.

The problem for More was that the movement for radical change
did seem to be prospering. By 1533 he had seen Cromwell's political
revolution triumph in England. With several decisive legislative
blows, Cromwell and his faction had severed England from the
common body of Christendom, reducing the *ecclesia Anglicana* to
political impotence, thus opening the door for the midday incursions
of heresy and despotism. Much of More's vehemence and relentless
ferocity sprang from one great perturbation underlying all the rest: the

---

[1] *Dialogue, CW* 6, pp. 146/34–147/1, 178–9.

threat of despair. The failure of his religious and political cause would mean the destruction of his entire understanding of providence and the nature of things. Because his intellectual security depended upon success, the prospect of defeat was fearsome to contemplate; but the unfolding of events in England after 1526 forced him to contemplate it.

The controversies reveal in More a struggle between two rival interpretations of what he saw happening around him. The first derived from the relatively optimistic assumption that 'neyther here-tikes nor deuyls can any thyng do but by goddes specyall suffer-aunce'.[2] When this thought was uppermost in his mind, More believed that the contemporary crisis was merely one of the recurrent tribulations by which God corrects his faithful and stirs them into spiritual alertness. As such, it would last only a short time, and then the situation would revert to its former state:

> what harme so euer such heretykes as goddes scourge be suffred to worke for the whyle, hys mercy shall not fayle in conclusyon, both to prouyde for the perpetuall saufgarde of hys catholyke chyrche (which he hath promysed neuer to forsake / but though he vysyt theyr iniquytees wyth the rodde of correccion, yet hys grace and good wyll he hath warraunted neuer to take from theym) and also shall of hys goodnes turne agayne frome theyr errours, some suche as those malycyouse archeheretykes deceyue / and them whose malyce he shall fynde vncurable he shall as an olde noughty rodde, before the face of hys faythfull chyldren of hys catholyke chyrche, when he hath beten and corrected them therwith, do as the tender mother doth, breke the rodde in peces and caste it in the fyre.[3]

God's providence would ensure that however many misbelievers sprang up, the true believers would always outnumber them, and that

> though the faythlesse be some tyme suffred to prosper in theyr malycyouse rage by some euyll softenesse of suche as sholde

[2] *Apology, CW* 9, p. 160/23–5.
[3] *Confutation, CW* 8, II, pp. 608/29–609/6. More uses the same figure in the *Responsio* (*CW* 5, p. 142/6–10) and the *Apology* (*CW* 9, p. 160/29–34).

resyste them . . . yet shall god alway sone after send down some good Moses from the mount, that shall wyth the corage of godly zele rere vppe the faythfull, and shewe the prowde faythlesse heretikes, how farre they be to feble and to few.[4]

This expectation was all very well in theory, being an inevitable conclusion of More's view of biblical history,[5] but in practice he found that the facts ran so counter to the theory that at times he wavered in his conviction of its truth.

As early as the *Dialogue Concerning Heresies,* he realized that Lutheranism was of a far different order from any other kind of heresy that had preceded it. Luther was far worse than Pelagius, for example, for whereas the latter had held that men could do good works sometimes without the aid of grace, the former argued that men could never do good with it.[6] As far as the sacraments were concerned, More believed that the Lutherans were the very first heretics who ever 'durst for very shame so boldely barke agaynst them'.[7] Such perversions of the true faith, More thought, made the new heretics 'double and treble more enemyes to grace' than had been any of the old.[8]

In addition to the more serious intrinsic heterodoxy of Lutheranism, More detected a much greater proclivity towards it in the English people than had ever existed before. He lamented the contrast between the old days, when 'deuocion was feruent in the people, and vertue plenteous in the church', and his own days, when one could not ignore 'how colde the charitie of christen people waxeth'.[9] Men could not keep their 'itching fingers' away from the poisoned books being brought into England, and they no longer abhorred 'the pestilent contagion of . . . smoky communicacion'. Many took up heretical books of a 'vaine curious minde, whom the diuel dryueth after forward, and fyrste maketh them dout of the trouth. And after bryngeth them oute of doute to a full beliefe of heresy'.[10] The fact that these books were forbidden, he continues, merely made men more

[4] *Confutation, CW* 8, II, p. 794/3–9.
[5] See above, pp. 151–2.
[6] *Dialogue, CW* 6, p. 396/7–16.
[7] *Confutation, CW* 8, I, p. 120/31.
[8] *Dialogue, CW* 6, p. 396/14–15.
[9] *Supplication, EW* 1557, p. 333 D.
[10] *Poisoned Book, EW* 1557, pp. 1035 D, 1036 E.

eager to buy and delight in discussing them; money from the large numbers sold financed the writing and printing of more, and so the gyre widened in a vicious spiral.[11] As well as the spread of misbelief, More also observed a 'decay from chastitye by declinacion into foule and filthy talking' which, begun a great time ago, had by then grown very far on.[12] In a very unpleasant metaphor from St Paul, he likened the creeping corruption to a 'corrupt canker'.[13]

In spite of repeated attempts to keep a sense of perspective by affirming that the true faith was nonetheless still as firmly rooted in England as it had ever been,[14] More could not prevent himself from fearing that the infection would become so widespread that the nation would sink beyond the point of recovery. His worst fears are summed up in the *Apology*:

> And veryly in thys declynacyon of the worlde, and by this great fall of faith, the olde feruour of cheryte so begynnynge to cole: it is to be fered at length, that yf it thus go forth and contynue, bothe the spyrytualtye from thapostles, and the temporaltye from the other dyscyples, maye fall so farre downe downe down downe, that as there was than one nought amonge twelue, so may there in tyme comyng yf these heresyes go forward, amonge twelue spyrytuall or peraduenture twenty temporall eyther, be founden at last in some whole cuntre scante any one good.[15]

More did add immediately that he did not think that that state of affairs had arrived in England or that it ever would, but the force of his fear saps this qualification of all conviction.

The catastrophic degeneration More foresaw was not in itself the only thing that tempted him to despair. He feared equally the consequences of God's anger.

In 1529 he prophesied direly that if Englishmen allowed Lutheranism to prosper, God would 'withdrawe his grace and let al runne to ruine'.[16] By the time he wrote the Preface to the *Confutation of Tyndale's*

---

[11] ibid., p. 1036 F–G.
[12] ibid., p. 1035 F.
[13] ibid., p. 1036 A.
[14] For example, *Poisoned Book, EW* 1557, p. 1035 G.
[15] *CW* 9, p. 70/13–21.
[16] *Supplication, EW* 1557, p. 313 D.

Answer in early 1532, he had started to feel that this divine repudiation of England had already begun:

> wysdome were it for vs to perceyue, that lyke as folke beginne now to delyte in fedyng theyr soules of the venemouse caryn of those poysened heresyes . . . our lorde lykewyse agaynwarde to reuenge yt wythall, begynneth to wythdraw hys gracyouse hande from the frutes of the erth, mynyshynge the fertylyte both in corne and catell, and bryngynge all in derth myche more then men can remedy or fully fynde out the cause. . . . I fere me surely that excepte folke begynne to reforme that fawte the soner / god shall not fayle in suche wyse to go forwarde, that we shall well perceyue and fele by thencrease of our gryfe, that all this gere hytherto is but a begynning yet.[17]

Such comminations as this become more and more frequent as the controversies proceed, and one senses behind them More's dismay at the progress not only of heresy, but also of the political revolution he was trying so energetically to oppose. His warnings grow even more portentous and threatening once he had given over the chancellorship. In the *Second Part* of the *Confutation* (written in late 1532), for example, he warned that God would devise some newer and 'more horryble' torment to punish Luther's form of misbelief than even the burning with brimstone by which he had punished Sodom and Gomorrah for the sin of the flesh.[18] About the same time, in his *Letter Impugning Frith,* More warned that 'euer hath God and euer will, by some way declare his wrath and indignacion agaynste as many as fall into such dampnable oppinions'.[19] And when he was in the thick of the political battle against the anticlerical bills of early 1533, he warned the clergy that should they begin to slacken in the summoning, arresting, interrogation, and further correction of heretics, 'god . . . wyll not fayle to make fall vpon them the terryble commynacyon and thrette that the spyryt speketh of in the Apocalyps vnto the byshoppe of Ephesye, *I wyll come and remoue thy candelstycke oute of his place'.*[20]

In his most desperate moments of anxiety, More was tempted to believe that the end of the world was near. This time, he feared, there

---

[17] *CW* 8, I, p. 3/15–31.
[18] ibid., II, p. 610/28ff.
[19] *EW* 1557, p. 834 H.
[20] *Apology, CW* 9, pp. 109/7–110/5; Revelations 2:5.

might be no providentially assisted recovery as there always had been in previous history; instead, God might let the world slide into its prophesied destruction, after which those who remained would 'be taken vpe . . . in the cloudes to mete our lorde in the ayer' at the second coming.[21]

His doubt is reflected in the number of instances when he contemplated whether events were matching up with the prophecy of the Apocalypse in the Book of Revelation. Without irrevocably committing himself, he tentatively concluded that they were. In book 4 of *A Dialogue Concerning Heresies,* for example, asserting that the Lutherans' outward manner of living makes them infinitely worse than the Pelagians, Manichees, or even the Mohammedans, he declares: 'If the world were not nere at an ende / and the feruour of deuocyon so sore coled that it were almost quenched among crysten people / yt coude neuer haue comen to passe that so many people sholde fall to the folowyng of such a bestly sect.'[22] More was not merely thinking metaphorically or rhetorically, for he elsewhere equates particular signs with precise events and persons. He regarded the inherent nature of Lutheran doctrines as certain evidence that 'now in these latter dayes the deuyll hath broke his chaynes, and of all extreme abomynacyon hathe set his poysoned barell a broche'.[23] No heretic had yet been suffered to perform miracles, 'but according to scripture, this would indeed happen when the great arch-heretic Antichrist himself came. More's metaphysical dismay is barely concealed in his admission that he thinks the time may have come: 'as helpe me god I fere [he] be very nere hys time, and that Luther is his very fore goar and his baptiste, to make redy his way in the deserte of this wreched world / and Tindale, frere Huskyn, and Swynglius, his very fals prophetes to preache for hym'.[24] More's sense in this passage of antichristian parody and perversion indicated that the world in his eyes was being turned almost literally upside-down.

As usual, he tried to correct the balance by affirming that 'bycause he [Antichrist] shall haue so many wayes to turne the peple wronge: god shall not suffer the wreche longe, but shall shorten his dayes / and . . . shall kyll hym wyth the spiryte or blaste of hys holy mouth'. But he acknowledges equally that before Antichrist's final destruction,

[21] *Confutation, CW* II, p. 794/20–23.
[22] *Dialogue, CW* 6, p. 374/12–15.
[23] *Confutation, CW* 8, I, p. 120/32–3.
[24] ibid., I, p. 271/11–15.

he would kill many of the faithful out of anger, and it was with that potential horror that More was most preoccupied.[25]

Later, in *A Dialogue of Comfort against Tribulation*, More would change his mind, concluding that the Day of Judgement was, in fact, still a long way off yet because of the absence of certain tokens,[26] but at the conclusion of his polemical effort he believed intensely and sincerely that it was about to occur. Unlike Tyndale and later protestant millennarians such as John Foxe, he did not believe that the unchaining of Antichrist would be followed by an earthly millennium; it was the end, not the beginning, that he thought was commencing by 1533.

It is distressing to observe the emotional depths to which More's experience in religious and political controversy sank him. That experience forced changes in his personality that threatened to destroy much of what was most attractive and admirable in him. Equally, it exposed chinks in his intellectual armour that in all the million words of the controversies he refused to acknowledge. Had he not stuck so stubbornly to the dogmatic assertion of what he was not in all respects emotionally persuaded he believed, then he might never have been reduced so low. As it was, one senses that, by the time his arrest and imprisonment relieved him of the polemical burden on 17 April 1534, More was near the point of collapse.

If his literary career had ended there, posterity would have been left with the cautionary exemplum of a man whose life had been an unmitigated tragedy – More is not remembered today for his controversial writings or his behaviour during the years when he wrote them. However, this period marks the nadir of his life and works, not the summit of their achievement. Moreover, had he not undergone it, he could never have attained the remarkable recovery to which his subsequent Tower works testify.[27]

[25] ibid., p. 271/19-23.
[26] *CW* 12, p. 193/28–9.
[27] For a similar estimation, see Lewis (*Essential Articles*, pp. 396–7).

PART THREE

The Tower Works

9

Calm Regained: *A Treatise upon the Passion*

By the end of the controversies More had become the victim of his own polemical engagement. Not having wished to be drawn into such combat in the first place, he tried, once he had been, to square his own philosophy to fit the pre-cast moulds of dogma.

It was an impossible task, for More was wrong in believing that his view of the world could be contained within dogmatic formulations. Dogma by nature is definitive, and More's whole earlier intellectual career had revolved about his recognition that life is characterized by ambiguity and paradox. There was thus a fundamental incompatibility between what he was trying to say and the way in which he was required to say it. Ironically, he found himself arguing rigidly and arbitrarily the need to be responsive and flexible, so that his very meaning was negated by the manner of expression he had chosen. Eventually he became imprisoned by his own rhetoric, having lost sight of the central meaning in his argument. In short, he lost his ability to imagine that contemporary history might be manifesting providence, whose workings he so earnestly extolled, in some creative rather than merely punitive way. The sixteenth-century reform and reformation eventually proved to be no temporary lapse from the preordained historical blueprint, but rather an intrinsic part of it; in the heat and contention of the controversies, More could neither see nor concede this.

He thus found himself, to his own surprise, swimming against the tide of history with no possibility of changing direction. As it became obvious that all he had stood for was about to be defeated in England, he was confronted with two alternatives: either to conclude that the end of the world was near, or else to modify his assessment of what was taking place. At first his pride prevented him from considering the latter, so that he was forced to conclude that Antichrist was about to appear and triumph. The effects on him of this belief, combined with the other psychological forces animating his polemic, were thoroughly destructive. As well, he had landed himself in almost every conceivable sort of trouble: political and emotional. By late 1533 More's story had all the ingredients of a catastrophe.

The most remarkable aspect of More's intellectual career was that he was able triumphantly to pull himself out of the slough into which he had fallen. His three so-called 'Tower works', *A Treatise upon the Passion of Christ, A Dialogue of Comfort against Tribulation* and *De Tristitia Christi,* mark the stages by which this recovery was achieved. They reveal first an attempt on More's part to disengage and distance himself from the storm and stress in which he had been involved, and then an attempt to approach its archetypal meaning. As his perspective narrowed from a consideration of universal human experience to that of Europe, England and Christendom, and finally to that of the individual, epitomized by Christ, he discovered that his own experience adumbrated the pattern of all human experience from the creation to the end of time. This realization turned his death from a consequence of defeat into an act of faith and a sign of victory, in his own mind.

The *Treatise upon the Passion* shows More's first steps towards rehabilitation. They involved both the repudiation of his polemical mode and also a revision of his sense of contemporary history.

It used to be thought that the *Treatise upon the Passion* was written in the Tower, an error arising from William Rastell's misleading rubric in his 1557 edition of More's English works and his assumption that the Latin *De Tristitia* was the continuation of the same treatise.[1] A letter written by More before 17 April 1534 to his secretary, John Harris, proves conclusively that most, if not all, of the work was written before More entered the Tower.[2] Indeed, there is good reason for suspecting that the *Treatise upon the Passion* is the promised second part of More's reply to George Joye's *The Supper of the Lord.*[3] In his *Answer to a Poisoned Book* More identified two courses in the heretical

---

[1] *EW* 1557, pp. 1270, 1349.

[2] Rogers, *SL,* no. 48, pp. 186–8. The letter contains instructions to correct an error in More's first draft concerning the Greeks' dating of Christ's paschal feast; this passage was incorporated into the text printed by Rastell, about halfway through the *Treatise upon the Passion* (*CW* 13, pp. 88/22–91/22). For further discussion, see Haupt, ibid., pp. xxxviii–xxxix, and Louis L. Martz, *CW* 12, p. lviii.

[3] See also Germain Marc'hadour, *Thomas More et la Bible* (Paris, 1969), pp. 72–3.

supper he believed 'Master Masker' (the anonymous Joye) had served up: his interpretations of Christ's words in John 6, and of Christ's maundy, the Last Supper. He declared that, as a result, 'I shall . . . deuide this worke of myne into twoo partes in lykewyse, of whych twain this shal be the first, wherin I shal detect and make euery man perceyue thys mans euyll cooquery in hys fyrst course', adding that he would later send forth his second part against the second course as well.[4] The *Answer to a Poisoned Book* became the first part, and the *Treatise upon the Passion*, together with its concluding section, *A Treatise to Receive the Blessed Body of Our Lord*,[5] became the second. Given that the *Answer to a Poisoned Book* was finished in December 1533,[6] it is likely that More wrote the *Treatise upon the Passion* between January and April 1534.

The question of the date and purpose of the *Treatise* is important, because they show that More chose willingly to confront the consequences of his polemical career before imprisonment and the prospect of death forced him to.

Significantly, even though the *Treatise* was written to oppose heresy, it was not designed to be polemical. More seems to have recovered a sense of what he had declared 20 years earlier in *Utopia* and the *Letter to Dorp*: that violent controversy is futile.[7] Instead of continuing to quote and refute his opponent piecemeal, More chose a new method altogether. The work is cast as a series of lectures, or 'homilies', aimed at instruction and moral edification rather than refutation or summary proof, for as More explicitly declared concerning the heretics: 'yet is it not my present purpose to dyspute the matter with them, but to shewe and set forthe the trouthe before the eyen of the reader, that he may rather of the trouthe redde, encrease in faith, and conceiue deuocion, than wyth muche tyme bestowed in the reading of their erronious fallacies, misse occupy his eares, and heape vp in his hart a donghyl of theyr dyuelyshe vanities'.[8]

He now sought to persuade indirectly, by placing the eucharist in

---

[4] *EW* 1557, p. 1038, D–F.

[5] On the possibility that the *Treatise on the Blessed Body* may have become detached from the *Passion* because it was written after More was imprisoned, see Martz, *CW* 12, pp. lxxxii–lxxxiii. For another explanation, see Clarence Miller, *CW* 14, II, p. 741n.

[6] For More's correction of the printer's erroneous date (Anno 1534), see his letter to Cromwell of 1 February 1533/4 (Rogers, *Correspondence*, p. 468/16–21).

[7] See above, p. 131.

[8] *CW* 13, p. 137/25–31.

the universal context which gave it meaning, and whose meaning it summed up.

More had already attempted this kind of thing in *A Dialogue Concerning Heresies*. There he had tried to prove that revelation was progressive, historical, and achieved through the evolving consensus of the church, by demonstating how the situation instituted by God at the Fall logically dictated that it should be. God had placed men in a condition of perpetual warfare between reason and sensuality, in which they were to be kept straining with the confession of their ignorance, being vouchsafed knowledge of the truth only when and as divine wisdom saw fit;[9] it followed unquestionably, therefore, that God would neither have enshrined all knowledge of things necessary to salvation in written scripture, nor have revealed even the meaning of scripture all at once. In the *Dialogue* this use of the historical perspective had been only fleeting, so that More's consideration took on the character of a digression; in the *Treatise upon the Passion*, on the other hand, it became the foundation of the entire book. As its subtitle · indicated, the work is 'a treatyse hystoricall': not just an exposition of the literal sense of the scriptural account of Christ's passion, but also a consideration of the place of the event in history. By adopting the historical perspective and homiletic form, More may have been reviving the method he had used in his youth to lecture upon Augustine's comparable historical meditation, *De civitate Dei*; if this were so, it would suggest further how thoroughly More was divesting himself of his polemical robes.

To begin his reconstruction of the historical context, More went back to the fall of the angels out of heaven. His purpose was to demonstrate the parallel between the angels and mankind for the sake of underlining the essential difference, because of which the latter could be redeemed, whereas the former could not.

The angels, More declared, having been created out of nothing by the 'mere liberal goodnes' of the Trinity, were left with free will and liberty either to turn towards God with praise and thanks, or else to decline 'into wretchednesse'.[10] Although a great multitude did turn to God through the instinct of grace, Lucifer was driven so crazed with pride and ambition 'that he boasted that he woulde be goddes felow in dede'. Thus he was suddenly cast out of heaven with 'an infinite

[9] *CW* 6, pp. 139/21–144/25.
[10] *CW* 13, p. 4/7–22.

number' of like traitorous angels and thrown down to hell.[11] Their punishment was dire, for 'the inflexible iustice of almighty God . . . depryued them from his grace for euer, and thereby from al hope and coumfort, of recouery of any maner atteining to the celestial glory, but for euer condemned to payn'.[12]

God, not willing to allow his enemies to frustrate his creative purpose, determined to create a new kind of creature to take the place of the fallen angels. This new kind, man, was given a mingled and tempered nature as a safeguard against Lucifer's pride, and was also bound in further with precepts and commandments, and the threat of punishment by death should he eat the fruit of the tree of knowledge.[13] Even though God gave them every assistance for resisting 'proud disobedience', the devil nevertheless succeeded in filling Eve's heart with 'the poyson of proud curious appetite'; Eve succeeded in infecting her husband, and together they duplicated the fall of the angels into ruin and confusion, being thrust out of paradise into 'the wretched earthe' as a result.[14]

Even then God would not endure his enemy, the devil, to rejoice in the subversion of mankind, for although Satan had deceived men into committing his own fault, there was a difference between their two cases. Whereas the evil angels had been self-tempted, man had been 'brought into sinne, not al of himself but by the suttle suggestion of his false enuious enemy'.[15] Moreover, Adam and Eve, unlike the angels, did not despair, and for that reason, after their repentance and plea to God for remission and mercy, he had forgiven them 'the eternalite of the payne dewe vnto theyr offence'.[16] Entering into counsel together, his justice and mercy between them determined upon a 'marvellous' plan for mankind's redemption. Intrinsically, such a prospect seemed impossible. The ransom had to be paid for the maintenance of God's justice by a man since men were they who most owed it, but because the whole human race was already 'al in one dampnacion, con-dempned al to bodely death', none of them could pay the ransom on behalf of the rest; even should one man wish to suffer willingly, his death could avail nothing to the rest because he had been doomed to

---

[11] ibid., p. 5/3ff.
[12] ibid., p. 6/14–18.
[13] ibid., pp. 11/19–13/2.
[14] ibid., pp. 13/12, 16/21, 19/6.
[15] ibid., p. 25/25–6.
[16] ibid., pp. 53/29–54/8.

die for his own part anyway.[17] The angels could not have helped, even had they wished to, partly because no creature could give satisfaction for deadly trespass done against the creator, and partly because men would then be more beholden to angel than God, and 'thoccasion therof had bene a very foule dysorder'.[18] God's solution to the dilemma, More continues, 'farre passed the wisdom of al the wise angels of heauen', for 'that excellent meane . . . of mans redempcion so by himselfe deuised, hymselfe moste graciously fulfilled' in the incarnate form of the second person of the Trinity.[19] Being conceived without sin, born without pain, and 'not bounden or subiect vnto deathe, neyther by nature nor sinne', Christ was able obediently to offer himself up as a 'pleasaunt acceptable sacrifice' to pacify the wrath and indignation of God.[20] And by so doing, he 'reduced mankinde (in such as wil take the benefite) to more ioy, more welth, and farre more honour to, than euer the fal of our first father lost vs'.[21]

By placing the passion in its universal context, More tried to show how it was the very linch-pin of the whole grand design of God as far as human destiny was concerned. Christ's death on the cross was the only means for men's salvation, and, he argued, God had never failed to give men sufficient knowledge of this fact to allow them to accept it if they chose. Revelation of the passion was given to Adam, Noah, Abraham and the old fathers who gave it to every generation before the written law. Afterwards it was given to Moses in the written law and then to the prophets who passed it down to every generation of the Jews until the coming of Christ himself.[22] In the centuries after the passion, knowledge had been carried in the beliefs of the church and scripture, and would continue to be so until Christ's faith had been preached to the ends of the earth.[23]

It was within this context that the eucharist assumed its crucial importance for More. Among Christians it was the essential instrument by which they were 'animated and quickened' by grace and 'more firmely knyt and vnyd quicke liuely membres in the spirituall

---

[17] ibid., p. 26/4–19.
[18] ibid., p. 26/20–32.
[19] ibid., p. 27/2–33.
[20] ibid.
[21] ibid., p. 28/1–3.
[22] ibid., p. 29/23–9.
[23] ibid., p. 173.

societie of sayntes',[24] so that the fruit of their good works might bear witness to their conscience.[25] But men could only receive 'the vertue and theffecte thereof' if they received the sacrament in the right faith: 'that is to wytte, that we verelye belieue, that it is, as in dede it is, vnder the fourme and likenesse of breadde, the very blessed bodye, fleshe and bloude of our holy sauiour Christe himselfe, the verye selfe same body, and the very selfe same bloude, that dyed and was shedde vppon the crosse for oure synne'.[26]

This was the essential proposition that the entire *Treatise upon the Passion* had been contrived to prove in answer to Joye's contention in the *Supper of the Lord* that the sacramental forms were mere signs, or tokens, which the elect received spiritually through faith. That More could bring himself to handle such a momentous doctrinal issue in a non-polemical mode testifies to the thoroughgoing change of disposition that had taken place in him.

Apart from this general strategy, the change is evident in other ways. At many points More allows for the same kind of speculative disagreement that he had depicted earlier in *Utopia* – concerning such matters as God's justice in allowing original sin to be inherited, the salvation of pagans, and the damnation of unbaptized infants.[27] Without conceding any justice to the heretics, he mitigated the intolerance that had helped bring them into being; for example, while he still condemned the posing of religious questions out of 'curious bold presumpcion', he now allowed that 'on the tother syde, where suche questions are not demaunded of frowardnesse, of a vayne pryde, nor of blasphemous purpose, it is not onely no displeasure to God, but is also a good occupacion of the minde'.[28] This belief had been one of the mainstays of his thought even as late as *A Dialogue Concerning Heresies,* but had been largely absent in the controversies from the *Confutation* onwards. One should not overestimate the issue – More's basic viewpoint had not changed – but the less truculent tone and attitude confirm the return in him to a more charitable mind implied by his choice of the homiletic genre. In the *Treatise upon the Passion* he had grown less concerned to make it appear as if the position he

---

[24] ibid., pp. 176/32, 177/6–8; 'vnyd' is the past particiuple of the obsolete verb 'uny', 'to join into one' (OED).

[25] *Treatise on the Blessed Body, CW* 13, p. 204/8–9.

[26] ibid., pp. 192/18, 195/24–9.

[27] *CW* 13, pp. 28–36.

[28] ibid., p. 28/16–29.

espoused involved nothing but complete certainties. He could admit, for example, that Jean Gerson had found it difficult to harmonize the chronology of the gospel accounts of the passion itself ('such doutes as he sometime moueth concerning the context of the stori').[29] He could also allow a greater diversity of opinions on certain matters, such as the question of whether man in his unfallen state could have resisted sin of his own nature. Declaring his own conviction that they could not, he adds immediately: 'How be if it any man affirme styflye yet, I wyll kepe no scoles vpon the matter nor almost in nothing els.'[30] It is almost as if More were consciously striving to prevent himself from slipping back into the dogmatic mire in which he had been immersed for the past six years.

As well as adopting a new tone and mode, More also sought to remedy some of the other faults in the controversies of which the reformers had complained. In the *Apology* he had recorded how some men complained that his books were too long and therefore too tedious to read.[31] His answer then had been sufficiently testy to suggest how cuttingly the quip hurt: 'Nowe where as these good blessed bretherne say, that my wrytyng is so long and so tedyouse, that they wil not ones vouchsaufe to loke theron / they shew them self that my wrytynge is not so longe as theyre wyttes be shorte.'[32] In the *Treatise upon the Passion,* however, he could finally bring himself to acknowledge the truth of the charge by attempting to avoid giving grounds for it. At the end of the 'Introduction', for instance, he declares that, although many other questions could be raised about the historical context of the passion, 'yet lest I shulde therwith make this worke to tedious, and the introduction lenger than the principal proces of the passion, we shall be content with these fewe, as those that moste properly perteyne vnto the matter'.[33] This concern with order and proportion makes for a welcome change from the digressiveness, diffuseness and sprawling anarchy of the later controversies; along with his equilibrium, More had recovered his sense of form.

The deeper cause of More's recovery underlying all these outward signs of it was his reassessment of the meaning of history.

The essence of More's view of history did not change – his account

[29] ibid., p. 50/15–16.
[30] ibid., p. 38/19–22.
[31] *CW* 9, p. 5/7–8.
[32] ibid., p. 7/28–31.
[33] *CW* 13, p. 49/1–5.

of biblical history is exactly consistent with that given in *A Dialogue Concerning Heresies* – but his precise application of it did. In the course of his systematic reconsideration of the instrumentality of the imperfect human situation in God's regenerative plan, his faith in providence seems to have revived. The consequences are seen most clearly in a new interpretation of contemporary events. Whereas in the controversies More had concluded that the end of the world must be near, he now pondered whether the events that had seemed so apocalyptic to him might merely be an intense manifestation of what had always been likely to occur in human history from the beginning. One need not wait until the prophesied advent of Antichrist to see evidence of antichristian persecution, because it had begun at the creation. Meditation on the Fall prompted More to this speculation:

> On which thing when I bethinke me, me thinketh I mai wel say the wordes of saint Iohn in the Apocalippes, wyth which he bewayleth this wretched worlde, by reason of that the diuel fell out of heauen thereinto: *Ve terre et mari, quia descendit diabolus ad vos, habens iram magnam sciens quia modicum tempus habet.* Wo to the earth and to the sea, for the dyuell is come downe to you, hauyng greate anger, knowyng that he hathe but a lyttle tyme. This wo well founde oure forefathers, when the diuell full of yre for hys owne fall, and enuye that they shoulde succede him, labored to bringe theym to the place of his final dampnacion: from which he saw wel he had but a litle time left, that is to wit the time of thys present worlde, which is transitorye and soone shall passe, and is a time in all together very short, from the first creacion to the final chaunge therof at the day of dome.[34]

Antichrist's persecution prophesied in the Book of Revelation would merely be a foreshortened, climactic epitome of this general persecution of the devil allowed through God's sufferance, and in his account of it in the *Treatise upon the Passion* More no longer gives any hint that he thinks it is about to occur. Indeed, his words anticipate his explicit declaration in *A Dialogue of Comfort* that the apocalypse is a long way off yet:[35]

> afterward when . . . [Christ's faith] is all preached rounde aboute vppon all partes of the earth, the tyme shall come whan it

[34] *CW* 13, p. 23/8–21; cf. *De Tristitia Christi, CW* 14, I, p. 555/4–11.
[35] *CW* 12, p. 194/28ff.

shal so sore decaye agayne, and the churche by persecucion so strayghted into so narow a corner, that in respect of the countreyes into whiche chrystendome hath been and shalbe delated and spred before, it shall seeme that there shall bee than no chrysten countreyes left at all. . . . But that tyme shalbe but short. For our sauiour sayth: *Propter electos breuiabuntur dies illi.* And than shal our lorde come soone after and finyshe thys presente worlde.[36]

Until that time Christendom would go on losing and winning many lands as part of the process by which the devil turns corn into cockle as fast as God turns it back into good corn again.[37] More had come to feel that the dictum that even the just man falls seven times a day and rises again might apply metaphorically, to some extent, to nations as well as individuals,[38] and that England was proving no exception to the general rule. Once More had restored his sense of the inevitable mutability of the process, he was able to cast off the near-despair that had intermittently gripped him; events no longer seemed to testify so conclusively to an imminent triumph of Antichrist.

Just as *A Treatise upon the Passion* testifies to More's thoroughgoing efforts to regain peace of mind and shed the contentiousness to which he had grown habituated, it also reveals that he had not as yet entirely succeeded in suppressing the old reflexes.

This appears first in his continuing habit of stinging political opponents under the cover of allegory. The council of Caiaphas and the Jews, for example, gave him the pretext for declaring his thinly veiled opinion of the deliberations of his enemies. He begins by condemning wicked assemblies in terms that evoke the king's Council and the Reformation Parliament:

> when men assemble theym together, to deuyse and counsayle about myschief and wrechednes, the mo that are at it, the wursse is the counsayle, and the lesse to bee regarded, be theyr personages in the syghte of the worlde, neuer so seemelye, and theyr authoritye neuer so great: as these that here assemble

---

[36] *CW* 13, pp. 173/24–174/3.
[37] ibid., p. 172/33–5; *Confutation, CW* 8, II, p. 1020.
[38] *Dialogue, CW* 6, p. 395/23–6.

about the death of Christ, were the chiefe heades and rulers of
the people, and specially the chiefe of the spiritualty.[39]

As well as obliquely criticizing the various anticlerical measures
devised to procure Henry VIII's divorce, which More had been
energetically, though covertly, opposing, this passage almost certainly
alludes to Cranmer, who had been appointed Archbishop of Canterbury on 10 January 1533, equating him with Caiaphas.

The success of his opponents obviously still rankled with More, for
he administers a further lash of the whip in an inset exemplum
describing how a young man came to gratify his lust for a certain
woman. If one substitutes Henry for the young man, Anne Boleyn for
the woman, and Cromwell as the 'wretch' who had urged him on, the
scene More intends to expose is clear:

There was once a yong man fallen in a leud mynde towarde a
woman, and she was such, as he coulde conceiue none hope to
get her, and therefore was fallynge to a good poynt in his own
mynde, to let that lewde enterprise passe. He myssehapped
neuertheless to shew hys minde to another wretche, whyche
encouraged hym to go forward and leaue it not. For begynne
thou once man the matter quod he, and neuer feare it, let the
dyuel alone with the remnaunt, he shall bringe it to passe in such
wyse as thy selfe alone cannest not deuise how.[40]

Recalling the council of the Jews, More adds bitterly: 'I trow that
wretch had learned that counsayle of these priestes and these
auncients, assembled here together against Christ at this counsayl.'[41]
Through the implied analogy, More is thus able to cast Cromwell in
the role of Judas, who 'came . . . to this assemblye that wee speake of
nowe, and vnsent for, presented hym selfe vnto them, to helpe forward
theyr vngracious counsayle'.[42] Although the soul of political discretion
as always, taking due care to blur the traces of his trail, More was
sufficiently human to seek revenge in these unflattering covert com-
parisons. His ensuing prayer makes one strongly aware of his own

[39] *CW* 13, p. 73/25–31.
[40] ibid., p. 78/5ff.
[41] ibid.
[42] ibid., p. 77/31–3. For the facts of Cromwell's rise, see Elton, *Reform and Reformation*,
pp. 136–8.

perilous political position at the time when the *Treatise* was being
composed: 'Gracious god giue me thy grace so to consider the
punyshement of that false great counsayle . . . that I be neuer to thy
dyspleasure partener, nor giue mine assent to folow the sinful deuice
of any wicked counsail.'[43] This prayer must have been given extra
point by the fact that the administration had stepped up its pressure
to make him conform with the Bill of Attainder of 21 February 1534
implicating him in the treason of the Nun of Kent. More's awareness
that his own arrest might be imminent would have heightened his
sense of the correspondences between his situation and that of Christ.
Nevertheless, the danger did not prevent him from making his
opposition plain in writing. Even if his later indictment were false in
the letter, it was certainly accurate in spirit.

Further vestiges of More's old controversial habits materialize
when he does slip helplessly into polemic near the end of the *Treatise*.
This occurs as he approaches its real goal and purpose: a proof that
the eucharist does contain the very body and blood of Christ. At first
when he recalls his opponents' views he tries to maintain a moderate,
relatively uncontentious tone. Without specifically mentioning names,
or even the word 'heretics', he states that 'there are in dyuers
countries of Christendome som . . . that labour in the blessed sacrament to subuert the very true christen faythe'; this they do by making
men believe that Christ named the bread and wine his body and blood
only as tokens 'for perpetuall remembraunce of hys passion'. Continuing to exercise self-restraint, More declares that he will not
dispute the matter with them, but will simply set forth the truth of the
matter before the reader's eyes. Nevertheless, recollection of the
polemical context of the *Treatise* leads him within a couple of lines to
intensify the 'erronious fallacies' of these unspecified dissenters into
the 'donghyl of theyr dyuelyshe vanities'.[44] And suddenly the reader is
plunged back into the world of the controversies as More finds the call
to battle irresistible. He gives first a catalogue of the 'special engines'
used by the heretics in furthering their 'craftye purpose',[45] then a
catena of patristic quotations in support of his own interpretation of
Christ's words at the Last Supper,[46] and finally a full-blown account

---

[43] *CW* 13, p. 75/22–5.
[44] ibid., p. 137/12ff.
[45] ibid., pp. 138–9.
[46] ibid., pp. 160–71.

of the growth of heresies.[47] The changes remind one that part of the original motive for this work had been to refute George Joye's sacramental heresies. Even though More's focus may have gradually shifted to the passion itself, he did not forget entirely his original intent.

Doctrinally, in fact, the *Treatise upon the Passion* and its concluding section of the final lecture, the *Treatise on the Blessed Body*, pick up where the *Letter Impugning Frith* and the *Answer to a Poisoned Book* left off: the sacrament contains the 'selfe same bodye and bloude in their proper fourme' that Christ offered on the cross;[48] the scriptural account of its institution is to be read literally, not figuratively;[49] Christ's body can indeed be in many different places at once because he said it would;[50] and his soul and almighty Godhead are also present in the sacrament.[51] In great detail More further considers its substance and accidents, outward sensible signs and inward insensible signs, and the manifold mysteries encompassed and signified by its many names.[52]

Although More does not labour to point it out, the final lecture on the manner in which the eucharist ought to be received is designed to counter Joye's claim that Christ's flesh is received only spiritually by the elect in whom faith has been confirmed by the Holy Spirit.[53] This subtext is given away by More's use of the term 'spiritually', which echoes Joye's terminology, when he first raises the question of receiving at the end of the *Treatise upon the Passion*.[54] When he resumed the topic in the *Treatise on the Blessed Body*, he replaced this word with another: 'virtually'.[55] The substitution allowed him not only to avoid the heretical implications vested in the reformers' use of the word 'spiritual' altogether, but also to recover his non-polemical frame of thought.

As it was, when More broke off the *Treatise upon the Passion* in the middle of the third lecture – possibly it was interrupted by his

[47] ibid., pp. 172–3.
[48] ibid., pp. 123/23ff, 147/10–23.
[49] ibid., pp. 138, 158–9.
[50] ibid., pp. 139, 147/27ff.
[51] ibid., p. 146/26ff.
[52] ibid., pp. 140–1, 152–6.
[53] *Supper of the Lord*, pp. 239–40. See also the passage quoted by More in *Poisoned Book, EW* 1557, p. 1110 D–E.
[54] *CW* 13, p. 174/32.
[55] ibid., p. 191/10. The change is discussed by Martz, *CW* 12, pp. lxxx–lxxxii.

summons to Lambeth and subsequent imprisonment on 17 April – he was in danger of lapsing into the old manner from which he was trying to extricate himself. The interruption may have saved him, for the new disposition struggling to be born in the *Treatise* had been more fully realized in the will than the deed.

10

The Great Turk: *A Dialogue of Comfort against Tribulation*

If we suppose that *De Tristitia Christi* was the last work More wrote, and allow sufficient time for him to have written it, then the *Dialogue of Comfort against Tribulation* must have been composed between June 1534 and the early months of 1535. By that time the fifth and six sessions of the Reformation Parliament had finally put the seal on the political changes he had been opposing: the clergy had been stripped of their independent right to try heresy by an Act establishing open trials,[1] and the breach with Rome had been confirmed in Acts restraining annates, abolishing Peter's pence, confirming the Submission of the Clergy, and transferring the pope's authority to issue dispensations to the Archbishop of Canterbury.[2] More's own near escape from inclusion in the Bill of Attainder against the Nun of Kent had also proven how mercilessly his opposition to the king's second marriage would be suppressed should he persist in opposing it as he fully intended. When, in mid-April, More was imprisoned after he had refused to take the oath accompanying the Act of Succession, execution had not yet been prescribed as the punishment for his offence, but it was a future possibility that he might well have envisaged (if he did not, others, such as Chapuys, certainly did).[3] He thus had every incentive for considering what the collapse of his world and his own ominous situation meant in philosophical and religious terms.

Such a consideration was indeed the prime cause and concern of the *Dialogue of Comfort*. Whereas in the *Treatise upon the Passion* More had contemplated universal history in its generalities, he now focused more narrowly upon the calamity he believed had descended upon

[1] Lehmberg, pp. 186–7.
[2] ibid., pp. 191–2.
[3] *LP,* VII, pp. 499, 500, 530.

Europe, and on the predicament of individual men and nations caught up in it. To this end he devised a fictional framework, consisting of the extended metaphor of the Great Turk, and developed a series of analogies within it that allowed him to identify and confront the objects of his perturbations. All of them, he saw, were aspects of the same universal reality of human experience: tribulation. Yet having confronted it, he found in tribulation a cause for hope rather than despair.

Scholarship occasionally shows a tendency to reduce the fictional frame to simple allegory, with the Great Turk representing Henry VIII, or the devil, or the Lutherans, or all three,[4] but to do so is to miss much of the basic point of the *Dialogue*. It is, in effect, far more than a merely partisan piece of anti-Protestant allegory designed to fortify Catholics against future persecution for the old faith. The allegory of the Turk is polysemous rather than simple, in the manner that More thought characterized scripture itself. More's own comments on scriptural exegesis in his *Letter Impugning Frith* provide an appropriate gloss for the way it works. There, he insists on the primacy of the literal sense in all instances where a literal reading can pertain; nevertheless, additional allegorical meanings can reside within the literal sense without replacing it.[5] In the *Treatise upon the Passion* he had demonstrated what he meant by giving elaborate figurative interpretations of literal biblical episodes, such as the bondage of the Israelites under the Pharaoh of Egypt, which 'signifieth the bondage of mankynde vnder the prynce of thys darke world', their delivery and safe passage through the Red Sea, which 'sygnifieth mankynd passyng oute of the dyuels daunger, thorowe the water of baptisme', and their 40 years wandering in the desert, in which 'is there sygnified and fygured, the long payneful wandering of men in the wylde wyldernes of this wreched world ere we can get hence to heauen'.[6] More's own work deliberately reproduced this kind of multilayered structure of meaning in order to achieve universality.

---

[4] Jones, pp. 122–3, 128. While this identification is indeed intermittently implicit, to exaggerate it in relation to the literal meaning is to distort.

[5] *EW* 1557, p. 835 C–D. More treated the same issue from the other perspective in *De Tristitia Christi*: 'we should not feel bound to consider only the facts of the account, though even these can teach us salutary lessons, but let us look further for the saving mystery of the spirit veiled beneath the letter of the story' (*CW* 14, I, p. 507/3–5).

[6] *CW* 13, p. 58/14–32.

At the literal level, the Turkish threat is presented *per se* in precise and accurate detail. Ever since the fall of Constantinople in 1452 and Athens in 1453, the expansion of the Ottoman Turks had instilled very real fear in the European imagination.[7] They had pillaged as far as Zagreb in 1470, and had repeatedly invaded Hungary in 1473, 1479 and 1493. Several decades later the threat had grown suddenly more menacing when Suleiman the Magnificent captured two of the most important bulwarks of Christendom: Belgrade in 1521 and the island of Rhodes in 1522. After the decisive battle of Mohács in 1526, the Turks seemed poised to invade the very heartland of Christianity.

It is in this context that More places his two Hungarian protagonists, Vincent and Anthony, as they await the final onslaught. Vincent describes the depth of their fear:

> sith the tydynges haue come hether so brymme of the great Turkes interprise into these parties here: we can almost neyther talke nor thynke of any other thyng els, than of his might and our mischefe. There falleth so contynually before the eyen of our hart, a fearefull imaginacion of this terryble thyng / his myghty strength and power, his high malice and hatryd, and his incomparable crueltie, with robbyng, spoylyng, burnyng, and layng wast all the way that his armye commeth / than kyllyng or carying away, the people far hens fro home.[8]

In a later passage Anthony further details the atrocities of the Turks: the exaction of annual tributes and taxes, the dispossession of Christians from their lands, the levying of children for Janissaries and the seraglio, and forcible conversion to Islam.[9] All these facts, together with accurate references to the internal struggle for the Hungarian crown between Ferdinand, Archduke of Austria, and John Zapolya, Voivode of Transylvania,[10] testify to More's precise knowledge of contemporary developments in the Balkans as reported to Wolsey in numerous official documents.[11]

[7] See C. A. Patrides, '"The Bloody and Cruell Turke": The Background of a Renaissance Commonplace', *Studies in the Renaissance*, 10 (1963), pp. 126–35; and R. J. Schoeck, 'Thomas More's "Dialogue of Comfort" and the Problem of the Real Grand Turk', *English Miscellany*, 20 (1969), pp. 23–37.

[8] *CW* 12, p. 6/19–27.

[9] ibid., pp. 190–1.

[10] ibid., p. 8/2–5.

[11] See Manley, *CW* 12, pp. cxxv–cxxvi.

Significantly, More sets the action in 1527–28 *before* the permanent occupation of Buda by the Turks in the spring of 1529. His use of the literal historical event as a framing fiction thus allowed for the creation of a double perspective: that of the Hungarians, Anthony and Vincent, who are struggling (like More had been from about the same date) to come to terms with the imminent invasion, literal and metaphorical, of their 'country', and that of the European reader who, with the advantage of hindsight, knows that the feared occupation had indeed occurred in the intimated fictional aftermath of the dialogue. Attention focuses, therefore, on the process by which the two protagonists strive to prepare themselves to confront the terrifying experience they fear is about to descend upon them, as the reader knows it will. In depicting that, More was also dramatizing how he himself had evolved out of the state of desperation into which he had been tempted to fall before the field had been won. In this way the *Dialogue* is contrived to provide a spiritual biography of More's response to his own particular circumstances at one level, while at the same time offering a universalized exemplum relevant to all comparable occasions of real or threatened tribulation when and wherever they may occur.

Clearly, the self-sufficient, literal Turkish/Hungarian context contains within it at least two other contexts: one similarly literal, and the other metaphorical. They exist as intermittently obtruded analogies to the main Turkish business, similar, for example, to the political and anagogical strands in the allegory of Spenser's *Faerie Queene*.

The second literal context concerns recent events in European politics. When Vincent expresses fear that 'no small part of our own folke that dwell even here about vs, are (as we here) fallen to hym [the Turk], or all redy confeteryd with hym', one detects a veiled reference to the unscrupulous pragmatism of the French. Throughout the 1520s Francis I of France was negotiating with the Turks to form an alliance against Charles V.[12] Vincent's remark could be applied equally to the political alliance between the English administration and anticlericalism that had recently achieved the legislative breach with Rome, so that when Anthony rejoins that the Turk 'hath . . . destroyid our noble yong goodly kyng', his observation, which applies literally to Louis II of Hungary, could bear upon Francis I of France and Henry VIII of England as well.[13] Another remark by Anthony allows for a

[12] ibid., p. 7/2–3. See Halil Inalcik, *The Ottoman Empire* (London, 1973), pp. 35–7.
[13] ibid., p. 8/2–3.

specific English inference when he claims that 'sinnes the title of the crowne hath comen in question, the good rule of this realme hath very sore decayed / as litle while as it is / And vndowtidly Hungary shall neuer do well, as long as . . . mens myndes harken after newelties, and haue their hartes hangyng vppon a chaunge.'[14] The word 'title' ambiguously raises the question of the 'style' being claimed for Henry as well as the question of the succession. More focuses attention on his own political plight in this context when he makes Vincent observe that good men will be deprived of their goods and bodies 'but yf we turn as they do, and forsake our saviour to / And than (for there ys no born Turke so cruell to christen folke, as is the false christen that falleth fro the fayth) we shall stand in perill yf we percever in the truth, to be more hardely handelyd and dye more cruell deth by our own countremen at home / than yf we were taken hens and caried into Turkey.'[15] Here the allegory could allude to More's sense of his own likely treatment should he persist in refusing to swear to the Oath of Supremacy. Sometimes it is difficult, in fact, to remember as one reads the *Dialogue of Comfort* that Anthony is merely sick and not, like More, in prison fearing the worst.

The political application of the fiction at this level merges with yet another, in which the Turks are likened to the heretics, without precisely being equated with them.[16] When Vincent refers to the growing leniency of his countrymen towards the Turks, his phrasing evokes the countless occasions in the controversies when More uttered the same lament with respect to the attitude of Englishmen to the heretics: 'my thinke I here at myn eare some of our owne here among vs, which with in these few yeres could no more haue born the name of a Turke than the name of the devill, begyn now to fynd litle faute therein'.[17] These lines recall, for instance, the opening of the *Answer to a Poisoned Book,* when More expressed incredulity that Englishmen were now prepared to countenance talk of heresy at their very tables, whereas before a man would have informed upon it 'all thoughe the thing touched hys owne borne brother'.[18] Throughout the contro-

[14] ibid., p. 192/12–16.
[15] ibid., p. 7/7–12.
[16] Manley concludes that More does equate Protestant with Turk (*CW* 12, p. cxxxiii), but I can find no evidence of any such precise identification. The passage at p. 192/3–9, for example, if read closely, does not do so. False Christians (e.g., p. 7/1–12) may be worse than Turks, but in the *Dialogue* they are not the same as them.
[17] ibid., p. 192/3–6.
[18] *EW* 1557, p. 1035 F.

versies More had stressed the analogy between the Lutherans and the Turks, particularly in respect of their infidelity and use of violence.[19] It is not surprising, therefore, that he should have allowed the analogy to surface on several occasions in the *Dialogue of Comfort*. Heresy, along with Henry VIII's political voluntarism and the violence of the Turks, was one of the many manifestations of the larger evil encompassing them all.

That larger evil was the devil himself, and the Great Turk is sometimes described in terms evoking him, as when More refers to 'this terryble thyng' with his 'high malice and hatryd, and his incomparable crueltie'.[20] The depersonalization of the phrase suggests rather more than the historical human figure of Suleiman the Magnificent at that point. The fear instilled by the Turk also makes him like the prophesied Antichrist, at least in the imaginations of the terrified Hungarians. More underlines this by alluding to Christ's reference to the forecast event in Luke 23: 28–30 when he describes their terror: 'These ferefull heps of perill, lye so hevy at oower hartes, whyle we wot not into which we shall fortune to fall, and therefore fere all the worst / that as our sauiour prophesied of the people of Ierusalem, many wysh among vs all redye before the perill come, that the montayns wold ouerwhelm them / or the valeys open and swallow them vpp and keuer them.'[21]

The Turk, together with all that allegorically he represents, is a manifestation of something still larger: the inescapable reality of tribulation in this world and the experience of it. Through the figure of the Turk, More sought to confront the meaning of everything in human experience generally that had the power to perturb the human mind.

The universality of More's concern is indicated in the simplicity of his definition: 'tribulacion semeth generally to signifie nothyng els, but some kynd of grefe, eyther payne of the body or hevynes of the mynd'.[22] The former he was about to suffer, the latter he had already

---

[19] See, for example, *Dialogue Concerning Heresies*, *CW* 6, pp. 411/17–412/20, *Supplication*, *EW* 1557, p. 300 F–G. In the *Debellation* he supported a crusade against the Turks just as fervently as he urged the bodily persecution of heretics (ibid., p. 1030 F).

[20] *CW* 12, p. 6/23–4.

[21] ibid., p. 7/13–18 and note (p. 336).

[22] ibid., p. 10/6–7.

suffered extremely. While book 3 of the *Dialogue of Comfort* progressively narrows its focus to concentrate on painful physical torture and death, it is not to be overlooked that the earlier books are largely concerned with mental and emotional tribulation. The task More had set himself was first to show how hope could be derived from the same experiential realities that can induce despair, and second, to show how he had been able to fortify himself in readiness to 'smyte the devill in the face with a firebrond of charitie'.[23]

Book 1 gives a largely theoretical exposition of how comfort can be achieved. The essential foundation for all hope, More declares, is faith, which is 'in dede the gracious gift of god himself'.[24] The pagan philosophers could never give adequate comfort against tribulation through their natural reasoning because they had no knowledge of the salvation in heaven to which all faith is directed: 'they neuer strech so ferre, but that they leve vntouchid for lak of necessarye knolege, that special poynt, which is not onely the chief comfort of all / but without which also, all other comfortes are nothing / that is to wit the referryng the fynall end of their comfort vnto god'.[25] Once men have attained 'faithfull trust' in God's promise through 'the true beliefe of Goddes woorde',[26] however, they are able to accept that 'by the pacient suffraunce of their tribulacion, they shall attayne his favour / and for their payne receve reward at his hand in heven'.[27]

After the foundation of faith has been laid, one can then understand that tribulation is providentially bestowed. As Anthony explains to Vincent, tribulation is an instrument to drive men *out of* spiritual discomfort and despair: 'And that is one of the causes for the which god sendith it vnto man / for albeit that payne was ordeynyd of god for the punyshment of synne . . . yet in this world in which his high mercye giveth men space to be better / the pvnyshment by trybulacion that he sendith, servith ordinarily for a meane of amendment.'[28] The thought here is exactly consistent with that in earlier works such as the *Dialogue Concerning Heresies*; tribulation is both a

[23] ibid., p. 318/18–19.

[24] ibid., p. 12/29. Someone concerned with the Corpus Christi MS upon which the Yale edition is based evidently thought More's view of faith too close to the heretical view for real comnfort, and so cut his discussion out of the manuscript altogether (see Martz, ibid., p. xxvii, and the textual collation, p. 12).

[25] ibid., p. 10/18–22.

[26] ibid., p. 13/18–20.

[27] ibid., p. 10/23–4.

[28] ibid., p. 17/15–21.

means of punishment for sin and also an instrument for regeneration. It serves to induce 'the obedient confirmyng of the mans will vnto god, and . . . thankes givyng to god for his visitacion',[29] and thus assists men to recover the obedience, devotion and sole dependence owed to God that they had betrayed at the original Fall. Tribulation cleanses and purges men of their sins as well, so that not only does the patient suffrance of it become 'a mater of merite and reward in heven', but it also serves to remit men's future pain in purgatory.[30]

As far as the particular type of tribulation was concerned, More believed that men could be absolutely certain that God allowed whatever they suffered for the best. This applied both to the pain and the comforting remedy God would always provide: 'let vs nothyng dowt / but that like as his high wisedome better seeth what is best for vs than we can see our selfe / so shall his souerayne goodnes give vs the thyng that shall in dede be best'.[31] All good men, he believed, were afflicted with one general kind of tribulation, consisting of 'the conflyte of the flessh agaynst the sowle / the rebellion of sensualitie agaynst the rule and gouernaunce of reson . . . lefte vs by godes ordynaunce to strive agaynst yt and fight with all and by reason and grace to master yt'.[32] Otherwise, men were afflicted variously and severally by diverse kinds of tribulation according to divine wisdom. These included loss of goods, physical sickness, bereavement, disease, mental perturbation, imprisonment, fear of death, and the severest form of all, the fear of damnation.[33]

One of the most grievous forms of tribulation was that of temptation, which More (for obvious personal reasons) held to be as frightening as bodily persecution itself: 'yf we well consider thes two thynges, temptacion and persecucion we may fynd that eyther of them is incident to the tother / For both by temptacion the devill persecuteth vs, and by persecucion the devill also temptith vs / and as persecusion is tribulacion to eueryman, so is temptacion tribulacion to euery good man.'[34] More considered the tribulation of temptation to be so important that he organized the whole of book 2 around an

[29] ibid., p. 71/4–5.
[30] ibid., p. 36/5–15.
[31] ibid., p. 21/26–9.
[32] ibid., p. 21/1–8.
[33] ibid., pp. 19/30–20/11.
[34] ibid., p. 100/11–16.

exposition of the four kinds of temptation metaphorically figured in the words of Psalm 90:

Scuto circumdabit te veritas eius / non temebis a timore nocturno / a sagitta volante in die, a negocio perambulante in tenebris, ab incursu et demonio meridiano: The trouth of god shall compasse the about with a pavice, thow shalt not be aferd of the nightes feare, nor of the arrow fleyng in the day, nor of the bysynes walkyng about in the darknesses / nor of the incursion or invacion of the devill in the mydde day.[35]

In book 2 these four forms of temptation are treated as four separate demons. *Timor noctu* he identified as 'the tribulacions by which the devyll thorow the suffraunce of god, eyther by hym selfe or other than are his instrumentes, temptith good folke to impacience / as he did Iob'.[36] Generally speaking, this impatience comprised all kinds of imaginary fears, as when 'in the night euery bush to hym that waxeth ones a ferd semeth a thefe'.[37] It also consisted of pusillanimity, excessively scrupulous conscience,[38] and the temptation to suicide.[39] *Sagitta volante in die* he identified as 'the arrow of pride, with which the devill temptith a man / not in the night / that is to wit in tribulacion and aduersite . . . but in the day that is to wit in prosperite'.[40] *Negotium perambulans in tenebris* was simply the demon of sensuality – the temptation 'to seke the pleasures of the flesh / in eatyng drinkyng and other filthy delite' – and the materialistic greed for wealth.[41]

To the fourth temptation, that arising from the incursion of the midday devil, or open persecution, More devoted the entire third book. Even physical torture, he asserted, was not to be feared, for God would never allow 'the devill with all his faythles tourmentours in this world' to beset any men with more torment than they could endure:

whan we be of this mynd / and submit our will vnto his, and call and pray for his grace: we can tell well inough, that he will

---

[35] ibid., p. 105/17–23. See also Joaquin Kuhn, 'The Function of Psalm 90 in Thomas More's *Dialogue of Comfort*', *Moreana*, 22 (1969), pp. 61–7.

[36] *CW* 12, p. 107/11–13.

[37] ibid., p. 109/27–8. Shakespeare uses a similar figure to illustrate the distorting power of the imagination in *A Midsummer Night's Dream* (V.i.21–2).

[38] *CW* 12, pp. 111–13ff.

[39] ibid., p. 122ff.

[40] ibid., p. 157/20–3.

[41] ibid., p. 167/6–8.

neuer suffre them to put more vppon vs / than his grace will
make vs hable to bere / but will also with their temptacion
prouide for vs a sure waye / For / *fidelis est deus* sayth saynt
paule / *qui non patitur vos temptare / supra id quod potestis sed dat
etiam cum tentatione prouentum vt possitis ferre* / God is (sayth thap-
postell) faythfull, which suffreth you not to be temptid above
that you may bere / but giveth also with the temptacion a way
out.[42]

Either God would ultimately protect men from such persecution,
having allowed them in the meantime to experience the dread of it so
as 'to drive vs to call for grace', or else the short pain he would allow to
be inflicted on their bodies would 'tourne vs to eternall profitt'.[43] If
men were surely grounded in faith and confirmed in the hope of God's
assistance, they could receive no harm from persecution: 'that that
shall seme harme / shall in dede be to vs none harm at all / but
good / For yf god make vs and kepe vs good men as he hath promisid
to do / yf we pray well therfor / than saith holy scripture / *Bonis
omnia cooperantur in bonum* / vnto good folke, all thinges turne them to
good.'[44] As More said elsewhere, a man might lose his head and take
no harm from it.

For More, the supreme exemplar of this truth was Christ himself at
his passion. Like any ordinary human being, Christ had experienced
'great horrour and . . . fere . . . in his own flesh agaynst his paynfull
passion'.[45] More believed that he had suffered in the Garden before
the crucifixion for the express purpose of providing comfort: 'In our
fere let vs remembre . . . [it] to thentent that no fere shuld make vs
dispayre.'[46] Meditation on Christ's agony could, with the assistance of
grace, lead a man to 'submit and conforme' his will to Christ's, just as
Christ had submitted his own will to his father'. As a result, one would
be 'comfortid with the secret inward inspiracion of his holy sprite' and
hence be able to 'dye for the truth with hym, and therby rayne with
hym crownid in eternall glory'.[47]

All the different structural patterns of the *Dialogue*, in fact, converge

[42] ibid., p. 247/13–21.
[43] ibid., pp. 247–8.
[44] ibid., p. 248/20ff.
[45] ibid., p. 245/18–19.
[46] ibid., p. 318/26–9.
[47] ibid., pp. 245/24–246/5.

upon the same point: More's demonstration that Christ's passion archetypally embodies the purpose of all human experience, individual and common, present, past and future. One pattern derives from the organization of the three books around faith, hope and charity respectively.[48] Book 1 declares the necessity for faith as the foundation of all comfort, book 2 shows how men can have sure hope of God's assistance, and book 3 illuminates the charity that allows a man to overcome his tribulation. The progression of the argument through these three Christian virtues serves to condition Vincent's mind and emotions to the point where he will be able to strike the devil blind with 'that fire of charitie throwne in his face' by pitying and praying for his killers should the worst come to the worst when the Turks come.[49] Psychologically, the movement through faith, hope and charity reproduces the mental process which, in More's view, can 'quicken' a man's willingness to imitate Christ even in his passion.

A second pattern organized around the different types of tribulation leads to the same point. Book 1 deals with tribulation one cannot avoid, and book 2 with tribulation one willingly suffers, temptation in particular. That in turn is subdivided into four types, three of which are dealt with in book 2, and the third of which (that deriving from physical persecution) is treated at length in book 3. Each pattern arrives at the vivid visual image of Christ suffering on the Cross:

> the scornefull crowne of sharp thornes beten down vppon his holy hed, so strayght and so diepe, that on euery part his blyssid blode yssued owt and stremyd down / his lovely lymmys drawen and strechid out vppon the crosse to the Intollerable payne of his forebeten and sorebeten vaynes and synewes / new felyng with the cruell strechyng and straynyng payne far passyng any crampe, in euery part of his blyssid body at ones / Than the greate long nayles cruelly dryven with hamers thorow his holy handes and fete / and in this horryble payne lyft vpp and let hang.[50]

To increase the force of this highly charged climactic image, it is reiterated proleptically in each of the two earlier books. On the first

---

[48] Manley expounds this pattern in detail (*CW* 12, pp. lxxxix–cxvii).
[49] *CW* 12, p. 318/18–24.
[50] ibid., p. 312/15–23.

occasion More sounds the same linguistic chords when he refers to 'all
the torment that he hangyd in / of beatyng / naylyng / and strech-
yng out all his lymmes / with the wrestyng of his synews / and
brekyng of his tender vaynes / and the sharpe crown of thorn so
prickyng hym into the hed that his blessid bloude stremyd down all
his face'.[51] On the second occasion More evokes the image for the sake
of parody, in Anthony's tale of the Carver's wife and her mock
crucifixion of her husband, to illustrate both the suicidal folly and the
delusion of seeking to imitate Christ presumptuously. After his wife
has scourged him and driven a crown of thorns on his head, the
Carver 'thought this was inough for that yere, he wold pray god
forbere hym of the remenaunt till good friday come agayne . . . he
longid to folow christ no ferther'.[52] In this way the structural patterns
work through progression, duplication and convergence to move the
reader imaginatively and intellectually into an apprehension of the
book's total meaning.

Through his systematic exploration of the nature and purpose of
tribulation, More was able to understand why God had allowed
history to unfold as it had. The assault of the Turks, the internal
dissension within Europe, the threat of antichristian despotism in
England, and the subversion of the church by heretics were merely
macrocosmic extensions of the persecution God had allowed the devil
to wage on mankind since the Fall, and all, he considered, was for the
best, being a manifestation of God's beneficiently wise providential
disposition.

More's deepened sense of God's way confirmed his growing belief
that the Apocalypse was a long way off yet. At the opening of book 3,
when fresh news has arrived of the Turkish advance, Anthony
reassures Vincent that even should Hungary and much of Christendom be lost to the Turks, Christ would not allow the enemy
completely to prevail. The historical rhythm of decay followed by
renewal would continue until the end of time:

> I nothyng dowt at al, but that in conclucion how bace so euer
> christendom be brought, it shall spring vp agayne till the tyme
> be come very nere to the day of dome / wher of some tokens as

[51] ibid., p. 67/10ff.
[52] ibid., p. 144/4–22.

me thinketh are not comen yet / But som what before that tyme
shall christendome be straytid sore, and brought into so narrow
a compas, that according to christes wordes / *Filius hominis quum
venerit putas inueniet fidem in terra* . . . for as apperith in thapocalips
and other places of scripture, the fayth shalbe at that tyme so far
vaded that he shall for the love of his electes, lest they shuld fall
and perish to, abbredge those dayes, and accelerate his comyng.

But as I say me thinketh I mysse yet in my mynde, some of
those tokens, that shall by the scripture come a good while before
that.[53]

The return of a more balanced historical perspective helped restore
More's equilibrium, and once that had happened, he was able to see
the escalation of heresy, too, in a new light. At one point in book 1,
Vincent questions whether the comforts Anthony has proposed may
have been put in doubt by the new doctrines. Many men, he declares,
'affirm for a suer trowth, that ther is no purgatory at all' and 'say ye
wot well also, that men merite nothyng at all / but god giveth all for
fayth alone'. If these two propositions are true, he continues, they
destroy the two main causes for comfort that Anthony has suggested.[54] Anthony's reply reflects a new attitude towards the
Lutherans in More himself and as such is worth quoting at length:

albeit that it is a right hevy thyng to se such variaunce in our
beleve rise and grow among our self / to the grete encouragyng
of the comen enymies of vs all / wherby they haue our fayth in
dirision and cach hope to ouerwhelm vs all / yet do there iij
thynges not a litle recomfort my mynd.

The first is, that in some communicacions had of late together,
hath aperid good liklyhod of some good agrement to grow in one
accord of our fayth /

The second, that in the meane while till this may come to pas,
contencions, dispicions, with vncharitable behaviour, is pro-
hibitid and forboden in effect vppon all partes / all such partes I
meane as fell before to fight for it.

The Third is, that all germanye for all their diuers opynions /
yet as they agre together in profession of christes name / so agre

---

[53] ibid., pp. 193/26–194/8.
[54] ibid., p. 37/11–16.

they now together in preparacion of a comen power in defence of christendome ageinst our comen ennymy the Turke / And I trust in god that this shall not onely help vs here to strength vs in this warr / but also that as god hath causid them to agre together in the defence of his name / so shall he graciously bryng them to agree together in the truth of his fayth.

Therfor will I let god worke and leve of contention.[55]

Several crucial things are to be noted here. More stresses the common bond uniting all Christians – the profession of Christ's name – rather than the doctrinal differences that divide them into orthodox and heterodox. He also expresses hope that the common Turkish threat might unite them all into one agreement as to the true faith. Finally, he deliberately and decisively repudiates the contention to which he had been accustomed, replacing it with a faith that God is in some way working in events. In spite of the view of a recent editor that Anthony's statements must be taken 'as somewhat satiric' and ironic,[56] there is nothing in tone or content to suggest that More himself did not firmly believe everything that he has Anthony say. The Peace of Nürnberg (1532), which had been reaffirmed in the Peace of Cadan on 29 June 1534 – the very time when More was writing the *Dialogue* –, had stressed the need for unity and the avoidance of controversy: 'Et quoniam causa controversiae religionis, multis laboribus frustra susceptis, non potuit ad aliquam concordiam reduci, ad animum revocavimus, id quod res est, non posse crudelitati ac tyrannidi Turcicae validus resisti quam si in Imperio communis ac firma pax constituatur.'[57] More chose to set an example himself by leaving off contention, as both the tone and matter of the *Dialogue of Comfort* attests. As in the *Treatise upon the Passion*, he forgets himself from time to time (as when his treatment of penance and bodily affliction momentarily opens the old wound of Luther's marriage),[58] but his overriding intent is clear – to adopt a more charitable form of behaviour and avoid 'contencions' and 'dispicions'. This is confirmed, for example, in his choice of the word 'christendom' for most of the occasions when formerly he would have written 'church' (which he

---

[55] ibid., pp. 37/24–38/18.

[56] Manley, *CW* 12, p. 349 (note to p. 38/3–5), p. 350 (note to p. 38/10–13).

[57] *Documents Illustrative of the Continental Reformation*, ed. B. J. Kidd (Oxford, 1911), pp. 302–3.

[58] *CW* 12, p. 93/26 *et passim*.

uses in the *Dialogue* on only two occasions, and then, one feels, inadvertently).[59] 'Christendom' allows conditionally for the inclusion of all those who, as More says, profess the name of Christ regardless of their particular disagreements; 'church', on the other hand, raises the whole divisive spectre which More was trying to lay to rest.

More's new spirit of charitable accommodation is seen even in Anthony's assertion of his own personal belief (and More's) that good works are necessary and meritorious: far the more part [of the reformers] are thus farr agreed with vs, that like as we graunt them that no good worke is ought worth to hevyn ward without fayth / and that no good worke of man is rewardable in hevyn of his own nature. . . . And as we graunt them also that no man may be proude of his workes for his own vnperfit workyng. . . . As we I say graunt vnto them these thynges / so this one thyng or twayne do they graunt vs agayne / that men are bound to worke good workes yf they haue tyme and power and that who so workith in trew fayth most, shalbe most rewardid.[60]

While More was not prepared to make any further concession in the matter than that, the concession itself testifies to the huge contrast with the inflexible dogmatism of the controversies. The *Dialogue of Comfort* is not a narrowly partisan or bigoted work, which makes it all the more erroneous to identify too precisely the Turk with the reformers.[61]

Once More had been able to step back from events, he seems, without repudiating one jot of his own personal commitment to Latin orthodoxy, to have been almost able to contemplate once again the possibility that he had put into the mind of King Utopus years earlier: that God might desire a varied and manifold worship, and therefore inspire different people with different views ('. . . nihil est ausus temere definire, uelut incertum habens, an uarium ac multiplicem expetens cultum deus, aliud inspiret alij').[62] More knew that if Christendom were to arise again into one accord of faith, as he hoped and expected, it would mean growing into a new consensus rather than returning to the old.

[59] ibid., pp. 75/10, 95/10.
[60] ibid., p. 39/3–17.
[61] As does Jones (pp. 122–3).
[62] *Utopia, CW* 4, p. 220/10–12.

One of the most striking features of the *Dialogue of Comfort* is its proof of the return of More's literary powers. The enforced leisure of imprisonment no doubt gave him time to create an intricately designed, resonant and polished fiction, just as the diplomatic stalemate in Bruges had previously done in 1515, but a far more potent cause was the recovery of his equilibrium and faith.

For the first time since *A Dialogue Concerning Heresies,* More chose the form of the dramatized dialogue – the vehicle of *Utopia*. Within the dialogue, the relation of More's two personae, Vincent and Anthony, to himself is just as complex as that of Morus and Hythlodaeus, and the Messenger and 'More' in the earlier works. It is wrong to make a simple identification of More with Anthony, the old wise man awaiting death, for More dramatizes his experience equally in Vincent, the perturbed and anxious nephew. If anything, Vincent represents the militant self, and Anthony the resolved self, and the depiction of both served to give More himself comfort just as much as he intended it to provide comfort for his family and readers.

The experience Vincent undergoes in the course of the dialogue exemplifies the effect that the book itself is designed to produce. As well, it epitomizes in a 'speaking picture' all that More is trying to say. In effect, he shows as much as he tells, just as he did in *Utopia,* and tried (less successfully) to do in the *Dialogue Concerning Heresies*. In Vincent he also projects the process by which he himself had managed to regain calm and purge himself of the despair with which he had been threatened at the end of his controversial effort.

At the outset, Vincent, too, is so gripped with 'fearefull imaginacion' and 'desperat dreade' that he, along with his family is in 'perill of spirituall drounnyng'.[63] He is so filled with fear that he is tempted to conclude that 'the gretest comfort that a man can haue, ys when he may see that he shall sone be gone'.[64] It is out of this state of spiritual despondency that he arises, by finding within the causes of his fear grounds for faith, hope and charity.

The wise counsel of Anthony provides the instrument by which he is able to confront his tribulation. Anthony himself has 'bene taken prisoner in Turkey ij tymes' earlier in his days;[65] metaphorically speaking, he has suffered the same imprisoning dread in which

---

[63] *CW* 12, pp. 6/14, 23, 9/12.
[64] ibid., p. 3/18–19.
[65] ibid., p. 3/25.

Vincent is now trapped, and thus, having learnt through experience how to overcome it, can now give and take counsel in the way he later urges all men to do who find themselves in a similar case.[66] His task is to make Vincent realize how he can come to embody the truth mystically signified in his name according to the words of St John (in the person of Christ) in scripture:

> *vincenti dabo edere de ligno vite* / To hym that ouercometh, I shall give hym to eate of the tree of lyfe / And also he that ouer-cometh shalbe clothid in whyte clothes / and I shall confesse hys name before my father and before his Angelles . . . feare none of those thynges that thow shallt suffre . . . but be faythfull vnto the deth / and I shall give the the crowne of lyfe. He that ouercometh shall not be hurt of the second deth . . . *vincenti dabo manna absconditvm, et dabo illi calculum candidum. Et in calculo nomen nouum scriptum quod nemo scit nisi qui accipit* / To hym that ouer-cometh will I give manna secret and hid / and I will give hym a white suffrage, and in his suffrage a new name wrytten, which no man knowith but he that receyveth it.[67]

The insistent repetition in these lines draws attention to the action of overcoming, and suggests that More chose the name 'Vincent' deliberately to underline Vincent's function as an exemplar of that process. By the end of the dialogue, Vincent has become fully prepared to fulfil the possibilities inherent in his name, and thus takes his leave to perform the same task that More himself has just completed: 'I purpose vncle as my pore witt and lernyng will serve me, to put your good counsayle in remembrauns, not in our own langage onely, but in the Almayne tong to.'[68] Without precisely duplicating it, Vincent's intention to translate his projected work evokes the subtitle of the *Dialogue of Comfort* itself: 'made by an hungaryen in laten, and translatyd out of laten into french, and out of french into Englysh'. Through a peculiar telescoping and inversion of the time scale, the past merges in the future as Vincent participates with Anthony, More and Christ himself in a timeless triumph of charity to which experience should serve to draw all good men.

[66] ibid., pp. 146/30–147/10.
[67] ibid., p. 309/12–23.
[68] ibid., p. 320/13–16.

In the course of contriving this drama, More depicted functionally one of the inadequacies he had come to recognize in his old polemical method. After the *Dialogue Concerning Heresies* his literary mode had rapidly disintegrated from representation into assertive diatribe. He must have soon realized that such rambling monstrosities as the *Confutation* were far less help to those in doubt or perplexity than they might otherwise have been had he chosen another method. Something of this realization is dramatized within the *Dialogue of Comfort*.

Book 1, declaring the facts and varieties of tribulation and the need for faith as the foundation for any comfort against it, is closest in manner to the controversies. It is largely theoretical and stark, with most of the talk going to Anthony, who assumes the role of a schoolmaster administering a lecture. Vincent's role is reduced to little more than that of a foil, rather like the Messenger in the last book of *A Dialogue Concerning Heresies*. The effect on Vincent is to make him feel importunate and insignificant, as if his very presence has been a burdensome encumbrance to the wise man: 'you haue evyn shewid me a sample of sufferaunce in beryng my foly so long and so paciently'.[69] He calls an end to the conversation, but nevertheless emboldens himself to request a further meeting.

In the intervening time, Vincent's guilt increases, until, as he charitably declares to Anthony on next seeing him, he had become convinced that any fault was his:

> after my departyng from you, remembring how long we taried together, and that we were all that while in talkyng / And all the labour yours in talkyng so long together without inter-pawsyng betwene / and that of mater studiouse and desplesaunt, all of desease and siknes and other payne and tribulacion: I was in good fayth very sory and not a litell wroth with my selfe for myn own ouer sight, that I had so litell considerid your payne.[70]

Admitting that he had indeed felt '(to sey the trowth) evyn a litell wery', Anthony reciprocates this charitable gesture by confessing that he, too, had felt some remorse after Vincent's departure: '[I wished] the last tyme after you were gone . . . that I had not so told you styll a

[69] ibid., p. 77/7–8.
[70] ibid., p. 78/10–16.

long tale alone / but that we had more often enterchaungid wordes / and partid the talke betwene vs, with ofter enterparlyng vppon your part.' Anthony, however, will not let Vincent take all the blame: 'in that poynt I sone excusid you, and layd the lak evyn where I found yt / and that was evyn vppon myn own nekke'.[71] It occurred to him that they had been like a nun and her brother: after a long absence abroad, the brother had returned to visit his sister at her convent, but as soon as they met at the locutory grate, she had immediately launched into a sermon on the wretchedness of the world, the frailty of the flesh, and the subtle sleights of the wicked fiend, with plenty of unsolicited counsel besides; eventually, she began to find fault that her brother was not delivering 'some frutfull exortacion', at which he upbraided her: 'By my trouth good sister / quoth her brother I can not for you / for your tong haue neuer ceasid, but said inough for vs bothe.'[72]

In the exchange between Vincent and Anthony, and in this merry tale, More ironically scrutinizes the habit of mind into which he had slipped in his polemical writing. Vincent identifies, in passing, the gloomy oppressiveness of his works once he had lost his sense of humour, perspective and proportion; Anthony, on the other hand, identifies the obsessiveness that can mar the determined expression of a fixed personal viewpoint. More may still have felt that such a hammering method was justified with heretics, as distinct from the non-heretical audience for whom he now wrote, but his professed readiness in word and deed to leave off contention altogether suggests that he had come to accept that it was intrinsically faulty. In any case, the whole episode symbolically figures forth the moment when More steps down from his polemical soapbox, being prepared to re-enter into dialogue, and kissing goodbye at the same time to the hubris that had animated his controversies.

More probes the sigificance of this change of method still further by dramatizing its subsequent effects on the two protagonists.

Vincent is at once drawn out of himself, and reciprocates in kind with another merry tale – about the kinswoman who was content to let her husband have all the words, so long as she spoke them all herself.[73] Just as importantly, he feels that he need no longer forbear boldly to show his folly or be so 'shamfast'. He therefore proceeds to declare

---

[71] ibid., p. 79/20–8.

[72] ibid., p. 80/1–23.

[73] ibid., p. 81/1–18. This is the first of the numerous tales bearing upon Dame Alice More.

more openly and honestly what he really thinks, as when he admits that he finds Anthony's earlier statement that men should in no way seek comfort in any worldly or fleshly thing 'somwhat hard'.[74] Vincent's new honesty in turn induces Anthony to modify the rigidity of his own position. On the matter of mirthful recreation, he admits that he 'dare not be so sore as vtterly to forbyd yet', even though he maintains his prior conviction (and More's) that men should not need it.[75] Even while soberly affirming that he will not be so partial to his own fault ('my selfe am of nature evyn halfe a giglot') as to praise it, he proceeds immediately to tell a very funny story of a holy father's devious strategy to get his sleeping congregation to listen to his sermon.[76] Thereafter, the merry tales flood back with a profusion and inventiveness not seen since the earlier *Dialogue Concerning Heresies*. By book 3 the old literary More had been fully reborn.

More could very well have laid down his pen after finishing the *Dialogue of Comfort*. He had recovered his composure, faith in providence, and had attained a deeper sense of what had happened, was happening, and might be about to happen. His writing of the book had also been a means of offering comfort to others while at the same time being his own means of gaining it. More had little to do but wait, seeking in the meantime to exploit whatever possibility of defence the law of the land still held out to him.

He did not, however, finish there. Both the *Treatise upon the Passion* and the *Dialogue of Comfort* had pointed to Christ's passion as the epitome of the meaning of things, but neither had fully explored the passion itself. As More's trial and likely execution drew near, it still remained to him to consider the extent to which the journey through Cedron to the Mount of Olives might image his own. In his next and final work, *De Tristitia Christi*, he found that his own passion was indeed comprised within the other, and in so doing he discovered that his experience mirrored that of the whole world as he had come to understand it.

---

[74] ibid., p. 82/8ff.

[75] ibid., p. 83/7ff. In 'A Godly Meditation', written in the margins of More's prayerbook while he was in the Tower, More himself prayed for grace 'To abstayn from vayne confabulations / To estew light folysh myrth and gladnesse / Recreationys not necessary, to cutt off' (*CW* 13, p. 227/11–14).

[76] *CW* 12, pp. 83/4, 84/5ff.

11

The Image of History: *De Tristitia Christi*

Both the *Treatise upon the Passion* and *A Dialogue of Comfort against Tribulation* had looked towards the crucifixion as the central event in human history. It was logical, therefore, that More should have returned to a consideration of the circumstances leading up to Christ's death as his own approached.

De tristitia, tedio, pauore, et oratione Christi ante captionem eius ('On the Sadness, Weariness, Fear, and Prayer of Christ before His Capture'),[1] in fact, picks up the gospel narrative practically at the point where the eucharistic *Treatise upon the Passion* had left off. It is also cast in much the same form, being an exegetical commentary whose function is both homiletic as well as devotional, and public as well as private.[2] As literature, *De Tristitia Christi* does not rate very high, at least not in comparison with the *Dialogue of Comfort*: its digressions are too disparate to contribute to any satisfyingly unified effect, and its recurrent, rather bilious diatribes against heresy and heretics actively shatter the decorum of its conception.[3] Understandably, the growing pressure and stress on More tended to unseam the fabric of composure he had achieved during the time when he wrote the *Dialogue of Comfort*. The earlier work had been produced in the mood in which More could rejoice that imprisonment had given him something close to the

[1] Clarence H. Miller demonstrates how More's revisions in the Valencia holograph show him formulating the title with care and precision (*CW* 14, II, pp. 739–40, and the commentary, p. 789). The previous titles under which the work was known, the *Expositio passionis Domini* of the 1565 Louvain *Opera omnia* and Philip Hallett's *History of the Passion*, are spurious.

[2] For the relation between the exegetical and devotional elements, see Haupt, *CW* 13, pp. li, lxxxiiiff., and Miller, *CW* 14, II, p. 742, and the same author's essay, 'The Heart of the Final Struggle: More's Commentary on the Agony in the Garden', in *Quincentennial Essays on St Thomas More*, ed. Michael J. Moore (Albion, North Carolina, 1978), pp. 112–13.

[3] See, for example, *CW* 14, I, pp. 259, 347, 355–9, 389, 393–5, 445–9 and 509ff.

monastic cell he had always yearned after. More had then said: ' "me thinckethe god makethe me a wanton, and settethe me on his lappe and dandlethe me" '.[4] There is no such feeling reflected in *De Tristitia Christi*, which registers the agony of its subject, and is marked by stressful outward manifestations of it.

However, even though More's final work is not his best, thematically it is the logical, climactic conclusion to his whole opus. In it he realized once and for all the full implications of his world view: first, that in universal terms the passion was an archetype, or *typum*, for all human experience, and second, that in personal terms its pattern was being reproduced in his own life.

The archetypal, exemplary nature of the passion, More believed, had been determined by divine providence: 'it was by His own marvelous arrangement that His divinity moderated its influence on His humanity for such a time and in such a way that He was able to yield to the passions of our frail humanity and to suffer them with such terrible intensity'.[5] Christ chose to experience 'not only the pain of torture in His body but also the most bitter feelings of sadness, fear, and weariness in His mind', partly for the sake of performing his redemptive sacrifice for mankind, and partly 'to admonish us how wrong it is for us either to refuse to suffer grief for His sake . . . or to tolerate grudgingly the punishment due to our sins'.[6] By so doing, he provided an exemplum of profound anguish ('tam nouo tam miro tam immensae anxietatis exemplo') capable of consoling men against future fear and alarm.[7]

God's eternal providence ('eterna dei prouidentia') had also seen to it that the very placenames connected with Christ's passion had been bestowed in such a way as to embody a figurative significance.[8] These placenames symbolically suggested the nature of human history at large and also the pattern of emotional experience likely to be encountered by every individual who enters it. After the last supper,

[4] Roper, p. 76.

[5] 'ipsius . . . admirabili dispensatione contigit / quod eius deitas tantisper in humanitatem sic temperauit influxum / ut hos humane fragilitatis affectus admittere tam atrociter et subire posset' (*CW* 14, I, pp. 87/5–89/1).

[6] ibid., pp. 95/7–97/4.

[7] ibid., p. 237/6.

[8] ibid., p. 23/1–4; cf. p. 15/1–8, where More affirms that the evangelists must have been moved by the Holy Spirit to record these names. More's etymology for 'Cedron' is idiosyncratic and spurious; see Miller, *CW* 14, II, p. 1005 (note to p. 17/1).

Christ had set off on a journey to the Mount of Olives across the stream Cedron to the outlying estate named Gethsemani. 'Cedron', More (erroneously) declared, meant 'sadness' and 'blackness' in Hebrew; 'Gethsemani' meant 'fertile valley' or 'valley of olives'.[9] The names were thus providentially intended to remind men that while they are exiled from God, before they could reach the fruitful Mount of Olives and pleasant estate of Gethsemani, 'fertile in every sort of joy' ('omni iucunditate pinguissimam'), they must first cross over Cedron, 'a valley of tears and a stream of sadness whose waves can wash away the blackness and filth of our sins' ('uallis lachrimarum et torrens tristitiae / quae sua inundatione possint peccatorum nostrorum nigredinem et sordes abluere').[10] The sadness and tribulation of Cedron refer to transitory states of suffering, but also to the perpetual, historical condition of the world itself, which is a purgatorial vale of tears, as More recurrently affirmed. God had created it, he said, to be a 'place of labour and penance ('laboris et penitentiae locum'), not a 'joyful haven of rest' ('quietem leticiam celum'), and if men sought heaven on earth, they would exclude themselves from true felicity, signified by the Mount of Olives, forever.[11]

Other details of the passion illuminated the essentially dolorous nature of the human situation for More. The fickleness of the Jews, for example, who joined with the gentiles in arresting Christ like a thief only days after they had welcomed him into Jerusalem like a king, reminded him of 'the constant revolutions and vicissitudes of the human condition' ('assidue se uertentem humanarum rerum uicissitudinem').[12] More believed that Christ had taken care to provide this contrast as a warning to Christians not to trust in fortune or pursue the mutable glory of this world ('huius mundi despuendam gloriam').[13]

He again extended the meaning of the passion to history at large in expounding Christ's words to his captors, ' "This is your hour and the power of darkness." ' At the most immediate level, these words referred specifically to the malice of the high priests, scribes, pharisees

[9] ibid., pp. 13, 17.

[10] ibid., pp. 17/6–19/5.

[11] ibid., pp. 19/6–21/3.

[12] ibid., p. 367/5–6.

[13] ibid., p. 369/8. The *contemptus mundi* here recalls the *Rueful Lamentation* and the *Verses for the Book of Fortune,* but with the difference that More no longer held the things of the world to be intrinsically contemptible, only the excessive desire for them. In Augustinian terms, he held that they were to be *used,* not *enjoyed.* For More's discussion of the good use of wealth and place, see *Dialogue of Comfort, CW* 12, p, 179ff.

and elders in betraying Christ, to their self-deception in ascribing his death to their own strength, and to the relatively short time they would be suffered to prevail.[14] Figuratively, however, More took Christ's statement as referring to the whole span of time in which the prince of darkness would be permitted to persecute the faithful; namely, the whole time of this present world. This is indicated by the allusion to the Apocalypse he makes Christ utter as he warns his captors not to take pride in their apparent power: 'For the span of time allotted to your wanton arrogance is not endless but has been shortened to the span of a brief hour for the sake of the elect, that they might not be tried beyond their strength' ('Non enim sempiternum seculum est / quod uestrae libidini permittitur / sed instar horae breuis *propter electos tempus abbreuiatum* / ne ultra tentarentur quam possent ferre').[15] Christ's imagined words here echo Matthew 24: 22, which More had persistently associated with the raging persecution prophesied in the Book of Revelations: 'Et nisi breuitati fuissent dies illi, non fieret salua omnis caro: sed *propter electos breuiabuntur dies illi*.'[16] The verbal allusion therefore suggests how Christ's resurrection, by which the malice of the Jews would be frustrated in the short term, betokened in the larger context of universal history the church's final victory over the devil when it would arise triumphant in heaven at the end of time: 'when they have taken up their cross to follow me, when they have conquered the prince of darkness, the devil, when they have trod under foot the earthly minions of Satan, then finally, riding aloft on a triumphal chariot, the martyrs will enter into heaven in a magnificent and marvelous procession.'[17]

Heaven, nevertheless, had to be earned, and the sleep of the disciples during Christ's agony impressed More as typical of the spiritual negligence into which all men are prone to lapse. It also struck him with the ironic discrepancy between what men commonly are and what they are called to be, and with the paradox that God draws priceless treasures of the faith out of such unpromising material. More makes Christ himself ironically comment on these facts on two occasions. The first is when he addressed the sleeping

[14] *CW* 14, I, pp. 537–8.

[15] ibid., p. 555/5–7. My italics.

[16] My italics; cf. *Treatise upon the Passion, CW* 13, p. 173/24ff., and *Dialogue of Comfort, CW* 12, p. 193/30ff.

[17] 'eoque modo cum cruce sua me sequuti / deuicto tenebrarum principe diabolo / subpeditatis sathane terraceis satellitibus / triumphali curru sublimes / pompa mirabili / martyres intrabunt celum' (*CW* 14, I, pp. 553/3–5).

Peter by his former name, 'Simon' – or 'Cephas'. As More explains, 'Simon' in Hebrew means 'listening' and 'obedient', whereas Peter was neither listening nor obedient, for he went to sleep against Christ's express wishes. By satirically exposing the gap between Peter's behaviour and the virtues signified in his name, Christ was emphasizing not only the contrast between Peter and himself, but also the contrast between the negligent Peter and the future glorious martyr who would be killed by the as yet unborn Nero.[18] The second occasion on which Christ uses irony is when he addresses the sleeping apostles after rousing them for the third time: ' "Sleep on now", He said, "and take your rest." ' Here, More asserted, Christ had granted permission to sleep in such a way as to show clearly that he meant to take it away: they might sleep on if they could, but they would certainly not be able to.[19] Thereafter, they would confront temptation and the open assaults of Satan, and would finally pour forth tears in their prayers and shed blood in the agony of their suffering.[20]

The sleep of the apostles thus signified for More the condition of spiritual sloth out of which life itself is designed to drag men. Upon contemplating it, he reaffirmed the conclusions he had reached in the *Dialogue of Comfort*:

> such is God's kindness that even when we are negligent and slumbering on the pillow of our sins, He disturbs us from time to time, shakes us, strikes us, and does His best to wake us up by means of tribulations.
>
> But still, even though He thus proves Himself, to be most loving even in His anger, most of us, in our gross human stupidity, misinterpret His action and imagine that such a great benefit is an injury.[21]

Paradoxically, the pain of tribulation can achieve joy, and also be the means by which the timorous sheep may overcome the rampant lion even while being ripped to pieces by it.

[18] Cf. ibid., p. 545/7–8.

[19] ibid., pp. 287/4–291/9.

[20] ibid., pp. 551/6–553/2.

[21] 'quae dei bonitas est necligentes nos / et peccatorum puluino indormientes / agitat interdum quatit et concutit / ac tribulationibus satagit expergifacere.

Atqui quum ea re se probet (etiam si iratum) tamen amantissimum / plerique tamen / homines stultissimi / aliorsum rem accipimus / et beneficium tantum / maleficij loco ducimus' (ibid., p. 203/1–6).

More reserved his final expression of this paradox for his exposition of the episode in which Mark describes how a young man avoided capture by fleeing away naked, leaving his garment in his would-be captors' hands. Figuratively, this episode suggested to More how readily the soul can escape from the clutches of wicked men and the snares of the devil, 'for the body is, as it were, the garment of the soul' ('siquidem uestimenti uice corpus anime est'). Just as clothes are worth much less than the body, so too the body is worth much less than the soul, and one should be prepared to shed the one just as eagerly as the other to avoid falling into sin.[22] By drawing an analogy between the young man's shedding of his clothes and the way a snake sloughs off its skin, More was able to suggest the integral part tribulation plays in this process:

> if we patiently endure the loss of the body for the love of God, then, just as the snake sloughs off its old skin (called, I think, its 'senecta') by rubbing it against thorns and thistles, and leaving it behind in the thick hedges comes forth young and shining, so too those of us who follow Christ's advice and become wise as serpents will leave behind on earth our old bodies, rubbed off like a snake's old skin among the thorns of tribulation suffered for the love of God, and will quickly be carried up to heaven, shining and young and never more to feel the effects of old age.[23]

As in the *Dialogue of Comfort,* More's treatment of tribulation directs attention to the ultimate heavenly reward to be achieved by patiently suffering it.

As More's exegesis of the passion proceeded, he grew increasingly aware of the correspondences between it and his own situation. This awareness obtrudes in isolated instances, as when he muses that 'it was not yet summer when Christ left the supper and went over to the

---

[22] ibid., pp. 605/7–611/4. More saw Joseph's flight from Potiphar's lecherous wife as a typological prefiguration of the episode of the young man (pp. 611–13).

[23] 'Sin ob amorem dei patienter sustinemus amittere quemadmodum anguis pellem ueterem quem opinor senectam uocant spinis et tribulis adfricatam exuit et relinquens in sepibus nitidus et iuuenescens egreditur ita nos christi consilium sequente prudentes scilicet sicut serpentes effecti corpus hoc uetustum uelut anguinam senectam inter spinas tribulationis effricatum ob amorem dei relinquentes in terris nitidi nimirum et iuuenes nunquam post illa sensuri senium propere subuehemur in celum' (ibid., pp. 615/5–617/5).

mount'.[24] More inferred this from the fact that the servants were warming themselves around charcoal fires in the courtyard of the high priest. It seems a gratuitous detail until one recalls that at the time when More was writing *De Tristitia Christi* it was not yet summer in England either. The correspondence in chronology helped underline the parallel More detected as he contemplated in Christ's sadness a reflection of his own.

He detected another specific parallel in one of the causes of Christ's grief. Apart from dread at the thought of his approaching ordeal – 'infensos hostes / uincula / Calumnias / blasphemias / uerbera / spinas / clauous / crucem / et dira per horas multas continuata supplicia' – Christ had been tormented by the thought of his disciples' terror and the loss of the Jews: 'discipulorum terror / perditio Iudeorum'.[25] More, one senses, saw this as reflecting both his private concern for the perturbations of his family, and also his public, intellectual concern for the slide of the English into heresy and schism. It comforted him that Christ had had to confront the same perplexity at the course history was about to take that he had experienced.

Even the *adulescens* is described in terms that turn him into a mirror of More himself. When all the disciples had run away, the young man had remained alone out of love of Christ. More's observation of this fact ties up with his earlier denunciation of the successors of the apostles – the bishops of his own day who were proving themselves equally cowardly. Too many of them, More considered, were 'numbed and buried in destructive desires . . . drunk with the new wine of the devil, the flesh, and the world . . . [asleep] like pigs sprawling in the mire' and negligent in fulfilling the duties of their office, 'like a cowardly ship's captain who is so disheartened by the furious din of a storm that he deserts the helm, hides away cowering in some cranny, and abandons the ship to the waves'.[26] He was acutely aware that he was performing the role that the bishops should have enacted but (apart from Fisher) had not. More, like the young man, found himself alone after the others had fled, the difference being that in order to avoid being forced 'to do or say anything which might impugn the honor of Christ',[27] More had to relinquish not simply a linen garment, but his own body.

[24] ibid., p. 9/2ff.
[25] ibid., pp. 47/3–49/1.
[26] ibid., pp. 263/1–3, 265/1–3.
[27] ibid., p. 611/3–5.

In the wider context, the most important reflection in the passion of More's personal situation was Christ's human fear, as the true title of the work suggests. Probably to his own surprise, More found himself being called to enact the role of a martyr. He knew, however, that he was not the heroic kind of martyr who rushes forward eagerly to embrace death, but rather the kind who creeps out hesitantly and fearfully ('cunctanter et timide proripeat').[28] While More considered Christ's anguish salutary for both kinds, he found it particularly pertinent to himself, for he saw in it 'the loving shepherd lifting the weak lamb on his shoulders, playing the same role as he himself does, expressing his own feelings'.[29] Christ chose to experience weariness and unequalled fear to fortify people like himself, More thought, who were convulsed with terror at the prospect of physical pain. To such a person as this, Christ wanted his deed to speak as if with his own voice:

'O faint of heart, take courage and do not despair. You are afraid, you are sad, you are stricken with weariness and dread of the torment with which you have been cruelly threatened. Trust me. I conquered the world, and yet I suffered immeasurably more from fear, I was sadder, more afflicted with weariness, more horrified at the propect of such cruel suffering drawing eagerly nearer and nearer. Let the brave man have his high-spirited martyrs, let him rejoice in imitating a thousand of them. But you, my timorous and feeble little sheep, be content to have me alone as your shepherd, follow my leadership; if you do not trust yourself, place your trust in me. See, I am walking ahead of you along this fearful road. Take hold of the border of my garment and you will feel going out from it a power which will stay your heart's blood from issuing in vain fears. . . .'[30]

[28] ibid., p. 249/8–9.

[29] 'Nam hic uidebit pastorem pium ouiculam imbecillam in humeros suos attollere / ipsius personam gerere / ipsius affectus exprimere' (ibid., p. 253/6–8).

[30] 'Confortare pusillanimis et noli desperare. Times tristaris tedio et pauore concuteris crudeliter intentati supplicij. Confide. Ego uici mundum qui plus supra modum timui / plus tristatus sum plus affectus tedio plus ad contuitum appetentis tam dirae passionis inhorrui. Habeat fortis / quos imitari se gaudeat magnanimos martyres mille. Tu timidula et imbecillis ouicula / uno me contenta pastore me ducem sequere / de te diffidens in me spera. En ego te in uia ista tam formidolosa precedo. Meae uestis fimbriam apprehende. Inde uirtutem exire senties / qui hunc animi tui in metus uanos effluentem sanguinem sistet salubriter' (ibid., pp. 101/8–105/3).

In the emotional and mental agony of Christ in the Garden, More recognized what he himself was suffering.

More's final preoccupation in *De Tristitia Christi* was to contemplate the meaning of his own impending death. As it drew nearer he did everything in his conscientious power to avoid it,[31] not only because of his terror of physical pain, but also because he knew he was walking a tightrope between exposing himself to death for Christ's sake, which was meritorious, and committing suicide, which was damnable. In one half of his mind, one senses, More, in spite of his shrinking from the means of it, positively desired to be a martyr; that would answer to all the ascetic yearnings he had chosen to suppress in his earlier career, for, by making the ultimate self-sacrifice, he could, in the words of his 'Godly Meditation', 'by the tyme agayn that I byfore haue loste'.[32] Yet he also realized that while exposing oneself to death was 'a deed of preeminent virtue' when God secretly prompted one to do so it was otherwise not a very safe thing, spiritually, to do.[33] Christ had left men free, and had even enjoined them, to flee from punishment whenever this could be done without injury to his cause.[34] Almost all the apostles, and almost all the martyrs in succeeding centuries had fled 'until such a time as the hidden providence of God foresaw was more fitting' ('tempus quod occulta dei prouidentia magis prouidit idoneum').[35] More therefore had to make quite certain that no legitimate avenue of respite remained open to him, and that is the reason for the rigorous scrupulosity of his silence and legal defence.

Consequently, once More saw that circumstances were carrying him inexorably towards the fatal eventuality he both longed for and feared, he grew convinced that his death would not fail in some way to work to God's greater glory according to the providential disposition of the divine will:

[31] On More's silence, his trial, and the intricacies of his legal defence, see J. Duncan M. Derrett, 'The Trial of Sir Thomas More', *Essential Articles*, pp. 55–78; and G. R. Elton, *Policy and Police: The Enforcement of the Reformation in the Age of Thomas Cromwell* (Cambridge, 1972), pp. 383–425.

[32] *CW* 13, p. 227/10.

[33] 'Offerre se pro christo morti quum res aperte postulat aut quum occulte stimulat deus / egregie uirtutis opus esse. . . . Alioqui uero nec satis tutum reor' (*CW* 14, I, p. 241/7–9).

[34] ibid., p. 63/2–4.

[35] ibid., pp. 63/4–65/1.

He keeps hidden the times, the moments, the causes of all things, and when the time is right He brings forth all things from the secret treasure-chest of His Wisdom, which penetrates all things irresistibly and disposes all things sweetly. And so, if anyone is brought to the point where he must either suffer torment or deny God, he need not doubt that it was God's will for him to be brought to this crisis. Therefore, he has very good reason to hope for the best.[36]

More was prepared to die because the interaction of circumstances and his own conscience blocked him off from all the routes of escape he felt obliged to attempt.[37] Like Christ, he wished, if possible, for the cup of his imminent fate to be taken from him, yet he was also prepared to imitate Christ in subordinating his own will obediently to what he took to be the will of God.[38] Finally, having committed the matter to the divine will, More was prepared 'to trust the whole outcome to God, who desires our welfare no less than we ourselves do and who knows what is likely to produce it a thousand times better than we do'.[39] One scholar has recently claimed that 'in the last analysis, More did not die for any principle, or idea, or tradition, or even doctrine, but for a person, for Christ'.[40] That is largely true, but I would also add that his death was his supreme affirmation of his belief in providence: it was the final act required by More of himself to verify once and for all the view of things he had spent his whole life formulating. As with Shelley, one feels, More had to die to satisfy the requirements of his own myth.

---

[36] 'Ille tempora momenta causas omnium rerum habet abstrusas / et quando conuenit ex archano sapientiae sue cuncta depromit armario quae penetrat omnia fortiter et disponit omnia suauiter. Quisquis igitur in eam conditionem deductus est / ut aut sustinendum ei supplicium sit / aut denegandus deus / hic se non dubitet in has angustias deo uolente deductum. Habet ergo magnam bene sperandi materiam' (ibid., pp. 67/6–69/5).

[37] More urged others to avoid capture by fleeing if they could do so in conscience (ibid., pp. 589–91). Of Tunstal, for example, he prophesied: 'if he live, he may do more good than to die with us' (*LP*, XIV, II, p. 750). For Tunstal's later career, see Morley Thomas, 'Tunstal – Trimmer or Martyr?', *Journal of Ecclesiastical History*, 24 (1973), pp. 337–55.

[38] *CW* 14, I, pp. 111/6–113/2.

[39] ibid., p. 177/5–7.

[40] Miller, 'The Heart of the Final Struggle', p. 123; cf. *CW* 14, II, pp. 774–6.

De Tristitia Christi ends just after More has begun to treat the last topic he proposed to cover, the capture of Christ,[41] with the words: 'tum demum primum manus iniectas in Iesum' ('only then, after all these events, did they lay hands on Jesus').[42] William Rastell detected an occult correspondence between More's fate and Christ's at this point, as his prefatory words in the 1557 edition suggest. More, he declares, 'coulde not atchieue and finishe the same, as he that ere he could goe thorow therwith, (eauen when he came to thexposicion of these wordes, *Et iniecerunt manus in Iesum*) was bereaued and put from hys bookes, pen, inke and paper, and kepte more strayghtly than before, and soone after also was putte to death hymselfe'.[43] More, in effect, did not need to finish *De Tristitia*, for its ending was left implicit, and soon to be literally supplied when More's own execution super-imposed the image of his own passion upon that of Christ. As with the *Dialogue of Comfort*, More had allowed the literary work to merge with the historical reality surrounding it.[44]

[41] See More's notes for the final section in the Valencia MS, fol. 115ᵛ (*CW* 14, I, p. 465).

[42] ibid., p. 625/7–8.

[43] ibid., II, p. 1077; cf. *EW* 1557, p. 1350 C. The date when More's writing materials were seized was 12 June 1535, less than a month before he was beheaded on 6 July (*CW* 14, II, p. 738 and note).

[44] More's execution was a serious political miscalculation on the government's part, for it aroused much disaffection. Almost immediately, discontent was channelled into the Pilgrimage of Grace, in which a strong More connection has been traced; among other things, the rebels demanded stronger measures to arrest the spread of heresy, the suppression of heretical writings (including those attacked by More), and, generally, 'a change in the king's proceedings from revolution to reaction' (see G. R. Elton, 'Politics and the Pilgrimage of Grace', in *After the Reformation*, ed. B. Malament (Philadelphia, 1980), pp. 25–56, esp. pp. 42–50).

Conclusion

The impact of More's spectacular death, then as now, overshadowed the view of things he had evolved in the course of his life and had laboured continuously to express in his writings. Even when More was systematically restored in the reign of Mary, his books were republished not for their actual intrinsic matter, but for the doctrines they could be taken to embody in the minds of the counter-reformers. As the biographies of Roper and Harpsfield testify, the myth-making possibilities in More's life and death were far more important to his followers than the particular intricacies of his thought.

The significance of his death, however, cannot be objectively grasped without knowledge of the personal philosophy that eventually led him to it. From the beginning, the *modus vivendi* he chose for himself implied an incipient *modus moriendi,* and, indeed, perhaps More found it psychologically necessary to die. In the face of a deeply sprung recoil from the world's frustrations, mutability, injustice, tribulation, and its even more satanic allurements, More restrained his urge to flee it by persuading himself that its storms and trials were providentially instrumental to the gaining of heaven. But this sense of the world's instrumentality gave him no permanent feeling of location in it, even though he threw himself into the active life with energy and commitment. The idea that men do not really have their dwelling here on earth, but are only pilgrims seeking to reach their true, otherwordly home was a venerable commonplace of medieval Christianity, but in More's case one feels that it was peculiarly intense. He seems never to have fully accepted his own decision not to become a withdrawn ascetic, and in spite of the fact that he had provided an elaborate philosophical justification for his participation and success in the competitive (and lucrative) world of the Court, he needed confirmation of its truth. Once he had been drawn into the realm of religious and political reform, he resisted change because he needed to believe that God intended the world to be in the same irremediably militant condition in which he found himself. When change began to appear inevitable, he shifted his attempt to demonstrate the nature and workings of providence as he understood them away from the contemporary world to himself. In effect, More (consciously or unconsciously) turned himself into the exemplar and proof of the validity of his own view. Through literal self-sacrifice he could proclaim himself ultimately right in the face of manifest defeat. Thus, in some respects he needed and longed to die as much as he shrank from it. Perhaps, unwittingly, he even contrived it.

The stakes of this final throw were enormous. If he succeeded, More knew that he would not only gain immortality in this world and the next, but also justify his past actions and beliefs; however, if he lost, and his sacrifice proved to be wilful self-destruction, his reward would be damnation. If history has continued to admire More for one thing above all else, it is for the courage with which he staked everything on his end – even if, with Halle, one finds it hard to decide whether that courage made him 'a foolishe wyseman, or a wise foolishman'. One thing is certain: having convinced himself of the soundness of his motives, More put his understanding of the providence he believed in to the supreme test.

Works Cited

Adams, R. P. *The Better Part of Valour: More, Erasmus, Colet and Vives on Humanism, War, and Peace, 1496–1535* (Seattle, 1962)

Augustinus, Aurelius. *The City of God*. Trans. John Healey, with an Introduction by Ernest Barker (London, 1931)

Bacon, Francis. *Essays*. Ed. M. J. Hawkins (London, 1972)

Barker, Arthur E. '*Clavis Moreana*: The Yale Edition of Thomas More', *Essential Articles*, pp. 215–28 (reprinted from *Journal of English and Germanic Philology*, 65 (1966), pp. 318–30)

Barnes, W. J. 'Irony and the English Apprehension of Renewal', *Queen's Quarterly*, 73 (1966), pp. 357–76

Baumer, Franklin Le Van. 'Christopher St German: The Political Philosophy of a Tudor Lawyer', *American Historical Review*, 42 (1937), pp. 631–51

Bevington, David M. 'The Dialogue in *Utopia*: Two Sides to the Question', *Studies in Philology*, 58 (1961), pp. 496–509

Boke of the fayre Gentylwoman, that no man shulde put his truste, or confydence in: that is to say, Lady Fortune: flaterynge euery man that coueyeth to haue all, and specyally, them that truste in her, she deceyueth them at laste (London, 1538)

Bridgett, T. E. *Life and Writings of Sir Thomas More* (London, 1891)

Byron, Brian. *Loyalty in the Spirituality of St Thomas More* (Nieuwkoop, 1972)

Campbell, W. E. *Erasmus, Tyndale and More* (London, 1949)

Chambers, R. W. *Thomas More* (London, 1935)

Chaucer, Geoffrey. *The Complete Works of Geoffrey Chaucer*. Ed. Walter W. Skeat (London, 1912)

Coulton, G. G. 'The Faith of St Thomas More', *Essential Articles*, pp. 502–12 (reprinted from *Quarterly Review*, 265 (1935), pp. 327–43)

Cross, Claire. *Church and People, 1450–1660: The Triumph of the Laity in the English Church* (London, 1976)

Dean, Leonard. 'Literary Problems in More's *Richard III*', *Essential Articles*, pp. 315–25 (reprinted from *PMLA*, 58 (1943), pp. 22–41)

Derrett, J. Duncan M. 'The Trial of Sir Thomas More', *Essential Articles*, pp. 55–78 (reprinted from *English Historical Review*, 79 (1964), pp. 449–77)

Dickens, Arthur Geoffrey. *The English Reformation* (London, 1964)

Donne, John. *Essays in Divinity*. Ed. Evelyn M. Simpson (Oxford, 1952)

Donner, H. W. 'St Thomas More's Treatise on the Four Last Things and the Gothicism of the Transalpine Renaissance', *Essential Articles*, pp. 343–55 (reprinted from *English Miscellany*, 3 (1952), pp. 25–48)

Dorsch, T. S. 'Sir Thomas More and Lucian: An Interpretation of *Utopia*', *Archiv für das Studium der neueren Sprachen und Literaturen*, 203 (1966–67), pp. 345–63

Duhamel, P. Albert. 'Medievalism of More's *Utopia*', *Essential Articles*, pp. 234–50 (reprinted from *Studies in Philology*, 52 (1955), pp. 99–126)

Elton, Geoffrey R. 'The Evolution of a Reformation Statute', *English Historical Review*, 64 (1949), pp. 174–97

Policy and Police: The Enforcement of the Reformation in the Age of Thomas Cromwell (Cambridge, 1972)

'Politics and the Pilgrimage of Grace', in *After the Reformation: Essays Presented to J. H. Hexter*. Ed. B. Malawent (Philadelphia, 1980), pp. 25–56

'The Real Thomas More?', in *Reformation Principle and Practice: Essays in Honour of Arthur Geoffrey Dickens*. Ed. Peter Newman Brooks (London, 1980)

Reform and Reformation: England 1509–1558 (London, 1977)

Reform and Renewal: Thomas Cromwell and the Common Weal (Cambridge, 1973)

Review of the Yale edition of the *Confutation*, *English Historical Review*, 89 (1974), pp. 382–7

'Sir Thomas More and the Opposition to Henry VIII', *Essential Articles*, pp. 79–91 (reprinted from *Bulletin of the Institute of Historical Research*, 41 (1968), pp. 19–34)

Studies in Tudor and Stuart Politics and Government. 2 vols. (Cambridge, 1974)

'Thomas Cromwell Redivivus', *Archiv für Reformationsgeschichte*, 68 (1977), pp. 192–208

The Tudor Constitution: Documents and Commentary (Cambridge, 1960)

Erasmus, Desiderius. *Opus epistolarum*. Ed. P. S. Allen, H. M. Allen, and H. W. Garrod. 12 vols. (Oxford, 1906–58)

Fenlon, D. B. 'England and Europe: *Utopia* and its Aftermath', *Transactions of the Royal Historical Society*, 25 (1975), pp. 115–35

Fish, Simon. *A Supplicacyon for the Beggers* (Antwerp, 1528)

Fisher, John. *The English Works of John Fisher, Bishop of Rochester*. Ed. John E. B. Mayor (London, 1876)

Fortescue, John. *The Works of Sir J. F., Knight, Chief Justice and Lord Chancellor to King Henry the Sixth*. Ed. Thomas (Fortescue), Lord Clermont. 2 vols. (London, 1869)

Fox, Alistair, 'Richard III's Pauline Oath: Shakespeare's Response to

Thomas More', *Moreana*, 57 (1978), pp. 13–25

'Thomas More's *Dialogue* and the *Book of the Tales of Caunterbury*: "Good Mother Wit" and Creative Imitation', in *Familiar Colloquy: Essays Presented to Arthur Edward Barker*. Ed. Patricia Brückmann (Ottawa, 1978)

Foxe, John. *The Acts and Monuments of John Foxe*. Ed. George Townsend. 8 vols. (London, 1846)

Friedberg, E. A., ed. *Corpus iuris canonici. Editio Lipsiensis 2. Post A. L. Richteri curas ad librorum manu scriptorum et editionis Romanae fidem recognovit et adnotatione critica instruxit A. Friedberg*. 2 vols. (Leipzig, 1879–81)

Froude, James Anthony. *History of England from the Fall of Wolsey to the Death of Elizabeth*. 12 vols. (London, 1856–70)

Greenslade, S. L. 'The Morean Renaissance', *Journal of Ecclesiastical History*, 24 (1973), pp. 395–403

Greg, W. W., ed. *The Book of Sir Thomas More*. Malone Society Reprints (Oxford, 1911)

Guegen, John A. 'Reading More's *Utopia* as a Criticism of Plato', in *Quincentennial Essays on St Thomas More: Selected Papers from the Thomas More College Conference*. Ed. Michael J. Moore (Boone, North Carolina, 1978)

Guy, John A. *The Public Career of Sir Thomas More* (Brighton, 1980)

Haas, Steven W. 'Simon Fish, William Tyndale, and Sir Thomas More's "Lutheran Conspiracy"', *Journal of Ecclesiastical History*, 23 (1972), pp. 125–36

Halle, Edward. *The Union of the Two Noble Families of Lancaster and York, 1550*. Scolar Press reprint (Menston, 1970)

Haller, William. *Foxe's Book of Martyrs and the Elect Nation* (London, 1963)

Hanham, Alison. 'Fact and Fantasy: Thomas More as Historian', in *Thomas More: The Rhetoric of Character*. Ed. Alistair Fox and Peter Leech (Dunedin, 1979)

Richard III and His Early Historians, 1483–1535 (Oxford, 1975)

Harpsfield, Nicholas. *The Life and Death of Sir Thomas More, Knight, Sometymes Lord High Chancellor of England*. Ed. E. V. Hitchcock with an Introduction by R. W. Chambers (London, 1932)

Harris, Barbara. 'The Trial of the Third Duke of Buckingham: A Revisionist View', *American Journal of Legal History*, 20 (1976), pp. 15–26

Headley, John M. 'The *Nos Papistae* of Thomas More', *Moreana*, 64 (1980), pp. 89–90

'Thomas More and the Papacy', *Moreana*, 41 (1974), pp. 5–10

Herbrüggen, H. Schulte. 'More's *Utopia* as Paradigm', *Essential Articles*, pp. 251–62 (reprinted from *Utopie und Anti-Utopie* (Bochum-Langendreer, 1960), pp. 16–37)

'Sir Thomas Mores Fortuna-Verse: Ein Beitrag zur Lösung einiger Probleme', in *Lebende Antike: Symposium für Rudolf Sühnel*. Ed. Horst Meller and Hans-Joachim Zimmermann (n.p., 1967), pp. 155–72

Hexter, J. H. *More's Utopia: The Biography of an Idea* (Princeton, 1952)

Holeczek, Heinz. *Humanistische Bibelphilologie als Reformproblem bei Erasmus von Rotterdam, Thomas More und William Tyndale*. Studies in the History of Christian Thought, vol. 9 (Leiden, 1975)

Hollis, Christopher. *Saint Thomas More* (London, 1961)

Hume, Anthea. 'English Protestant Books Printed Abroad, 1525–1535: An Annotated Bibliography', *CW* 8, II, pp. 1063–91

Inalcik, Halil. *The Ottoman Empire: The Classical Age, 1300–1600*. Trans. N. Itzkowitz and C. Imber (London, 1973)

Johnson, Robbin S. *More's Utopia: Ideal and Illusion* (New Haven, 1969)

Jones, Judith P. *Thomas More*. Twayne's English Authors Series, no. 247 (Boston, 1979)

Joye, George. *The Supper of the Lord*. Ed. Henry Walter (Cambridge, 1850)

Kautsky, Karl. *Thomas More and His Utopia*. Trans. H. J. Stenning with an Introduction by R. Ames (New York, 1959)

Kelly, H. A. *Divine Providence in the England of Shakespeare's Histories* (Cambridge, Mass., 1970)

Kidd, B. J., ed. *Documents Illustrative of the Continental Reformation* (Oxford, 1911)

Kincaid, Arthur Noel. 'The Dramatic Structure of Sir Thomas More's History of King Richard III', *Essential Articles*, pp. 375–87 (reprinted from *Studies in English Literature*, 12 (1972), pp. 223–42)

Kuhn, Joaquin. 'The Function of Psalm 90 in Thomas More's *Dialogue of Comfort*', *Moreana*, 22 (1969), pp. 61–7

Kullnick, Max. 'Th. Morus, Picus Erle of Mirandula', *Archiv für das Studium der neueren Sprachen und Literaturen*, n.s., 121 (1908), pp. 47–75; 122 (1909), pp. 27–50

Lehmberg, Stanford E. *The Reformation Parliament, 1529–1536* (Cambridge, 1970)

'Sir Thomas More's Life of Pico della Mirandola', *Studies in the Renaissance*, 3 (1956), pp. 61–74

Letters and Papers, Foreign and Domestic, of the Reign of Henry VIII. Ed. J. S. Brewer *et al.* 21 vols. (London, 1862–1932)

Levine, M. 'The Fall of Edward, Duke of Buckingham', in *Tudor Men and Institutions*. Ed. A. J. Slavin (Baton Rouge, 1972)

Lewis, C. S. 'Thomas More', *Essential Articles*, pp. 388–401 (reprinted from *English Literature in the Sixteenth Century Excluding Drama* (Oxford, 1954), pp. 164–81, 191–2)

Lupton, J. H. *A Life of John Colet* (London, 1909)

McConica, James K. *English Humanists and Reformation Politics* (Oxford, 1963)
  'The Recusant Reputation of Thomas More', *Essential Articles*, pp. 136–49
  (reprinted from *Reports of the Canada Catholic Historical Association*, 30
  (1964), pp. 47–61

MacDonald, William W. 'Saint Thomas More and the Historians', *American
  Benedictine Review*, 21 (1970), pp. 428–38

Malament, B., ed. *After the Reformation: Essays Presented to J. H. Hexter*
  (Philadelphia, 1980)

Marc'hadour, Germain. *Thomas More et la Bible* (Paris, 1969)
  *L'Univers de Thomas More: Chronologie critique de More, Erasme, et leur époque,
  1477–1536* (Paris, 1963)

Marius, Richard. 'More the Conciliarist', *Moreana*, 64 (1980), pp. 91–9
  'Thomas More's View of the Church', *CW* 8, III, pp. 1269–364

Mason, H. A. *Humanism and Poetry in the Early Tudor Period* (London, 1959)

Miller, Clarence. 'The Heart of the Final Struggle: More's Commentary on
  the Agony in the Garden', in *Quincentennial Essays on St Thomas More*. Ed.
  Michael J. Moore (Albion, 1978)

More, Thomas. *The Complete Works of St Thomas More*. 14 vols. Various editors
  [for complete details see Abbreviations]; (New Haven and London,
  1963–)
  *The English Works of Sir Thomas More, Reproduced in Facsimile . . . with a modern
  version of the Same.* Ed. W. E. Campbell, 2 vols. (London, 1931)
  The Latin Epigrams of Thomas More. Trans. and ed. L. Bradner and C. A.
  Lynch (Chicago, 1953)
  St Thomas More's History of the Passion. Ed. Philip Hallett (London, 1941)
  Utopia. Trans. and ed. Paul Turner (Harmondsworth, 1965)
  *The Workes of Sir Thomas More Knyght, Sometyme Lorde Chauncellor of England,
  Wrytten by Him in the Englysh Tonge.* Ed. William Rastell (London, 1557)

Muscatine, Charles. *Chaucer and the French Tradition: A Study in Style and
  Meaning* (Berkeley, 1969)

Nicholson, G. D. 'The Nature and Function of Historical Argument in the
  Henrician Reformation' (Ph.D., University of Cambridge, 1977)

Oakley, Francis. 'Headley, Marius and the Matter of More's "Conciliarism"',
  Moreana, 64 (1980), pp. 82–8

Pastor, Ludwig. *The History of the Popes from the Close of the Middle Ages.*
  40 vols. Ed. Frederick Ignatius Antrobus *et al.* (London, 1938–53)

Patrides, C. A. '"The Bloody and Cruell Turke": The Background of a
  Renaissance Commonplace', *Studies in the Renaissance*, 10 (1963),
  pp. 126–35

Pollard, A. F. 'The Making of Sir Thomas More's *Richard III*', *Essential
  Articles*, pp. 421–31 (reprinted from *Historical Essays in Honour of James
  Tait*. Ed. J. G. Edwards *et al.* (Manchester, 1933), pp. 223–38)

Pollock, F. and F. W. Maitland. *The History of English Law Before the Time of
  Edward I.* 2nd edn, 2 vols. (Cambridge, 1968)

Raitiere, Martin N. 'More's *Utopia* and *The City of God*', *Studies in the Renaissance*, 20 (1973), pp. 144–68

Rerum Anglicarum scriptorum veterum (Oxford, 1684)

Reynolds, E. E. *The Field is Won: The Life and Death of Saint Thomas More* (London, 1968)

— *Saint Thomas More* (London, 1949)

Rogers, Elizabeth Frances, ed. *The Correspondence of Sir Thomas More* (Princeton, 1947)

— ed. *St Thomas More: Selected Letters* (New Haven and London, 1961)

— 'Sir Thomas More's Letter to Bugenhagen', *Essential Articles*, pp. 447–54 (reprinted from *The Modern Churchman*, 35 (1946), pp. 350–60)

Roper, William. *The Lyfe of Sir Thomas More, Knighte*. Ed. Elsie Vaughan Hitchcock (London, 1935)

Routh, E. M. G. *Sir Thomas More and His Friends, 1477–1535* (Oxford, 1934)

Saint German, Christopher. *Salem and Bizance* (London, 1533)

Scarisbrick, J. J. *Henry VIII* (London, 1968)

— 'Thomas More: The King's Good Servant', *Thought: Fordham University Quarterly*, 52 (1977), pp. 259–65

Schoeck, Richard J. *The Achievement of Thomas More: Aspects of His Life and Works*. English Literary Studies, no. 7 (Victoria, 1976)

— 'Thomas More's "Dialogue of Comfort" and the Problem of the Real Grand Turk', *English Miscellany*, 20 (1969), pp. 23–37

Schuster, Louis A. 'Thomas More's Polemical Career, 1523–1533', *CW* 8, III, pp. 1135–268

Seebohm, Frederic. *The Oxford Reformers, John Colet, Erasmus, and Thomas More*. 3rd edn (London, 1911)

Skinner, Quentin. *The Foundations of Modern Political Thought*. 2 vols. (Cambridge, 1978)

Stapleton, Thomas. *The Life and Illustrious Martyrdom of Sir Thomas More*. Trans. Philip E. Hallett (London, 1929)

Starkey, Thomas. *A Dialogue between Reginald Pole and Thomas Lupset*. Ed. K. M. Burton with a Preface by E. M. W. Tillyard (London, 1948)

Strype, John. *Ecclesiastical Memorials; Relating Chiefly to Religion and the Reformation of it, and the Emergencies of the Church of England, under King Henry VIII, King Edward VI, and Queen Mary I*. 6 vols. (Oxford, 1822)

Surtz, Edward L. *The Praise of Pleasure: Philosophy, Education and Communism in More's Utopia* (Chicago, 1957)

— *The Praise of Wisdom: A Commentary on the Religious and Moral Problems and Backgrounds of St Thomas More's Utopia* (Chicago, 1957)

Sylvester, R. S. and G. Marc'hadour, eds. *Essential Articles for the Study of Thomas More* (Hamden, Conn., 1977)

Sylvester, Richard S. 'Roper's Life of More', *Essential Articles*, pp. 189–97 (reprinted from *Moreana*, 36 (1973), pp. 47–59)

— ed. *St Thomas More: Action and Contemplation* (New Haven, 1972)

Thomas, Morley. 'Tunstal – Trimmer or Martyr?', *Journal of Ecclesiastical History*, 24 (1973), pp. 337–55

Thompson,Craig R. 'The Humanism of More Reappraised', *Thought: Fordham University Quarterly*, 52 (1977), pp. 231–48

Thompson, Sister M. Geraldine. 'As Bones to the Body: The Scope of *Inventio* in the *Colloquies* of Erasmus', in *Essays on the Works of Erasmus*. Ed. Richard L. DeMolen (New Haven, 1978)

Tromly, Frederic B. ' "A Rueful Lamentation" of Elizabeth: Thomas More's Transformation of Didactic Lament', *Moreana*, 53 (1977), pp. 45–56

Tyndale, William. *An Answer to Sir Thomas More's Dialogue, the Supper of the Lord after the True Meaning of John VI. and I. Cor. XI, and William Tracy's Testament Expounded by William Tyndale, Martyr, 1536.* Ed. Henry Walter (Cambridge, 1850)

The Works of the English Reformers: William Tyndale, Robert Barnes, and John Frith. 3 vols. Ed. Thomas Russell (London, 1831)

Vergil, Polydore. *The Anglica Historia of Polydore Vergil.* Ed. D. Hay. Camden Series, vol. 74 (London, 1950)

Three Books of Polydore Vergil's English History, Comprising the Reigns of Henry VI, Edward IV, and Richard III. Ed. Henry Ellis. Camden Society (London, 1844)

White, Thomas I. 'Aristotle and *Utopia*', *Renaissance Quarterly*, 29 (1976), pp. 635–75

Whiting, B. J. *Proverbs, Sentences, and Proverbial Phrases from English Writings Mainly Before 1500*(Cambridge, Mass., 1968)

Willow, Sister Mary Edith. *An Analysis of the English Poems of St Thomas More* (Nieuwkoop, 1974)

Index